PRAGUE'S 200 DAYS

By the same author

The Red Phoenix: Russia Since World War II

An Introduction to the Soviet Economy

Tsars, Mandarins, and Commissars: A History of Chinese-Russian Relations

China

The Soviet Economy Since Stalin

Russia's Soviet Economy

Soviet Union: Communist Economic Power

Russia's Postwar Economy

Seasonal Migratory Agricultural Labor in the United States

Editor

Russia Enters the 1960's

The Many Faces of Communism

Prague's 200 Days

The Struggle for Democracy in Czechoslovakia

HARRY SCHWARTZ

FREDERICK A. PRAEGER, *Publishers*
New York • Washington • London

FREDERICK A. PRAEGER, PUBLISHERS
111 Fourth Avenue, New York, N.Y. 10003, U.S.A.
5, Cromwell Place, London S.W. 7, England

Published in the United States of America in 1969
by Frederick A. Praeger, Inc., Publishers

Library of Congress Catalog Card Number: 69–19700

Printed in the United States of America

For Gloria and Denise

Preface

The "Czechoslovak spring" of 1968 was one of the most heartening and yet most tragic events in many years. No believer in the freedom and self-determination of nations could fail to be inspired by the spontaneous and courageous attempt at self-liberation Czechoslovakia made in the incredible "200 days" from January 5 to August 20, 1968. No one could fail to be devastated by the brutal invasion that was a callous effort to destroy the dreams and hopes of the Czechoslovak people. This book is an attempt to tell the story of Czechoslovakia's finest hours as simply and as accurately as possible, together with the background of this historic and unexpected lunge for freedom. An effort has also been made to recount the incredible tale of the unity and bravery with which the Czechoslovak people at least partially defeated the goals of the brutal attack on their national sovereignty. I can make no claim to complete objectivity, but even though I am an admirer of the brave people of Prague, I have tried to take into account all the relevant facts and to consider the warts as well as the halos in Czechoslovakia. No doubt future historians with more evidence, more memoirs, and diplomatic archives now secret at their disposal will correct some of the judgments made here. But the story is too fascinating and too important for its recounting to wait until every detail has been clarified, especially when the main contours of what happened are so clear.

The idea for this book was born during my visits to Czechoslovakia during February and March and late July, 1968. I received many kindnesses and much information from Czechs and Slovaks who, in the present situation, must remain nameless. However, I can acknowledge my indebtedness to the generosity of many fellow journalists in Czechoslovakia: Jonathan Randall, Henry Kamm, and Richard Eder of *The New York Times,* Anatole Shub of *The Washington Post,* Osgood Carruthers of the *Los Angeles Times,* and Richard Davy of *The London Times.* Dr. Ernst Kux of the *Neue Zuercher Zeitung* was good enough to share his abundant knowledge of Czechoslovakia with me when he visited the United States after the invasion. Gene Mater of the Free Europe Committee made an immense contribution to this book by providing translations prepared by his colleagues of many Czechoslovak newspaper and magazine articles and summaries of day-to-day developments in Czechoslovakia. Dr. J. F. Brown of Columbia University was good enough to read the manuscript and offer many helpful suggestions. Ruth B. Schwartz showed the patience of Job in accepting the many inconveniences the writing of this book caused her. My employers, *The New York Times* and the State University of New York, bear no responsibility for the views expressed here. Full responsibility for these views and for any errors is mine alone.

HARRY SCHWARTZ

Scarsdale, New York
December 26, 1968

Contents

Contents

I

BACKGROUND

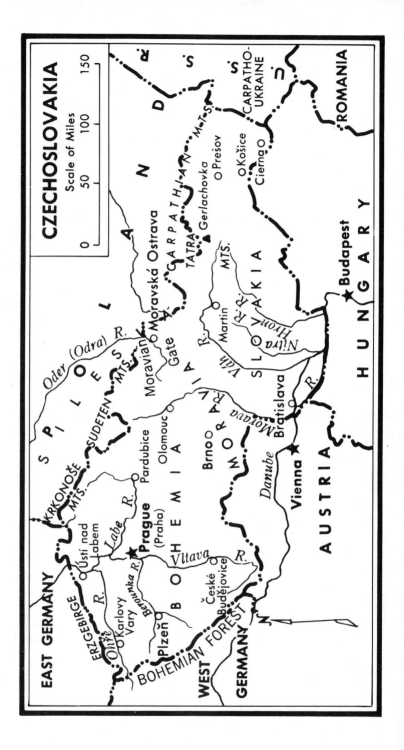

1

1948–1966:
The Roots of the Crisis

Every adult in Prague was a rumormonger in the early weeks of 1968, just after Alexander Dubcek had replaced Antonin Novotny as First Secretary of the Communist Party of Czechoslovakia. No longer afraid of the secret police and happy that old "Frozen Face" Novotny, still President at the time, was obviously on his way out, everyone in the old Bohemian capital seemed to have his own theory about the key element in the palace revolution just consummated. Five of these theories struck me as particularly interesting.

Most titillating was the view that the keystone of Novotny's downfall had been the love affair between Zdena Hendrych, daughter of the chief Party ideologist and Presidium member Jiri Hendrych, and the young writer Jan Benes. "You see," one man explained to me, "this silly girl told Benes everything her father told the family, and then stole secret documents from her father's files for him as well. Then Benes passed them on to somebody in the West. Of course the secret police traced it all finally and clamped down on the stupid wench. She was lucky not to go to jail along with Jan Benes. But her father couldn't believe his daughter had betrayed him and saw the whole thing as a Novotny scheme to frame him. So when the crisis came in the Presidium, he voted against Novotny. That made possible the five-to-five tie in the Presidium that forced the issue to the Central Committee, where the radicals took over and Novotny lost."

Another school of thought traced the dictator's downfall to the day in October, 1964, when he dared hang up his telephone while Leonid I. Brezhnev was talking to him from Moscow. "Novotny was angry about the removal of Khrushchev," an informant related. "He had gotten along well with the old man and was grateful to him for more than one favor. Besides, Novotny took it as a personal insult that he had had to learn about Khrushchev's fall from a news broadcast, and wasn't tipped off in advance. So when Brezhnev called up to explain things, Novotny was very annoyed and finally slammed down the receiver on him. The Russians don't forget such insults. Last December 8, when Brezhnev responded to Novotny's call for help and came here to look over the crisis, he didn't really mind the prospect of Novotny getting thrown out. Once he decided it was just a power struggle and anybody who succeeded the President would be just as reliable, he stopped worrying. That's the reason he said, 'This is your own affair. Settle it among yourselves,' and went home."

"It's all a Slovak plot," one Czech confided in me. "Sure, Novotny was an idiot and it's a good thing we're getting rid of him. But those hillbillies from Bratislava have been trying to get control of this country ever since the days of Masaryk. They're jealous that we Czechs are smarter, better educated, and richer than they are. They like to talk about Vlado Clementis and the other Slovak victims of the Stalinist period, but you don't hear them talking about Siroky, Bacilek, and the other Slovaks who trampled over everybody in the bad old days. And they're always complaining about being discriminated against, as though we Czechs haven't been bled for twenty years to give Slovakia much more than its fair share of money for investment and education. I don't remember that Dubcek was any great liberal during all the years he was boss in Slovakia. Now he's wormed his way into Novotny's job, the Slovaks will run this country and everything will go to hell. You just watch."

But a worried Slovak I met had just the opposite point of view: "Those slimy Czechs have trapped Dubcek. First they ruined the country and now, when the situation has become impossible, they give Dubcek the top job. You can bet that if they had thought things could be improved they would have put one of their own men in. They'll let Dubcek take the blame for everything that's wrong, and they'll go around saying, 'We told you so. Those Slovaks are simply incompetent.' "

Finally, a cab driver gave me what he claimed was the dominant opinion among ordinary workers. "The Jews have taken over again. Before the Nazis, the Jews controlled all the money and all the jobs here. When the Communists took over in 1948, the real boss was Slansky and his Zionist clique. Now they've made a comeback. Dubcek is just a dumb Slovak figurehead. Watch television and you'll see that Eduard Goldstuecker is on almost every night. He used to be ambassador to Israel, you know. Listen to the radio and you'll hear Milan Weiner trying to brainwash us. And now that Jew Ota Sik is going to run the economy."

*   *   *

On the morning of October 24, 1949, a handsome, vigorous man of 47 sat in his Manhattan office anxiously pondering an article near the bottom of the front page of that day's *New York Times*. Written from Paris by the newspaper's chief foreign correspondent, C. L. Sulzberger, the dispatch reported that the Communist government in Prague was thinking of purging Dr. Vladimir (Vlado) Clementis, its foreign minister, who was also the head of its delegation to the United Nations and the highest-ranking Slovak in the Czechoslovak Government. Dr. Clementis, the article added, was considered "somewhat too independent-minded" and too much of a "Slovak nationalist by his superiors." Suspicions were being voiced in Prague, Mr. Sulzberger reported, that Dr. Clementis had been cleared too easily by British intelligence in 1940 when he fled to London after the fall of France. After all, he was known to be a Communist, and a true Party member should have had more trouble with the British in those days when the Soviet Union was a great, good friend of Nazi Germany. The man reading the article, Dr. Clementis, understood all the implications of those words, for he was well acquainted with the history of Soviet purges and knew that a major one was going on in his own country at that very time. He knew, too, that his predecessor, Jan Masaryk, had met a violent death and that many people believed Masaryk had been thrown to his death from that window, rather than suicidally jumping as the official version claimed.

When a *Times* reporter called to ask for his reaction to the Sulzberger report, Dr. Clementis instructed his secretary to say that he was "not interested" in it. Since Dr. Clementis was a trained lawyer, skilled in several languages, and extremely intelligent, his noncommittal reaction actually spoke volumes. He did not, after all, deny the report, call it nonsense or a "bourgeois fabrication," or make any of the other standard responses open to him. The reason was simple: Clementis knew that there was more than enough in his record to hang him if his enemies in Prague got the upper hand. Merely the fact that he had denounced the Stalin-Hitler Pact of 1939 at the time, he must have known, would provide sufficient material for the Stalinist witch hunters in Eastern Europe, who then were busily sniffing out "Titoist traitors."

So Clementis dallied at his post in New York, finding one reason or another not to return home. Finally, President Klement Gottwald sent Mrs. Clementis as his envoy to Manhattan. She brought a message that Sulzberger's and similar reports were tricks of the capitalist intelligence agencies and that her husband and their family had nothing to fear. So Clementis returned home.

Then on March 14, 1950, it was officially announced that Clementis had resigned as foreign minister "at his own request." Two months later, his successor, also a Slovak, Foreign Minister Viliam Siroky made a speech accusing Clementis of "bourgeois nationalist deviationism." Siroky revealed that Clementis' self-criticism had not been accepted because he "still did not understand the gravity of his mistakes and shortcomings." Clementis, Siroky added, was also a "class enemy" and was not alone in his misdeeds. An entire group of Slovak intellectuals was involved, notably two men recently deposed from their key jobs in Slovakia: Gustav Husak, chairman of the semi-autonomous Slovak government structure, and Ladislav (Laco) Novomesky, Slovakia's Commissioner for Education. Early in 1951, Clementis was arrested. He was never a free man again.

Clementis' downfall undoubtedly gave pleasure at the time to the Czechoslovak Communist Party's Secretary General, Rudolph Slansky. Second in public stature only to President Klement Gottwald, Slansky had gone far since joining the Party in his late teens, some three decades earlier. A thin, intense man, he basked in the reputation of being Moscow's most devoted servant in Prague. He had been one of the founding members of the Cominform in the fall of 1947 and had delivered the chief Prague eulogy to Stalin on the latter's seventieth birthday in December, 1949. His cup seemed full in the summer of 1951, when, six months after Clementis' jailing, he celebrated his fiftieth birthday. He received the Order of Socialism and a telegram of congratulations from the Party's Central Committee. Czechoslovakia's Minister of Information wrote a highly laudatory article hailing Slansky as "a close and faithful collaborator of Klement Gottwald." Two weeks later, the workers of a major airplane factory voted to rename their plant the Rudolf Slansky Aircraft Works because they "wished thus to express their gratitude and love to Comrade Slansky." But Slansky was a Jew in a country where anti-Semitism is hardly unknown, and in 1948, it is said, he had tried to challenge Gottwald, going so far as to criticize the latter for waiting until 1948 to seize power rather than doing so in 1945.

The first shadow over Slansky's future came, ironically, on that same fiftieth birthday. In Moscow, strangely and ominously, the Soviet press ignored the anniversary. The shadow darkened on September 6, when, without any advance warning, Slansky was removed as Secretary General. There were accusations that he had made mistakes in picking Party officials and had interfered in Government policy. At first it seemed that he had only suffered a demotion. He was named a Deputy Premier, and his name was publicly listed fourth in the Party hierarchy, rather than second as earlier. In November, 1951, the state publishers issued his collected works under the title *For the Victory of Socialism*. *Rude Pravo*, the Party newspaper, hailed these writings as "a further important help for studying the history of our Party and for improving the ideological level of Party members."

Less than two weeks later, however, Deputy Premier and Communist Party Secretary Rudolf Slansky was arrested. The official communiqué asserted that "hitherto unknown circumstances have recently been established which prove that Rudolf Slansky has been guilty of many anti-state activities." Now Slansky and Clementis were prisoners together.

A year later, in November, 1952, Slansky, Clementis, and twelve other defendants—all former high officials of the Party or the Government—were placed on trial. All the accused pleaded guilty and confessed at length to being traitors, Titoists, spies for the United States and, in the case of the eleven defendants who were Jews, agents for international Zionism. In his testimony, Slansky woodenly declared, "I was never a true Communist," and said that at the height of his power he had given key jobs to "capitalist Jewish emigrants who had returned to Czechoslovakia as imperialist agents." From murder to economic sabotage to treason—there was almost no crime that the accused did not claim to have committed. Another defendant, former Deputy Foreign Minister Arthur London, asserted he had assigned Trotskyites as Czechoslovak diplomats in Moscow and other Eastern European capitals and had then used the Czechoslovak diplomatic pouch to send espionage materials to the British left-wing Labor Party parliamentarian Konni Zilliacus, who allegedly was a key man in the spy ring. Another defendant, Andrei Simon—originally named Katz—declared in his peroration: "In what countries do anti-Semitism and Nazism flourish? In the United States and Britain. In what country are there laws against anti-Semitism and Nazism? In the Soviet Union. And I worked for the spy services of the United States and Britain against the Soviet Union. I belong on the gallows and deserve the highest punishment."

Every effort was made to squeeze the maximum propaganda value out of the trials, both within Czechoslovakia and abroad; even the defendants' families were pressed into service. Mr. London's wife assailed her husband as "a traitor to his Party and his country." She was happy, she said, that "the treacherous gang has been unmasked and rendered harmless," and she appealed "for a just punishment for the traitors." The son of Ludvik Frejka, another Jewish defendant, wrote a widely publicized letter to the trial judge:

Dear comrade, I ask the heaviest penalty, the penalty of death for my father. Only now do I see that this creature, whom one cannot call a man because he did not have the slightest feeling of human dignity, was my greatest and vilest enemy. . . . Hatred toward my father will always strengthen me in my struggle for the Communist future of our people. I request that this letter be placed before my father and that, if the occasion permits, I may tell him all this myself.

While the trial was under way, in meetings held all over Czechoslovakia—in factories, schools, and elsewhere—demands for the death penalty for the defendants were made. Predictably, these demands were granted. Slansky, Clementis, and nine of their fellow defendants were sentenced to death and, on the morning of December 3, 1952, were hanged in Prague's Pankrac Prison. The other three accused men—London, former Deputy Foreign Minister Vavro Hajdu, and former Deputy Foreign Trade Minister Eugen Loebl—were sentenced to life imprisonment. The greatest purge trial since Andrei Vyshinsky's performances in Moscow in the mid-1930's was over. Every Czech and Slovak got the point: If such high-ranking Party and Government officials could be destroyed, no one who incurred the regime's displeasure was safe. An entire nation was terrified and remained so for many years.

Sixteen years later, in mid-1968, Eugen Loebl described how his confession had been obtained. He had been arrested in January, 1949, and was not amnestied until May, 1960. Of his eleven years in jail, five had been spent in solitary confinement. From 1960 to 1963, he had worked as a warehouse clerk, but in 1963 he was rehabilitated and made Director of the Bratislava branch of the Czechoslovak State Bank. Here is an extract of his description of the jail regimen that produced his confession:

I had to stand during the examinations and I was not allowed to sit down in the cell. The interrogations lasted on the average

sixteen hours a day; there was an interval of two hours . . .
[when he went to sleep]. Every ten minutes the warder pounded
on the door, and I had to jump to attention and report.
"Detainee number fourteen seventy three reports: strength one
detainee, everything in order." Naturally, the first two or three
nights I could not fall asleep again after the first awakening.
Later I was so tired that as soon as I lay down after making the
report I fell asleep. I was awakened thirty or forty times every
night. Sometimes when the loud bangs on the door did not
wake me, the warder came into the cell and kicked me. Another instrument was hunger. . . . The combination of linger-
ing hunger, of constantly disturbed sleep, of standing up the
whole day, and walking in hard leather slippers—all this was
unspeakable torture. After two or three weeks my feet were
swollen; every inch of my body ached at the slightest touch.
Washing became a torture; every step was concentrated pain.
The interrogation—three officials alternated—was a never-end-
ing stream of abuse, humiliation, and threats. Sometimes I had
to stand a whole day with my face to the wall. My nerves were
worn ragged by the constant repetition of the same questions.

Nothing was publicly known then of this and other besti-
alities that produced the "confessions" on which the outcome of the Slansky-Clementis trial was justified. On the
contrary, at that time, to have participated in the arrangements for this purge was considered a mark of great political
merit. It was natural, then, for the Minister of National Security, Karol Bacilek, to praise publicly those allotted the
greatest political credit for the affair. He wrote in *Rude
Pravo* on December 18, 1952:

Without the great assistance of Comrades Gottwald, Zapotocky,
Dolansky, Kopecky and most of all, of Comrade Novotny
[later Party First Secretary and President of Czechoslovakia]
. . . we would not have succeeded in clarifying in such a short
time many well-camouflaged problems or in securing a successful outcome of the investigation. Further, . . . Comrade Siroky

[later Premier] himself personally helped to evaluate the materials.

Trials of smaller fry followed in the same pattern during 1953 and 1954. Husak, Novomesky, Goldstuecker, and others confessed on schedule, but they were lucky and received prison sentences only. Like Loebl, they lived to play new roles in the latest chapter of their country's history.

All the confessions were fantasy, of course, and all the convicted men innocent. Only in 1968 did the world finally learn why the trials had taken place. Anastas Mikoyan came to Prague in 1951, a former secret police chief recalled seventeen years afterward, and "complained that, while Poland and Hungary were then staging trials against 'Titoist' elements, there were no such trials in Czechoslovakia, although the center of Titoism was supposed to have been here." The same witness claimed that Gottwald at first opposed the idea of trials but surrendered when Mikoyan phoned Stalin and was told that Prague too must have its trials.

Even in 1952 it was evident that one man in Prague benefited mightily from Slansky's downfall. Antonin Novotny was a poorly educated former mechanic who had earlier risen relatively slowly in the Party hierarchy. Novotny succeeded to Slansky's posts in the Party Secretariat and Presidium in 1951. Bacilek's words quoted above suggest strongly that Novotny was rewarded for his services in helping fabricate the judicial lynching of Slansky, Clementis, and their co-defendants.

Cold in personal relationships and the antithesis of an intellectual, Novotny was above all a man of the Party apparatus, skilled in manipulating others through the Party machine. When Gottwald died unexpectedly early in 1953, Novotny became boss of the Party bureaucracy and, therefore, of the entire country. Four years later, he added the title of President to his name, making his primacy plain to all. His very dullness must have made him particularly attractive to Moscow; he was a plodder who would take orders and obey them, not a flashy, charismatic figure who might develop real popular support and begin harboring dangerous ideas of independence.

The trials of 1952–54 were merely the visible tips of the Stalinist icebergs that chilled and terrorized Czechoslovakia in the years after the 1948 Communist take over. Tens of thousands of obscure figures were sent to jail for real or imagined political opposition. All opposition parties were destroyed and replaced by a group of puppet parties retained to give the illusion that the Communists did not have a monopoly of all power. Czechoslovakia's economic and cultural ties with the West were severed, and the Iron Curtain descended. Schools, newspapers, theaters, films, radio, and television were turned into propaganda media on the Soviet model. Libraries were purged, and millions of books with dangerous "bourgeois" ideas were converted to pulp. A network of secret police informers, covering every street and every apartment house, kept the populace under constant, vigilant surveillance. Czechoslovakia was the last of the Eastern European countries to fall under Communist rule, but its masters sought to make up for lost time by the thoroughness, speed, and fidelity with which they reproduced Stalin's Soviet patterns.

The arrests and trials of the late 1940's and early 1950's were designed to terrorize the population and prevent any organized action against the regime. Genuine anti-Communists were the first victims after February, 1948, but then the hunt was directed at "potential enemies," including numerous members of the Communist Party. Among the favorite victims were Jews, partisans who had fought the Germans in Czechoslovakia during World War II, soldiers who had fought with Western forces, and even those who had fought with the Soviet armies in the last years of the war.

Perhaps most ironic was the fate of Ludvik Svoboda. An obscure refugee lieutenant colonel who had fled Hitler's take over of Prague, he was picked by the Russians in the early 1940's to head the Czechoslovak forces formed in the Soviet Union. Svoboda's troops fought alongside the Red Army in the Ukraine, where he got to know Nikita Khrushchev. After the war, he became the "non-Party" defense minister under President Eduard Benes and, by keeping his troops idle, gave passive assent to the 1948 coup that resulted in the Communist Party's seizure of power. However, in the early 1950's he, too, was imprisoned, despite his numerous Soviet decorations and his past contributions. Released, he became a bookkeeper on a collective farm until one day Nikita Khrushchev, visiting Prague, expressed a wish to see his "old friend Svoboda." After a frantic search Svoboda finally was found and presented to the visitor from Moscow. Rehabilitation occurred instantly, of course, and after Khrushchev left, Svoboda became head of a military academy. Most other victims did not have such an influential friend, so their sufferings had no such happy ending.

The Sovietization of Czechoslovakia's economy was thorough and ultimately disastrous. A major structural transformation was carried out in the classic Stalinist fashion. By 1960, as a result, it could be argued that Czechoslovakia was closer to Moscow's heavy industry ideal than the Soviet Union was itself. In that year, the share of Czechoslovakia's total output devoted to consumption was down to little more than 40 per cent, a level of Spartan austerity greater than the Soviet Union's at the time. Before World War II, Czechoslovakia had been famous for its consumer goods, its glassware, ceramics, textiles, and its shoes. The Communists cut -these "useless" industries back sharply and lavished investment on steel, machinery, and chemical plants—the underpinning for Czechoslovakia's important armaments industry. In effect, Czechoslovakia became a processing appendage of the Soviet economy, receiving from Moscow iron ore, petroleum, and other raw materials and sending back to the Soviet Union and the rest of Eastern Europe heavy machinery and other manufactured goods.

What made all this bearable for some years was the fact that Czechoslovakia had started out as the wealthiest of the Kremlin's Eastern European colonies. Moreover, it had suffered relatively little destruction during World War II. The country had an important layer of fat, which cushioned the impact of policies that increasingly emphasized investment at the expense of consumption and that also made Czechoslovakia a milch cow to be exploited for the benefit of Indonesia, Ghana, Egypt, Cuba, and the other underdeveloped countries Moscow wooed. An important additional cushion was provided by the property of the expropriated middle and upper classes, whose houses, furniture, and other belongings were divided up, in effect, by the rest of Czechoslovak society. Finally, Prague's economic policies carried an egalitarian bias, tending to raise the wages of the poorest-paid workers while sharply restricting increases for the better-paid groups. There was a great semi-equalization of living standards that benefited the formerly disadvantaged, but it steadily reduced incentives for large numbers of skilled workers. The result was a tendency to relax and try to get by with a minimum of effort. The tendency was summarized in the popular saying that socialism had some disadvantages, but it was better than having to go to work. All this was bearable in the 1950's because Czechoslovakia was largely cut off from the West. Nevertheless, there was much grumbling under the surface, and, in mid-1953, this erupted into protest demonstrations, but these were put down quickly.

In 1956, a series of major shocks rocked Eastern European Communist rule. They began with Khrushchev's denunciation of Stalin in February and ended with the Hungarian Revolution in October and November. Eastern Europeans

paid bitter tribute to the solidity of the Prague power structure when they said that in 1956 the Hungarians had behaved like Poles, the Poles like Czechs, and the Czechs like
dogs. Put another way, Czechoslovakia's stolid political sta-
bility in 1956 kept Poland and Hungary separated and
helped keep Warsaw from exploding while Moscow put out
the flames in Budapest with minimal difficulty and risk of
contagion northward.

Prague did not escape all tremors in 1956, of course, but
Party boss Novotny, Premier Siroky, and their colleagues
were able to get by with a few verbal self-criticisms and mild
confessions of error. Novotny, for example, admitted there
had been a mistaken "atmosphere of untouchability around
Comrade Gottwald" and a deplorable "propagation of the
idea 'Gottwald thinks for us.'" Premier Siroky declared that
there had been "certain manifestations of anti-Semitism" in
the Slansky trial, and he regretted that the "secondary issue"
of Titoism (by 1956, Khrushchev had already publicly apologized to Tito and admitted that the Yugoslavs were innocent of the charges of treason leveled against them earlier
in the 1950's) had been introduced into the trial. Some of the
defendants in the earlier trials—Novomesky and London, for
example—had been released, the Premier revealed. But
Slansky and Clementis had been guilty as charged of being
foreign agents, and their convictions had been justified.
Rude Pravo, the Party organ, fell into line by admitting that
Czechoslovak security police had been guilty of "breaches of
Socialist legality," of using "illegal methods" to get confessions, and that hundreds or possibly thousands of persons had
suffered. But it was all Rudolf Slansky's fault, the newspaper
assured its readers, and only during his period of power had
such awful things happened. Novotny himself assured the
nation that "I personally was not at that time a member of
the highest Party leadership."

This obvious lack of high-level enthusiasm for probing

the past too deeply helped give the whole operation an aseptic atmosphere calculated to produce minimal repercussions. But since at least one scapegoat was necessary, Novotny settled on Gottwald's son-in-law, the then First Deputy Premier and Minister of Defense, Alexei Cepicka. So the whole matter was tidily and neatly taken care of.

Some of Czechoslovakia's writers showed more sense of personal guilt, admitting they had sacrificed the truth to "agree with the official line" and complained that "supervisory committees rode herd" on their writings. One of the few who seemed willing to articulate the enormity of what had happened was the novelist Ladislav Mnacko. He spoke openly of the police dossiers with their detailed information on every citizen and suggested that these materials be burned in town squares to the sound of "happy merriment." He referred publicly to the fiasco of a huge iron and steel combine planned for Slovakia but then abandoned despite a tremendous capital investment. He referred also to the jailing of innocent people as scapegoats for the blunder. Mnacko appealed to his country's journalists: "You are the public conscience. You are the public's control. Do not dare to treat truth as deplorably as you once did."

Nothing came of this feeble beginning. The Hungarian Revolution showed the dangers of washing too much dirty laundry in public, and Khrushchev even spoke kindly of Stalin, a signal to go slow in raking up the crimes of the past. In Moscow, Stalin's mummy remained next to Lenin's in the Red Square mausoleum; in Prague, Stalin's statue continued to tower over the city; and in all Czechoslovakia, censors, secret police, and informers continued to work as usual.

*   *   *

Journalists reporting on Communist nations know that one of the barometers of the situation in a particular country at a given time is the willingness of its cab drivers to talk politics with their passengers. By that criterion, Prague, when I visited there in mid-1962, was one of the most fear-ridden cities I have ever seen. It was not unusual for a driver to draw a finger across his throat when I tried to learn his views. Some asked me indignantly if I were a *provocateur* trying to send them to jail.

A similar atmosphere then reigned in the American Embassy in Prague, where officials refused to exchange anything but commonplaces until they had taken me to a special room protected by esoteric electronic devices against the microphones that were believed to be everywhere else in the building. Once they could speak freely, the attachés concentrated on one question: "Why don't you correspondents tell the West that this is the most Stalinist country in Eastern Europe? The situation is worse here than in Moscow." They professed to see no hope or signs of change for the better, but a Labor M.P. from London I met then was better informed. Over cocktails in the lounge of the Alcron Hotel—a hostelry famed for the sensitivity of the microphones in the rooms of the correspondents who live there—he boasted that this was his tenth or twelfth visit to Prague as a member of a British peace delegation. He now had many important friends in the city, he confided, and they had told him that Novotny was on his way out. "There's a new generation getting top jobs around here," the Englishman concluded, "and they're not going to leave these Stalinists in power much longer."

My British friend was on the right track. In 1962 and 1963, Novotny had to repel the most powerful challenge to his rule since he had succeeded Gottwald a decade earlier. Not inappropriately, the first public indication that something was happening behind the scenes came in October, 1962, when the huge statue of Stalin was pulled down from its hill-top perch. Yet it was symptomatic of Czechoslovakia's Stalinist backwardness, even as compared with the Soviet Union, that the statue did not come down until a full year after the Twenty-second Congress of the Communist Party of the Soviet Union, in Moscow, in October, 1961, had voted to remove Stalin's remains from the Red Square mausoleum.

The Twenty-second Party Congress was the immediate source of Novotny's troubles because it revived the whole issue of Stalinist despotism and the need to complete the rectification of past injustices. Precisely because so little had been done along these lines in Czechoslovakia in 1956, Novotny was the most vulnerable of the Eastern European rulers before the onslaught of those who wanted radical changes. And, in Czechoslovakia, it soon became clear, there were many with such desires.

One reason for change was the deteriorating economic situation in 1962 and 1963. The outward sign of this during my visit to Prague was the long lines in front of butcher shops. But more than a shortage of meat was involved. The penalty was being paid for mistakes made over many years of centralized, Soviet-style economic planning, a reckoning hastened by unusually bad weather and other chance factors. In effect, during 1962 and 1963, Czechoslovakia suffered the Communist equivalent of a Western depression. Production of key commodities declined; the standard of living fell; and all over Czechoslovakia people were beginning to ask what had gone wrong and what needed to be changed.

There was also pressure from increasing contact with the West, its ideas, and its wealth. By the early 1960's, Czechoslovakia, following the Soviet example, was annually admitting tens of thousands of Western tourists and letting thousands of Czechs and Slovaks visit Western Europe. With the increasing exchange of people came increasing demand for access to Western books, magazines, newspapers, and ideas. The regime began to retreat, slowly but surely. In this changing situation, Eduard Goldstuecker (sent to jail early in the 1950's as a co-conspirator of Slansky but by the early 1960's freed and working as a professor of German literature at the Charles University) was able to fight for and win the battle to have Franz Kafka's writings legalized and published in Kafka's native land. It was indicative of the improving atmosphere that in February, 1963, Goldstuecker was able to demand publicly in Prague's *Literarni Noviny* that Czechoslovakia

> . . . must fulfill one very important condition: to see to it that even the weirdest imagination could not apply any of Kafka's visions of bureaucratic chicaneries and cruelties to our public affairs. If the history of our time has proved something beyond a shadow of doubt, it is that it was fatally wrong to believe that a new and higher social order could be created without the benefit of humanism and justice and that great human achievements in any field could be indefinitely loudly advocated in theory, while being trampled upon in fact.

The deeper meaning of Goldstuecker's words must have been apparent to the great majority of his original readers, who knew that nine years earlier he had been sent to prison after "confessing" that he was a traitor and a spy.

From Slovakia came the greatest pressure on Novotny, as well as the most passionate demands for change and for full public admission and rectification of the injustices of the 1950's. The Slovak element in the entire story is so important that a brief digression seems justified here.

*   *   *

The Czechs and Slovaks are closely related in origin. Both groups are Western Slavs, and their languages, though different, are sufficiently similar so that each group can understand the other. The division between them is historical. For a thousand years, until World War I, the Slovaks were a peasant people living under Hungarian rule and under pressure to become Hungarians. Their modern sense of national identity and their codified literary language are products of the nineteenth century. There are 4 million Slovaks and almost 10 million Czechs, but until comparatively recently Slovakia had relatively few trained, competent teachers, doctors, scientists, engineers, and skilled industrial workers. During the millennium before World War I, Czech culture developed in close association with German culture. Roughly 550 years ago, Jan Hus, a Czech, pioneered the revolt against medieval Catholicism, and the valor of his followers, the Hussites, became legendary throughout Europe. The great majority of Slovaks has traditionally been devoutly Catholic. For a time, the Czechs were predominantly Protestant. Although most were reconverted to Catholicism in the seventeenth century, Czech Catholicism has never been like the burning faith of the Slovaks. In the Austro-Hungarian Empire, the Czechs were often the petty bureaucrats and the railroad conductors, as well as the possessors of a well-developed bourgeoisie and intelligentsia.

When Thomas Masaryk—with Woodrow Wilson's help—merged these two related peoples, both Czechs and Slovaks were acutely conscious of their differences. It was almost as though the United States was being formed today by combining an all-white nation with a Negro nation. The Slovaks—some of whom I've heard refer to themselves disparagingly as "white niggers"—feared from the start that they would be dominated and forced to assimilate by the culturally and numerically superior Czechs. In the 1920's and 1930's, many Slovaks believed they were discriminated against by the dominant Czechs and denied full autonomy. Hitler skilfully used this antagonism to help him destroy Czechoslovakia in the late 1930's, replacing it with a puppet Slovak national state, which won formal recognition from many countries, and a Czech "protectorate" ruled directly from Berlin.

Initially, during and after World War II, Czechoslovakia's Communists catered to Slovak nationalism, seeking supporters in Slovakia by making extravagant promises of national

autonomy and independence. But once Gottwald had assumed undisputed control he—and Novotny after him—
steadily centralized more and more power in Prague. The
earlier promises were forgotten, and the formal institutions
of Slovak home rule became ever weaker. As they did, Slovak
resentment rose. Nor were the Slovaks placated by the real
efforts Prague made to industrialize Slovakia and raise its
educational level. They felt these efforts were inadequate,
especially since the economic and cultural gulf between Slovaks and Czechs remained wide. Moreover, many Slovaks felt
that their representatives at the highest levels of the Communist Party and the state were really traitors—Slovak Uncle
Toms, so to speak—who had sold out to the Czechs. The
chief targets of this criticism in the late 1950's and early
1960's were Premier Viliam Siroky and Slovak Communist
Party boss Karol Bacilek. This feeling was stronger against
Bacilek because he had been born and raised a Czech and
had adopted Slovak nationality only as an adult.

To many of the rebellious Slovaks in the early 1960's
the dead Vlado Clementis and the freed, but still not rehabilitated, Gustav Husak and Laco Novemesky were heroes
precisely because they had been punished for Slovak nationalism. Full exoneration of these men—and explicit, complete repudiation of the trials of 1952–54—was a burning
Slovak political demand. At the Congress of the Czechoslovak Communist Party late in 1962, the Slovaks, with the
support of Czech liberals, pressed for and won creation of
an official Party commission to study the trials of the early
1950's and report on their validity. It was a major victory.
Its consequences produced major political turmoil throughout 1963 and almost brought down Novotny then.

The first hint of the political repercussions of the investigation came on March 7, 1963. An official announcement
declared that the President of Czechoslovakia's Supreme
Court, Dr. Josef Urvalek, had resigned for "reasons of

health" and would devote himself to research on legal problems of the judiciary. A decade earlier, Urvalek had been the Vyshinsky of the Slansky-Clementis trial, the chief prosecutor who had abused and ridiculed the luckless defendants, and had called for the death sentences that destroyed eleven of the fourteen accused.

An even bigger surprise came the following month. The Slovak Communist Party met, removed its First Secretary, Karol Bacilek, and named in his place an obscure young *apparatchik*, Alexander Dubcek. Few outside of Slovakia knew much about Dubcek then, but one point was clear: He was a young man in his early forties and thus had had nothing to do with the trials of 1952–54; his hands were clean.

Even as these personnel changes began, Slovak intellectuals initiated a literary cannonade against Novotny and his collaborators. The Slovak Writers Union made its weekly, *Kulturny Zivot,* into a dissident political organ, which turned a spotlight on all the many festering sores in the nation's life. It assailed the "cult of the plan" and the mismanagement of the national economy. On the pretext of examining political liberalization in Hungary, it hinted that Czechoslovakia needed a similar wave of reform. Under the cover of refuting dogmatists in Poland, it demolished many ideas defended by Novotny. It explored the continuing impact of the personality cult in different areas and, in one article, charged that a "barracks" form of collective life had developed in Czechoslovakia. Whether exposing the shockingly low level of university education or the disregard for the alarming pollution of Czechoslovakia's rivers, it hammered home the message that callous incompetents were at the helm of the nation.

In this same spirit, the Union of Slovak Writers turned the readmission to its ranks of Laco Novomesky, in April, 1963, into a political demonstration against the injustices and lies of the past. Novomesky himself, in his speech of thanks, stressed that his own rehabilitation could not end the fight against a system that had victimized many thousands. Speaking to a group that included many whose writings had lied in the past, Novomesky warned that only by writing the truth could Slovak intellectuals regain the trust and confidence of their audience.

Novomesky's appeal for the truth was answered the very next month when the Slovak Journalists Congress produced the most sensational explosion yet in this insurrection of Slovak intellectuals. This was a speech by Miro Hysko pointing directly, explicitly, and by name at Premier Siroky as the man who had begun, inspired, and directed the entire criminal campaign against Slovak nationalism that had claimed the innocent Clementis' life. Hysko did not stop with Siroky. He spoke also about "the shameful role played in this by our press and by ourselves as journalists." Perhaps most remarkable was his conclusion, a demand that Czechoslovak journalists stop being the mindless puppets of the Communist Party, which told them how and what to write. Instead, he urged, "the socialist journalist should respect only directions which are not in conflict with the fundamental principles of socialist morality." This was heresy.

In an earlier period, Novotny and Siroky could have shut off such subversive ideas by a simple order to the censor. But now they and their supporters had to debate rather than command, and much evidence soon accumulated that among the intelligentsia, at least, the dissidents enjoyed the most sympathy. In view of later developments, it is interesting that most of this 1963 offensive of the Slovak rebels occurred after Alexander Dubcek took command of Slovakia's Communist Party. Publicly, Dubcek deplored the extremes to which the dissidents were going. About Hysko's speech Dubcek complained that the speaker "could have written his position to the Party Central Committee. Did he need the Congress of Slovak Journalists to express his opinions?"

This was soft criticism compared to what more enthusiastic supporters of Novotny and Siroky were saying. Even then it occurred to some foreign observers that it was strange the new Slovak Party chief was not doing more to silence these dangerous voices. The question was asked by some whether Dubcek was Janus-faced, trying to keep in Prague's good graces while *sotto voce* encouraging the heretics. Certainly, Dubcek stopped much short of the position taken by another Slovak Party Secretary, Vasil Bilak, who demanded that the press follow the Party line or take the consequences. If newspapers and magazines "persevere in expressing incorrect views," Bilak wrote, "then administrative intervention is necessary in the interest of the author and of the press itself. The press does not and cannot replace the Party, nor can it assume the Party's tasks because it is its instrument. Whoever loses sight of this basic principle excludes himself from the family of socialist journalists."

While the war of words continued, dramatic political developments gave evidence that the Novotny forces were being forced into retreat after retreat. In June, 1963, Dubcek told a Party gathering in Bratislava that Clementis, Husak, Novak, and others of that group had been illegally convicted and that those who remained alive were being re-admitted to the Communist Party. Two months later, Rudolf Slansky was declared juridically innocent of the crimes for which he had been convicted and executed, though his memory was denied political rehabilitation. The whole fabric of the great 1952 purge trial had been repudiated, after years during which Novotny and his entourage had persistently denied any need for such a reversal. Who would pay the political price for this blunder? The answer came a month later, in September, when the hated Siroky lost his post as Premier. In his place, Novotny installed the 40-year-old Jozef Lenart, a young Slovak whose hands—like Dubcek's —were free of any complicity in the frame-up of 1952. By sacrificing his closest collaborator of many years, Novotny hoped to save himself. The maneuver worked—for four years and four months.

Even the sacrifice of Siroky might not have saved Novotny if other factors had not contributed as well. It is perhaps more than coincidence that the President suffered his greatest political weakness in mid-1963, when the economic situation was at its worst, when the regime had to order "meatless Thursdays" to help cope with food shortages. But in 1964 and 1965, the economic situation had improved. During 1963–64, too, Khrushchev made very plain that he supported Novotny. In gratitude for that aid and out of fear of what the Brezhnev-Kosygin group might do, Novotny made public his unhappiness after Khrushchev was purged in October, 1964. Most important, perhaps, Novotny reached a modus vivendi with the intellectuals. The censors became more tolerant in considering material bordering on ideological heresy. The boundaries for permissible experimentation by writers, artists, and musicians were expanded, as were opportunities to go abroad, to see the West, and to exchange ideas with Western intellectuals. Tensions continued, of course. There were cases in the mid-1960's of individual films and books being banned, and there was much resentment early in 1966 when the literary magazine *Tvar* was forced to discontinue publication. However, until mid-1967, the regime avoided any major confrontation with the writers, and relatively free expression remained the rule.

An unexpected by-product of this new atmosphere was the impact on the young. Western rock 'n' roll, under the name of the Big Beat, took young Czechoslovakia by storm, complete with native singers and combos. By 1964, an officially sponsored International Jazz Festival was held in Prague, even though Moscow frowned on such "bourgeois" music.

Prague also became the beatnik and hippy capital of Eastern Europe, and the sight of young people flaunting their alienation by wearing *Texasski* (blue jeans), sandals, and bizarre hair styles became common in the city streets. The new trends sweeping the younger generation became vividly evident on May 1, 1965, when American poet Allen Ginsberg was elected *Kraj Majales* (King of the May Day Festival) and, for his coronation address, chanted a Buddhist hymn, accompanying himself with small cymbals. The regime deported Ginsberg a few days later, but not before he had had the opportunity to address numerous groups of young people on his ideas about the sexual revolution and the need to expand consciousness. Nothing comparable to the way Ginsberg took Prague's youth by storm had ever happened before in a Socialist nation loyal to conservative, puritanical Moscow.

The new atmosphere was most evident in the eruption of artistic brilliance that won international attention in the early and mid-1960's. By early 1967, British drama critic Kenneth Tynan hailed Prague as "the theatre capital of Europe," while the film world was shouting the praises of such remarkable Czechoslovak films as *The Shop on Main Street, Loves of a Blonde, Closely Watched Trains,* and *The Fifth Horseman Is Fear.* Dramatist Vaclav Havel and film directors Jiri Menzel, Milos Forman, and Jan Nemec suddenly became figures of world importance in their professions. International fame in varying degrees came also to other Prague institutions: to Jan Grossman's Balustrade Theater; to the Semafor, a theater of musical satire whose presiding geniuses were Jiri Suchy and Jiri Slitr; to the Viola Cafe, which advertised "wine and poesy"; and to the Laterna Magica, with its ingenious combination of filmed and live actors. After almost two decades of being regarded as a cultural desert, Prague was transformed in a few years into one of the capitals of avant-garde culture. The enormous success of Czechoslovakia's pavilion at Expo '67 simply proved that the nation's creative talent appealed to the masses as well as to the more finicky tastes of the international cultural elite.

Indicative of how much ideological censorship was eased in 1963 and the years immediately following was the fact that Vaclav Havel's two major plays, *The Garden Party* and *The Memorandum,* were produced and performed before appreciative Prague audiences. Both were examples of the theater of the absurd, but no censor could have been so obtuse as to miss the fact that the barbed satirical shafts were aimed at targets within Czechoslovakia. *The Garden Party* (1963) is an allegory about the conflict between the Stalinist "Union of Organizers" and the anti-Stalinist "Commission of Liquidators," ridiculing both groups of bureaucrats, whom the author depicts as cliché-spouting windbags. There is even a Khrushchev-like figure who tosses off synthetic folk sayings such as "He who argues with a mosquito net will never dance with a goat near Podmokly." The author's thinly veiled point is that there is no hope in either group of Communist politicians, the old dogmatists or the new revisionists. In *The Memorandum,* the rulers of a huge bureaucracy impose an artificial language, Ptydepe, on their subordinates and thus paralyze and prevent original thinking. Few could miss the analogy with the Marxist-Leninist jargon the Communists had imposed on Czechoslovakia.

An anti-Stalinist literature also appeared during this period of thaw, though it had far less impact on the outside world than the drama had. The most important of the new books, the extremely popular *Belated Reportages* of Ladislav Mnacko, recounted the sufferings and trials of loyal Communists during the darkest years of the 1950's; Ladislav Bublik's novel *The Spine* related the ordeal of a purge victim. Neither of these books, nor any of the others in this genre, approached the artistic merit of Soviet writer Alexander Solzhenitsyn's novel *One Day in the Life of Ivan Denisovich,* but they broke the old taboos and did much to educate the mass of Czechs and Slovaks about the horrors that had taken place in their country a mere decade earlier.

The heyday of the regime's truce with the writers and artists was in 1963 and 1964; the atmosphere tended to get colder in the years afterward. But never during the rest of Novotny's reign did conditions again resemble what had been the norm of the 1950's, nor was any immediate attempt made after 1965 to match the Soviet retrogression, which silenced Solzhenitsyn and sent Andrei Sinyavsky, Yuli Daniel, and other writers to jail. The thaw in Prague elevated the status of the nation's intellectuals at home and abroad, winning them confidence, trust, and prestige that were to have important consequences later.

The Novotny regime showed greater humility and flexibility during the first half of the 1960's because of economic setbacks as well as political difficulties. As the 1950's ended, Prague's rulers entertained very high hopes for rapid economic expansion in the years immediately ahead. *Pravda* (the Bratislava organ of the Slovak Communist Party) reflected those hopes when it reported on January 3, 1960, that by 1965 "Czechoslovakia will be far ahead of the United States, Great Britain, the German Federal Republic, and France. She will be a model for these states, not to speak of other capitalist countries, insofar as living standards are concerned." Reality soon mocked these expectations. Stagnation, not rapid growth, was the key characteristic of the Czechoslovak economy in the first half of the 1960's. This bitterly disappointed the Novotny leadership, encouraging critical scrutiny of what was wrong and prompting greater willingness to consider even radical reform proposals. Prague's readiness to ponder such ideas reflected also the fact that in Moscow Nikita Khrushchev and, after his political demise, Leonid I. Brezhnev and Aleksei Kosygin were evidently encouraging a Soviet economic reformer, Yevsei G. Liberman.

Czechoslovakia's economic troubles in this period had two main sources. First, the country's industrial plant was grossly maladjusted in terms of its markets at home and abroad. Stalin had conceived of Czechoslovakia as a great arsenal of Soviet socialism that would supply weapons and machines for the less-developed countries of Eastern Europe, for the Soviet Union, and for the underdeveloped nations. In time, however, many of Czechoslovakia's customers in Eastern Europe also industrialized and reduced their orders for Prague's wares. Even worse, there were increasingly frequent complaints about the poor quality and technological obsolescence of Czechoslovak equipment. Rumania was the most vocal critic, but throughout Eastern Europe the feeling grew that Prague's wares were more expensive and of poorer quality than competitive merchandise available from the West. Only the Soviet Union's willingness to buy Czechoslovakia's excess output saved the day, because Moscow paid with oil, iron ore, and nonferrous metals, without which the Czechoslovak economy could not have functioned. From the giant neighbor to the east came also a substantial proportion of the wheat for the bread of the Czechs and the Slovaks. But, by the mid-1960's, complaints were coming from Moscow, too,—hints that Soviet economists were beginning to think it would be more profitable to end this trade of first-class foods and raw materials for second-class machinery. After all, Soviet economists argued, the oil and iron Czechoslovakia was getting could be sold to the West for hard currency, and the machinery bought from Prague could be manufactured at lower cost and with better quality in Moscow's domain.

Inefficiency and mismanagement were the second major source of Czechoslovakia's economic problems. Those directing the highly centralized planning mechanism in Prague were in the position of the blind leading the blind. They knew neither the pattern of genuine demand nor the true production costs of what they were ordering. In part, this came about because of the nation's Kafka-esque price system, which had no relation to economic reality and reflected accurately neither supply nor demand. Capital, though scarce, was allocated for the wrong purposes or remained frozen for many years at unfinished factory and other construction projects. The system of incentives encouraged factory managers to produce the same product for as long as possible and to strenuously resist technical change and improvement. The stultifying influence of monopoly was felt throughout the economy because the planning of production protected producers from the unwelcome competition of other Czechoslovak enterprises and of imports.

It is true that in most years the economic indicators gave the superficial impression of a healthy economy, reporting increased production and expanding foreign trade. These figures concealed the rising inventories of goods that could not be sold because they failed to meet even minimum consumer standards. The Czechoslovak economist Radoslav Selucky got at the root of many of these problems when he attacked the "cult of the plan" early in 1963. He pointed out that many people had lost interest in whether their activity or output met genuine needs. They were concerned only with fulfilling their planned assignments and getting their bonuses. Selucky wrote:

> What good does it do if the railroads fulfill all the transport indexes, when the transport of many products is itself unnecessary? What good does it do if productivity is higher in the case of washing machines than in the case of ice boxes, when the stores are full of the former while people are queueing up for the latter?

The effort to correct these weaknesses was led by Ota Sik, a Marxist economist who had been named Director of the Economics Institute of the Academy of Sciences in 1963.

Sik was influenced not only by Selucky and other radical economists at home but also by the Polish reformers between 1956 and 1958, by the experience of Yugoslavia's socialist market economy, and by the ideas of Libermanism in the Soviet Union. Moreover, Czechoslovakia had tried a pioneering economic reform—comprehensive decentralization—in the late 1950's. It had failed but did produce useful lessons. By 1965, Sik and his supporters had won official support for the idea that the country's economy had to be reorganized, that there had to be greater decentralization of economic decision-making, a more meaningful price system, and substantial use of incentives based on profit criteria rather than on planned production. The reforms agreed to by Novotny and his colleagues were vague, reflecting the bitter battle that had gone on behind the scenes. Conservatives thought Sik's ideas a betrayal of genuine socialism. Many officials in Czechoslovakia's economic system saw their jobs threatened by this meddlesome radical who stressed the need for initiative, for quick adaptation to changed demand and technology, and for introduction of Western management techniques. Those who felt threatened responded in classic fashion, seeking to sabotage the reform and to keep as much of the placid, comfortable old system as possible.

A skeptic might argue that the whole Czechoslovak debate over economic reform was old hat, repetition of similar battles in the Soviet Union and elsewhere in Eastern Europe. Much more impressive, therefore, were the discussions in the mid-1960's about possible changes in the fundamental political and legal institutions of Czechoslovakia, about how it might be possible to get a system of political pluralism within a one-party state. The leader in this discussion was the Slovak legal philosopher, Michael Lakatos, who advanced some very unusual ideas for a Communist theoretician. Every society, Lakatos maintained, faces a conflict between those who determine a nation's political line and those who must follow it, between "those who rule and those who are manipulated." The usual Communist talk about worker participation in government activity, Lakatos had no difficulty showing, is irrelevant or false since most worker participation has little to do with policy-making. What is really needed, he argued, is a legislature that genuinely determines a nation's political line—instead of just rubber stamping decisions of the Party high command—and the means of giving the population a real choice about the legislature's members. In actual Czechoslovak practice, he observed dryly, voting came down "to the right to elect the proposed candidate" who has been imposed upon the voters "from above." Lakatos did more than urge "a selection among several candidates." He stressed the importance of interest groups in a socialist society. He recognized that the interests of various groups conflict and argued that this conflict should be given normal expression in elections and legislative bodies.

Lakatos' ideas were far from the usual bland Soviet assumptions of inevitable social harmony in a socialist state. It is remarkable, therefore, that not only was Lakatos' heresy published but that he also received cautious and partial support from some important officials. Moreover, here is much in the record of Novotny's tenure to suggest that, as a practical politician, he instinctively understood the reality of contradictory group interests and sought to balance and conciliate those interests in his policies.

It was typical of the contradictions of the last years of Novotny's reign, however, that, when others sought to draw practical conclusions from such ideas, they met vigorous opposition and even repression. In December, 1966, for example, a Prague student, Jiri Mueller, addressed a national student conference with an appeal for major structural reform in the all-embracing and Party-dominated Czechoslovak Youth League. He proposed that the organization be broken down into separate groups of industrial, agricultural, and student youth, each of which would become a component member of the National Front—the nominal united front of all legal political organizations that, in theory, ruled the country. Each of these youth groups, Mueller suggested, should be allowed to engage in political activity and even to oppose the Communist Party if it felt such action necessary. Mueller was rebuffed, of course, and later he was expelled from school and drafted into the army as a private. Inevitably, he became a hero to many of Czechoslovakia's students, and his case served as another irritant to the nation's angry young people.

By 1966, in short, an attentive observer of Czechoslovak society and its trends could see that the point of no return had been reached in 1963. Many of the old controls remained, but the men who commanded them were uncertain about using force and aroused widespread resentment when they did employ power for repression. The blinders were gone from the eyes of a large and articulate section of the nation's most intelligent and ablest people. The stage had been set for a new chapter in Czechoslovak history.

2

January–October, 1967:
The Gathering Storm

It was not hard to detect a touch of complacency in President Antonin Novotny's traditional New Year's broadcast to the nation as 1967 began. He spoke for only twenty-three minutes, and virtually every word he spoke was predictable. He referred to the coming fiftieth-anniversary celebration of the Soviet Union's Bolshevik Revolution and Czechoslovakia's role in that celebration. He gave a stereotyped denunciation of U.S. actions in Vietnam and expressed a cautious wait-and-see attitude toward the new West German Government's efforts to improve relations with the nations of Eastern Europe. If there was a cloud on the horizon, his speech suggested, it came from the fears of those who thought the long-debated economic reform (finally going into effect that day, but in badly bowdlerized and truncated form) might lower living standards. Novotny was the essence of reassurance, telling his listeners that those doing "honest work" need have no fear, that only slackers and incompetents would

suffer. There were no surprises, no new violent denunciations
of internal foes, no hints of the dramatic events that would
occur in a few months.

For the moment, at least, Novotny seemed satisfied with
the results of the centrist policies he had been following since
the early 1960's. He had made concessions, effected a controlled release of tensions, permitted liberalizing reforms in
many areas; yet he remained in power and controlled the
Communist Party, the secret police, and the armed forces.
He had also retained Moscow's confidence, while on every
side he could point to winds of change blowing through
Czechoslovak life.

An adult education lecture in Prague on January 18 illustrated the new paths that were being broken. More than one
thousand citizens packed a hall to hear experts discuss and
answer questions about love, sex, infidelity, contraceptives,
impotence, the rising divorce rate, homosexuality, psycho-
analysis, and similar topics banned from public discussion
during the puritanical past years. When the meeting formally
closed, moreover, the audience remained, as a repairman
and occasional poet took the speaker's stand to deliver a
speech assailing the failures of parents in raising their children. Mothers should not have to work in factories, he
declared. Instead the state should pay them a living wage for
raising their children; such activity is also a form of production, he maintained, and one for which the socialist state
ought to pay. Nothing like this meeting had taken place in
Prague for twenty years.

By the beginning of 1967, too, Czechoslovakia's isolation
from the rest of the world had ended. In 1966 alone,
3,500,000 foreign tourists had visited the country, including
755,000 from the West. In that same year, almost 2,000,000
Czechs and Slovaks had gone abroad, more than 200,000 of
them to the capitalist world. It was very expensive to go
abroad because the rate of exchange was 36 crowns—a half-

day's wages for many—to a dollar, but every year, more and more people were passing the frontier, enjoying the sea at Dubrovnik in Yugoslavia, marveling at Rome's architectural and cultural masterpieces, gaping at West Germany's material abundance. Europe's waiters already knew Czechoslovak tourists well enough to detest them because they rarely tipped. True, even in Prague, one could not buy Western newspapers and magazines—except for technical publications and Communist Party organs, but everyone had to admit that the press and radio and television had increased their foreign coverage and had made it more objective. Even the reportage from the Soviet Union had lost some of its sycophantic character. In April, 1967, for example, when Soviet astronaut Vladimir Komarov crashed to his death in the *Soyuz-1* spaceship, Prague's *Ceteka* news agency criticized the brevity of the official *Tass* announcement, and the Czechoslovak radio correspondent in Moscow said that humanity would pay tribute to all the fallen heroes of space exploration "irrespective of whether they speak English or Russian."

The number of domestic forums for plain speaking about internal problems was also increasing. On January 30, 1967, radio station Czechoslovakia II began a series of discussion programs entitled "Club of Engaged Thinking." The first broadcast gave notice that old bonds were loosening. The participants spoke positively of the World War II contribution of the country's last "bourgeois" president, Eduard Benes; they agreed that the economic reforms being introduced would have to be accompanied by political reforms as well. In the new spirit of the times, the noted author Jan Prochazka—then a friend of Novotny and a candidate member of the Central Committee of the Communist Party—spoke bitterly and plainly in a radio broadcast for young people on March 10, 1967: "We have gotten off the track and we should now do something to get the country back on it," Prochazka told his audience, adding, "Our greatest wealth has always been the people, and it is these very people whom we treat worst. So that we may say that we are working full steam against our own future."

Even Czechoslovakia's traditionally rubber stamp National Assembly was beginning to show signs of life and an interest in replacing the old arbitrary ways by something approaching the rule of law. The new press law that went into effect on January 1, 1967, illustrated this fledgling trend. Enacted on the initiative of one of the National Assembly's committees, it put the existing censorship on a legal basis for the first time since the Communist Party had taken control almost two decades earlier. It authorized censorship only to protect state, economic, and official secrets, and it provided legal channels for editorial appeal against a censor's decisions. To many of those affected, of course, legalized censorship seemed no better than the earlier illegal censorship; nevertheless, the change was another symbolic step toward greater normality.

Nor could it be said that the Novotny regime was insensitive to the desire for better living standards. A Central Committee meeting early in May decided to cut investment expenditures in 1967 by 1 billion crowns and simultaneously called for increased imports of consumer goods so that citizens could have a more varied choice when they went to spend their wages. At the same time, maternal leave for working mothers was increased from twenty-two to twenty-six weeks, and plans were announced to introduce a five-day, forty-two-hour work week to replace the existing six-day, forty-six-hour work week.

The millennium had not yet arrived, even early in 1967. The chief Party ideologist, Jiri Hendrych, took the occasion of a Central Committee meeting in February to blast certain literary figures, whom he accused of spreading "non-socialist opinions and even propagating foreign ideology in cultural periodicals." He mentioned the Prague weekly *Literarni*

Noviny and the Brno monthly *Host do Domu* by name and hinted vaguely but ominously that action might be taken to correct the situation.

The secret police was still powerful and cooperated closely with its comrades in the Soviet KGB. Anyone who doubted this had been disabused in October, 1966, by the maladroit and embarrassing Kazan-Komarek case. Vladimir Kazan-Komarek, a naturalized American citizen who had fled Czechoslovakia in 1948, had gone to Moscow to attend a conference promoting American tourist travel to the Soviet Union. He took a Soviet Aeroflot plane for Paris, but the plane made an unexpected and unscheduled stop in Prague, where Kazan-Komarek was arrested on charges going back almost twenty years. Only after much diplomatic unpleasantness and after American travel agents had threatened to have their clients boycott Czechoslovakia was the Foreign Ministry able to have the victim of secret police "vigilance" expelled from Czechoslovakia, where he hadn't wanted to go in the first place.

However, these complex cross currents within Czechoslovakia were working against a wider background of developments outside the country. Even as Czech and Slovak intellectuals sought to take advantage of the widening area of Party toleration in 1966 and early 1967, they were dismayed by signs of retrogression in the Soviet Union itself. The Moscow trial and sentencing of Andrei Sinyavsky and Yuli Daniel early in 1966 had sufficiently disturbed the writers in Prague so that an informal delegation was sent to Moscow to voice such protest and concern as were possible. Then followed the muzzling of Alexander Solzhenitsyn, Russia's greatest living novelist; the prompt closing down in January, 1967, of Moscow's first public modern art show in four years; and the firing of Alexander Efros, the controversial and daring director of Moscow's Lenin Komsomol Theater. Liberals in Prague became alarmed further when

Moscow's conservatives ruthlessly steamrollered the proceedings at the Soviet Writers Congress late in May, 1967. It was
to this Congress that Solzhenitsyn wrote a long and eloquent
letter protesting against censorship and demanding that the
Soviet Writers Union protect the rights, freedoms, and lives
of Soviet writers. Solzhenitsyn's letter was suppressed. An
atmosphere of foreboding prevailed, therefore, as the progressive and liberal members of the Czechoslovak Writers Union
prepared for their own congress in June, 1967, the following
month.

May, 1967, was also the month that the Middle Eastern
crisis mounted rapidly. In the situation created by Nasser's
moves to cripple Israeli shipping and while Arab radios
broadcast exultant promises of Israel's annihilation, the Soviet
Union—with Czechoslovakia following obediently behind—
swung as usual to the support of the Arabs. The propaganda
line adopted in Prague equated Zionism with Nazism. It
branded Israel the aggressor, the violator of treaties, and the
nation that had to make concessions to achieve peace—that
is, it parroted the Moscow line and was indistinguishable
from similar automatic responses in Warsaw, Budapest, East
Berlin, and Sofia.

The Middle Eastern crisis had special importance for a
significant number of Czechoslovakia's intellectuals. Many
of them were well aware that by supplying military instruc-
tors and arms their country had played a key role in helping
create the state of Israel in the late 1940's. They remembered, too, that in the mid-1950's their country had begun
the arms deliveries to Egypt that played a role in bringing
about the Suez crisis and the Middle East war of 1956.
Moreover, there was a sense of guilt about the blatant anti-
Semitism—thinly disguised as anti-Zionism—of the 1952
Slansky trial, with its false charges of Israeli espionage and
its many Jewish victims. Finally, many Czechoslovak intellectuals identified with Israel because they saw it as a small

state threatened by overwhelmingly superior force, a state that might suffer the same fate small Czechoslovakia had undergone at the time of Munich and the ensuing Nazi take over. The result was widespread, if covert, sympathy for Israel even while all the newspapers, radio programs, and television broadcasts mechanically trumpeted the official pro-Arab line. Many who cared little about Israel were irked in their national pride at the spectacle of their government's slavish obeisance to the Soviet Union.

Inevitably, therefore, Israel's complete and devastating victory over its larger opponents had an exhilarating and intoxicating impact among the most independent-minded sections of Czechoslovakia's people. Many rejoiced at the Israeli victory because of the David-Goliath parallel and because Israel had in effect triumphed over the Soviet Union, chief political friend of Egypt and Syria and chief supplier of their missiles, planes, and tanks.

The Israeli victory was seen also as a major blow at Novotny, and questions began to be asked in many quarters: Did he have to follow the Soviet lead so slavishly? Did he have to make Czechoslovakia the very first country in Eastern Europe to break diplomatic relations with Israel once Moscow did so? What would be the cost to Czechoslovakia of the Israeli victory? The sophisticated independent thinkers in Prague and Bratislava knew that Israel had captured Czechoslovak as well as Soviet arms and other supplies from the Arabs. They were dismayed when the decision was announced to help Egypt and its allies recover economically and militarily as quickly as possible. Long weary of the insatiable appetite of the recipients of Czechoslovakia's foreign aid, many Czechs and Slovaks had no enthusiasm even for sending economic and military supplies to the North Vietnamese. It was with almost an audible groan that they contemplated the cost of helping to bail Egypt and Syria out of the consequences of their ignominious defeat.

None of this discontent received public expression, of course, but its existence was well known and irked the Arab representatives in Prague. The Egyptian ambassador could not contain his anger. In an official press conference, he denounced Czechoslovak journalists for not writing objectively about the Middle Eastern crisis and for what he considered their support of ,Israel. He declared that their attitude was understandable since "the Czechoslovak press remains infested with many Jews." The incident was passed over in official silence. The press did not mention the complaint, and no reproach was directed at the ambassador for his remarks. But as word of the affair got around, it added to the intellectuals' indignation at their country's undignified posture.

In this strained atmosphere, on June 27, 1967, the Czechoslovak Writers Union opened what was to become a historic congress, a key event in the polarization and mobilization of forces that would end Antonin Novotny's reign six months later.

For the most independent-minded writers of Czechoslovakia, the events in the Soviet Union and in the Middle East during the preceding months had opened the darkest perspectives. If their country was as subservient to Moscow in foreign policy as the previous weeks had shown, could it remain independent and separate in internal policy at a time when neo-Stalinism was clearly spreading over the Soviet scene? Were not all the gains of the years since 1962 in danger? Adding to the writers' apprehensions were signs that the Communist Party, even before the congress opened, was attempting to limit the area of discussion and to guard against excessive publicity of whatever might be said within the walls of the meeting hall. Knowing the risks they took, a handful of the boldest writers decided to counterattack, to make their literary congress a political forum to challenge the basic premises of the Czechoslovak state under Novotny.

Because of the secrecy with which the Czechoslovak press treated the meeting, it was several weeks before the outside world knew the full magnitude of the writers' revolt. But when they found out, foreign radio stations broadcasting in Czech and Slovak passed the information on to the people of Czechoslovakia. By mid-August, the information was sufficiently widespread so that *Rude Pravo,* the Communist Party organ, had to publish two articles discussing some of the dissidents' arguments and attempting to answer them.

The fireworks had begun on the first day of the meeting. The very first speaker, Milan Kundera of the Union's Presidium, assailed the decline of Czechoslovak literature to the level of propaganda. This so angered the Communist Party's ideological watchdog, Jiri Hendrych, that he interrupted the discussion to deliver an angry reply. But worse yet came. In a sensational speech, playwright Pavel Kohout, once one of the Party's most effective propagandists, but now an angry rebel, read to his colleagues the full text of Alexander Solzhenitsyn's eloquent attack on Soviet censorship. A year later, Kundera described what happened as Kohout spoke before the five hundred people present in the closed meeting:

> When . . . Pavel Kohout began to read Solzhenitsyn's letter in which this great heir of Tolstoy described the tragic lot of Soviet literature under Stalinism and under neo-Stalinist conditions, Jiri Hendrych turned purple in the face, rose from his seat in the first row on the dais, put his coat on over his white shirt adorned with suspenders, and perspiringly left the hall; on his way out, he passed Prochazka, Lustig, and me who were sitting in one of the back rows, and said the following memorable words: "You have lost everything, everything."

And, a piquant detail in view of what happened in August, 1968, Kundera revealed that at the time of the Congress Kohout's reading of Solzhenitsyn's letter was denounced by Moscow as an intolerable interference in Soviet affairs.

In his speech, Kohout also defended Israel against the Novotny regime's daily attacks and accusations. Israel was right to fire the first shot in the war, Kohout argued, because "a country as small as Israel cannot defend itself otherwise than offensively." To hammer home his point, he drew a parallel between Czechoslovakia in 1938 and Israel in June, 1967, claiming for each the right to defend itself in any way necessary. He went on to defend Israel's internal development, asserting, "In Israel they have made a garden out of the desert. . . . Nearly the whole system of agriculture is organized in a socialist or Communist manner." Later Jan Prochazka, a candidate member of the Communist Party Central Committee, expressed similar pro-Israel sentiments.

However, the issue of freedom was central in the speeches. A film critic, A. J. Liehm, demanded that cultural policy be freed from the "dictate of power and market." Others such as Alexander Kliment joined in to attack the primacy of politics and ideology over culture. The real bombshell, however, came from a 40-year old novelist, Ludvik Vaculik, a self-educated former shoemaker and long-time member of the Communist Party. His speech is a major document in the history of the struggle for intellectual freedom under Communism.

Vaculik begins with an analysis of the nature of power and with praise—startling, since he was a member of the Communist Party—for the system of checks and balances in "formal democracy." Then he draws a contrast between democratic countries and Czechoslovakia:

> This formal system of democracy does not produce too firm a government, but only the conviction that the next government might be an improvement on the preceding one. Thus the government falls but the citizen is renewed. And vice versa, whenever the government remains in power forever or for a long time, the citizen falls. When does he fall? I shall not

please our enemies and claim that the citizen falls at a place of execution. This fate is only in store for some dozens or for a few hundred citizens.

However, our enemies know that this suffices, because then follows the fall of the whole nation into fear, political indifference, civil resignation, petty everyday worries and small wishes, into dependence on minor and pocket masters, in a word, it falls into vassalage of a new and unprecedented kind which defies any explanation one might wish to give to a visitor from a foreign land. I believe that citizens no longer exist in our country. I have my reasons for this belief, reasons founded on my long experience working for newspapers and radio. I want to dwell on one new reason. This congress was not convened after the members of this organization had decided to meet but only after the master, having considered his problems, graciously gave his consent. In exchange, he expects, as he has been accustomed to for hundreds of years, that we should show reverence to his dynasty. I suggest that we should not.

Vaculik goes on to compare the Writers Congress with a playground at which those in attendance have received permission to behave as though they were genuine citizens with independence. He suggests, therefore, "let us act for three whole days as if we were adult and had come of age. Here I speak as a citizen of a state which I shall never renounce, but in which I cannot live contentedly." Only extensive quotation can give the flavor of Vaculik's view of his country after two decades of his Party's rule:

In our country, too, we have witnessed the selection of men on the basis of their usefulness to the regime. The regime's confidence was won by the obedient, by those who made no difficulties, by those who asked no questions which were not raised by the regime itself. . . . The fabric on which rested the material structure and personal culture of such human communities as parishes, plants, workshops was torn. Nothing was permitted to bear the stamp of a person's own work . . .

principals of schools who were working on their own methods of education were sacked, managers of tile factories who expressed a critical opinion about the surroundings of their factories were dismissed. Cultural and sports clubs and societies with a good reputation were dissolved, institutions which, for some people, represented the whole scale of continuity in their parish, region and state.

Benjamin Klicka, in his work *Wild Daja* said: "Remember, ability is an insult to your superior and therefore pretend to be as dumb as a doornail, if you want to live a long life and enjoy it in this land of ours." This quotation is forty years old and it was coined for a society prior to the social revolution. Yet, it seems to me that it only acquired its full validity in our country after this revolution and that everyone has found out for himself how true it is. . . .

Our government pleases the artists when it praises them for having, for instance, designed a good pavilion for the World Exposition. The government certainly likes to do this and such declarations also have a political aspect. And perhaps the government actually means it. . . . Such a pavilion which enjoys in a certain sense the rights of cultural extraterritoriality only shows what the same creative workers could do at home if they were allowed to do so, if they carried the same weight in their own land. Thus I must ask myself whether we all do not serve an illusion when we build beautiful pavilions representative of our culture? When we know that our best work is unwanted, that we do everything by the grace of God, that our time is running out and we don't even know the date. Everything that our culture has achieved, everything good that men have done or created in our country, all the good products, the good buildings, the well-conceived ideas from our laboratories, all this has been achieved in spite of the fact that our ruling circles have behaved in that way for years on end. It was done literally in spite of them. . . .

Just as I do not feel very secure in a cultural-political situation which the regime apparently can drive to a state of conflict, neither do I feel safe as a citizen outside this room, outside this playground. Nothing happens to me, and nothing has happened. That sort of thing is not done any more. Should I be grateful? Not so, I am afraid. I see no firm guarantee. It is true that I see better work in the courts, but the judges themselves do not see any hard and fast guarantees. I see that better work is done by the public prosecutor's office, but do the public prosecutors have guarantees and do they feel safe? If you would like it, I should be glad to interview some of them for the newspapers. Do you think it would be published? I would not be afraid to interview even the Prosecutor General and ask him why unjustly sentenced and rehabilitated people do not regain their original rights as a matter of course, why the national committees are reluctant to return them to their apartments or houses—but it will not be published. Why has no one properly apologized to these people, why do they not have the advantages of the politically persecuted, why do we haggle with them about money? Why can we not live where we want to? Why cannot the tailors go for three years to Vienna and the painters for thirty years to Paris and be able to return without being considered criminals?

There was more to Vaculik's shattering indictment. He asked where the guarantees were for the limited freedoms that had been given and then raised the question "whether the ruling circles themselves, the government and its individual members possess those guarantees of their own civil rights without which it is impossible to create . . . a policy." This was an obvious, if oblique, reference to the Government's puppet status vis-à-vis Moscow. Near the end of his speech, Vaculik summed up:

It is necessary to understand that in the course of twenty years no human problem has been solved in our country—starting with elementary needs such as housing, schools and economic prosperity and ending with the finer requirements of life which cannot be provided by the undemocratic systems of the world, for instance the feeling of full value in the society, the subordination of political decisions to ethical criteria, belief in the value of even less important work, the need for confidence among men, development of the education of the entire people. . . . By this I do not wish to say that we have lived in vain, that none of this has any value. It has value. But the question is whether it is only the value of forewarning. Even in this case the total knowledge of mankind would progress. But was it necessary to make a country which knew precisely the dangers for its culture into an instrument for this kind of lesson?

Vaculik's speech produced panic or near panic among both the conservatives and the moderates in his audience. He was going much further than merely asking the writers to break the truce with the regime that had given them a measured, but real, amount of freedom. In effect, he was calling for revolution, for the writers and other honest people to revolt not only against the masters in Prague, but against the real masters in Moscow. The frightened in Vaculik's audience began calling for an end to this dangerous political talk. Hendrych himself arose on the last day of the Congress to answer Vaculik, to accuse him and other malcontents of misusing the Congress, mistaking freedom for anarchy, and defaming Czechoslovakia's socialist system, its government, its Communist Party, and its domestic and foreign policy. But some in the Congress were not intimidated. Jan Prochazka, giving the closing speech, endorsed the freedom of discussion that had taken place, implicitly denied Hendrych's right to make a meaningful judgment about the Congress, and expressed solidarity with "all who fight against oppression, persecution, the poison of racism and anti-Semitism, against chauvinism and narrow-minded nationalism." In the context of what had gone before, Prochazka's stand on the side of the rebels was clear.

For Novotny, the writers' revolt, and the possibility that it might spread, was a nightmare become reality. Panicky countermeasures were taken immediately. A few days after the Congress, writer Jan Benes, jailed for many months on charges of passing information to the West, was put on trial. A codefendant tried *in absentia* was the exile Pavel Tigrid, whose name was given in the press as Tigrid-Schoenfeld to call attention to his Jewish origins. Actually, Tigrid had become a convert to Roman Catholicism a quarter of a century earlier during World War II. Benes was found guilty and sentenced to five years in jail, the first Czechoslovak to receive so harsh a sentence for a political crime since the worst days of the early 1950's.

An equally panicky effort was undertaken to prevent copies of the speeches Vaculik and his sympathizers had made to the Congress from reaching the outside world. The regime knew well that the dissidents had good relations with Western journalists and would try to see that their statements were reported abroad, so that Radio Free Europe, the Voice of America, the B.B.C., and similar transmitters could then inform the people of Czechoslovakia. The *Neue Zuercher Zeitung* correspondent Andreas Kohlschuetter was a prime victim of this effort to keep copies of the speeches from circulating. On July 20–21, he was detained at the Czechoslovak-Polish border for twenty-nine hours, interrogated repeatedly, and searched. On July 24, he was held for three hours on the Bavarian border, and all the written material he had with him was confiscated. The secret police effort was fruitless; too many citizens and noncitizens of Czechoslovakia were traveling to the West to prevent the transmission of these materials. But the fact that the effort was made spoke volumes about the fear at the highest levels in Prague.

The furor might have died down. For all their anger, Novotny and Hendrych delayed taking public action against Vaculik and the other dissidents. They obviously did not want to escalate the crisis. Then one of the writers, Ladislav Mnacko, struck on his own. Mnacko was perhaps the most popular reporter and novelist in the country; his books had sold more than 1 million copies in Czechoslovakia. His most recent fame had come from his reporting on his trip to Vietnam. Mnacko had a personal reason for anger against the regime: It had banned publication of his novel *The Taste of Power,* but more than personal reasons guided his move. In mid-August, he appeared in the West and announced he was going to Israel. Here is a part of his statement:

> I am going to Israel. It is my intention to register my protest against the policy of the Czechoslovak government by this journey. Since in Czechoslovakia one is prevented from speaking out about the Middle East crisis . . . I am compelled to choose this unusual way.
>
> It is impossible for me to support—even through silence— a policy which leads to the eradication of a whole people and to the liquidation of an entire state. The Czechoslovak government has promised its unconditional support to the Arab states and their leaders, although these Arab leaders have proclaimed their plans quite openly. They have said it, and they wanted it too: Destruction of the two and a half million people in Israel. . . .
>
> Generally speaking I have been unable to understand our policy toward Israel throughout the past. In the West this policy is described as "satellitism." I do not believe this is quite correct. We go beyond the bounds which are required in this respect. We do our job with great eagerness and great alacrity. I believe this is connected with our past which is not yet overcome. In our country the connotations of the political trials of the Stalin era were particularly unpleasant. The Slansky trial served the purpose of producing an anti-Semitic tide. This had, of course, nothing in common with Communist ideology. Its effects have not been reversed up to this moment. The Slansky trial itself and its consequences, the anti-Semitic tide, have not yet been fully discussed and fully explained. . . .
>
> The system in Czechoslovakia must be changed to a very considerable degree if we want to continue as a healthy socialist humanitarian country. This chaos, this system of rubber laws, these opportunities of circumventing the law, and whenever the rulers see fit, these possibilities of applying such laws

which do not fit at all in a particular case, this arbitrariness must be eliminated. In this respect, a good deal has already been achieved. However, there are no guarantees that excesses will not occur again.

Mnacko's statements, which were broadcast to Czechoslovakia by Western radios, were especially damaging for two reasons. First, he was particularly popular in Slovakia, where he was known as a Czech who wrote in the Slovak language. Second, he was not a Jew. Appalled at the political effect of his defection, the regime moved swiftly against him. Within a week of his first statement, Mnacko was deprived of his Czechoslovak citizenship, expelled from the Communist Party, and stripped of all his official literary prizes and honors.

Two weeks later, as September began, Novotny spoke out personally about these disquieting developments. "Liberalistic" and "objectivistic" tendencies were showing up in public life, he warned, along with "pacifism, recklessness, and carelessness." The Party had tolerated differences of opinion in the past, he said, but democracy and freedom had their limits, especially since some people had interpreted the Party's leniency as weakness and misused the situation. The Communist Party ruled Czechoslovakia, he warned, and it intended to preserve that rule by whatever measures were required. It was a speech breathing fire, delivered appropriately enough before an audience composed of graduates of Czechoslovakia's military academies.

Two weeks later came another sensation. Jan Prochazka, formerly Novotny's confidant and still an alternate member of the Party Central Committee, published a tribute to Thomas Masaryk on the thirtieth anniversary of the latter's death. Writing in *Literarni Noviny,* organ of the Writers Union, Prochazka noted that Masaryk "was even esteemed by his enemies" because of "his, now no longer known, respect and tolerance for opinions with which he did not agree. He won supporters without cajoling or threatening anyone." The contrast with Novotny was plain for all to see.

How could Prochazka's article pass the censor when the atmosphere was so strained? Only a few days earlier, the regime had been deeply upset by the publication in London of a supposed Appeal of Czechoslovak Intellectuals calling for help from the free world. The highest officials had been concerned with getting denials that the Appeal was genuine. Now Prochazka was sounding a theme from the appeal within Prague itself. Rumor in the city at the time held that the censors had been afraid to veto an article by a Central Committee member and had passed the issue up the chain of command until it reached Novotny's desk, where that worthy refused to read the article but said he trusted Prochazka. Whatever the explanation, Prochazka's essay was the last straw. On September 26 and 27, the Central Committee met and handed down punishment. Vaculik, Liehm, and playwright Ivan Klima were expelled from the Communist Party. Prochazka lost his place in the Central Committee. *Literarni Noviny* was taken away from the Writers Union and turned over to the Ministry of Culture because it had become "a platform for dissemination of liberalistic moods" and even for spreading "standpoints of political opposition."

The move caused a sensation. Not only was such punishment unprecedented, but the action regarding *Literarni Noviny* showed that the Government and the Communist Party had lost control of the Writers Union, that they could not install officials in that group who could be depended upon to make the weekly a politically reliable journal. It was a confession of weakness and declaration of open war against the intelligentsia. The extent of the conflict was revealed when the new *Literarni Noviny* first appeared; virtually all writers of any standing were boycotting the weekly. Even the paper's appearance was different because the artist who had designed the original newspaper's name plate insisted, successfully, that his colophon should not be used against his wishes.

At the time, the September crackdown on the writers and their union naturally occupied the center of attention. But another facet of the same Central Committee meeting was to prove even more important for Czechoslovakia's future. This was the public evidence of increasing Slovak animosity toward the Novotny group. Part of the evidence came in the discussion on the writers' case. A Slovak writer, Vladimir Minac, opposed any repression at all. He did make some derogatory remarks about Vaculik *et al.,* but he urged the need for increasing the freedom of all the people and assailed the hysteria that had, he said, been created around the Writers Congress. The revolt at that Congress had been primarily a Czech affair because the Slovak delegates had walked out in mid-session, showing they wanted to have nothing to do with it. Minac's speech suggested that the Slovaks were having second thoughts. His speech also raised the possibility that his conciliatory attitude—so different from the Novotny-Hendrych line—might have high-level political support in Bratislava, perhaps from Dubcek and other key officials there.

Even more important in this connection, however, was the open expression, at the September plenum, of acute Slovak discontent with the results of the economic reform. Dubcek himself enunciated this dissatisfaction. He pointed out that the economic plan for the year had envisioned that Slovakia would get 28 per cent of the nation's investments in 1967, but that in the first half of the year it had gotten only 21.9 per cent. He called for quick action to rectify the imbalance, asking for the creation of a central investment fund that would permit channeling more resources to Slovakia. In effect, he was charging that the greater independence for grass-roots decision-making under the New Economic Model introduced the previous January permitted the Czechs, who made the bulk of managerial decisions, to favor their own areas at the expense of Slovakia, although Slovakia had the bulk of the nation's unemployed manpower and other free resources.

Dubcek, of course, was not the only one dissatisfied with the workings of the New Economic Model, then, nine months after its initiation. Nothing seemed to be going right. When the reform began, for example, a major revision of wholesale prices was introduced. Through this revision, the Government sought to bring prices and costs closer together so as to exert more pressure for efficiency and cost cutting. By September, it was already obvious that the enterprises had grossly overstated their costs so that the new prices were, in the main, egregiously high. As a result, most of the nation's industry had large profits, which it could use for inflationary wage increases and for employing still more workers, though there was already excess employment. The Government had earlier asserted that it would let economic processes work themselves out without administrative interference, but it was exerting pressure on the enterprises to turn back their excess profits or face stiff penalties. The result was to enrage Sik and his supporters, who felt it essential to let economic forces work without such direct interference.

In foreign trade—so vital for a small country like Czechoslovakia—a major balance of payments crisis with the West seemed to be building up. The 1967 plan had envisaged an 11 per cent increase of sales to the capitalist nations; the reality through August was a 2 per cent decline. Meanwhile, exports to the Soviet Union and the other Communist states were booming, but these were soft currency areas with which Czechoslovakia already had substantial, favorable trade balances it could not turn into goods. In effect, Czechoslovakia was subsidizing its neighbors who would neither make their currencies convertible nor pay with goods Prague needed and wanted.

It was a situation ideally calculated to produce quarrels

and mutual accusations. The reformers charged that the difficulties had arisen because their ideas had been implemented too cautiously and with too many changes. The conservatives charged that the difficulties confirmed their earlier doubts and reservations. Inevitably, Novotny, the centrist, earned the ill will of both sides.

As autumn of 1967 began, therefore, Antonin Novotny had all the major elements of a political crisis on his hands: He had alienated much of the country's elite, especially the influential intelligentsia; the national economy was in a mess, and his efforts to improve it were seen as incompetent and viewed with suspicion by both conservatives and reformers; and the Slovak political machine that Alexander Dubcek directed was increasingly acting as an independent, opposition political force, demanding more concessions and taking fewer pains to hide its distaste for Novotny, whose image among Slovaks had always been that of Czech centralism incarnate.

Novotny must have known that his enemies were closing in, but he may have underestimated them because he was well aware of his assets. As far as he knew, he was still very much in Moscow's good graces. He had won the favor of East Germany's Walter Ulbricht by refusing to recognize West Germany, as Rumania and Yugoslavia had recently done (although he never went as far in his denunciations of West Germany as Ulbricht wanted). Most important, only little more than a year had passed since the last, the thirteenth, Congress of the Czechoslovak Communist Party. He had been in control then, and the Central Committee chosen at that time was packed with his supporters. Surely, he must have thought, he could repulse any challenges ahead. His three-month fight for political life, from mid- or late October until the battle was lost in late December and early January, testified that he wanted to hang onto his power, that he put up a stupendous battle, and that at times he came close to winning.

3

October 30, 1967– January 5, 1968: The Revolution

Skeptics jeer at the arcane arts of Kremlinology. They compare practitioners to readers of tea leaves, astrologers, and other snarers of the gullible. At times, the cynics' fire intimidates even the Kremlinologists themselves, causing them to lean over backward in rejecting the Kremlinologically plain significance of the materials available for probing Communist secrets.

Some such excessive caution is the only possible explanation for the fact that it was not until mid-December that the Western press and public opinion got their first inklings that Antonin Novotny was fighting for his public life and that his reign might end in days or weeks. In retrospect, there seems to have been an almost incredible failure to use available evidence. The situation was presented clearly enough, for those with eyes to see and minds to evaluate the signs, in the Czechoslovak press on November 19, the tenth anniversary of Novotny's accession to the Presidency. The two Communist Party organs, Prague's *Rude Pravo* and Bratislava's *Pravda,* marked the occasion with identical articles that emphasized objective developments—Party congresses, foreign-policy changes, and so on—and eschewed any praise of Novotny as a person. He was portrayed as an executor of Party policy, not as its creator. As if to emphasize that Novotny was being deliberately played down, the article declared at the end that "The role of important leading Party personalities is determined by the mission of the Party itself . . . ," implying that there was nothing unique about Novotny's contribution. For any signs of personal warmth toward Novotny one had to turn to the non-Party press. But there the careful reader could see the possible use of Aesopian language and symbols. Thus, the front page of one paper juxtaposed its tribute to Novotny with another article headlined "Hitler Number Two," dealing with the leader of West Germany's neo-Nazis. Another newspaper declared that all important events of the past decade carried the stamp of Novotny's personality—a tribute that could be read negatively as well as positively. Most telling of all, the Slovak daily press, except for the Party's Bratislava organ, ignored the anniversary altogether. One did not have to be very perceptive to suspect that Novotny was in serious trouble and that the opposition to him must be most powerful in Slovakia. Anyone who reached such a conclusion at the time was correct.

What had happened was that Novotny's attempt to walk a middle path between conservatives and reformers had finally failed. To the forces of change, he represented the key figure opposing much more radical and fundamental alteration of the nation's life than had yet taken place. Novotny's concessions had merely whetted their appetites and produced expectations that were periodically disappointed as, in the case of the writers and the economic reform, he took back with a second hand what he had given earlier with the first. The conservatives saw Novotny in a reverse mirror, as a dangerous adventurer who made too many concessions and then was maladroit when he finally came to his senses and retreated. By ironic accident, just as the high-level struggle over Novotny raged secretly behind the scenes, Czechoslovakia's public life was dominated by a student revolt that provided ammunition for both liberal and conservative opponents of the President. In effect, the luckless Novotny came under attack from both above and below and from both extremes of his Party's political spectrum. He tried to manipulate the individuals involved, appealing to one's cupidity and ambition and to another's jealousy of a Novotny opponent. He even appealed for and got the help of Leonid I. Brezhnev, First Secretary of the Communist Party of the Soviet Union, but that, too, proved a miscalculation. As so often in such political disasters, Novotny found it impossible to do anything right. The united front of his opponents brought about his downfall.

The full story of what happened in the Presidium and Central Committee of the Czechoslovak Communist Party during the ten-week struggle between October 30, 1967, and January 5, 1968, must be pieced together from many sources. The minutes of the key meetings have never been published for general circulation, and a definitive account must wait until that happens. Fortunately, there were enough loose tongues in Prague during late 1967 and early 1968 so that the essentials of the story can be put together.

It all began on October 30, when the Central Committee met to consider "the Party's position and role in the current stage of socialist society." In the previous two months, similar meetings had been held at local and regional levels to impress upon lower-echelon leaders that the disarray of the summer had to be ended and that Party control of all phases of the nation's life had to be strengthened.

Apparently the trouble began when Dubcek challenged

the resolution offered by Jiri Hendrych, the chief speaker. The proffered resolution, Dubcek charged, differed significantly from the earlier version to which all members of the Presidium—including Dubcek—had agreed. The discrepancy, Dubcek added, was typical of the kind of cheating Novotny and his supporters always indulged in when Slovakia was at issue. Novotny responded like a wounded bull. Losing his temper, he accused Dubcek and his followers of coming close to bourgeois nationalism. Novotny's fury at Slovak nationalism immediately united most of the top Slovak politicians around Dubcek. In the exchange that followed, Dubcek called for a radical change in the Party's structure, its methods, and its relationship with the state. He justified these changes not only in terms of Slovak ambitions but also in terms of the Party's need to regain the nation's confidence. As the debate proceeded, Dubcek's call for separating Party and state was seen as a means of clipping Novotny's wings, and some Czechs rallied to the banner first raised by the Slovaks. Calls for Novotny's resignation as Party boss were heard, but early the next afternoon, Novotny asked that the fiery debate be interrupted. He pointed out that he and other leading figures had to participate that afternoon in a previously scheduled ceremony honoring the fiftieth anniversary of the Bolshevik Revolution, a meeting that could not be postponed. It was agreed to resume the debate at another Central Committee meeting early in December. The battle had been joined, but the first round had been inconclusive.

The people of Czechoslovakia, of course, were kept in the dark. The statement issued at the end of the two-day meeting made no reference to the clash or to the vital issues raised, and no paper inside the country carried the report of the Yugoslav news agency, which called the meeting "perhaps the most important one in the last decade."

On October 31, the very same night that the Central Committee ended its meeting, a major new factor entered the situation. It arose during a meeting in a dormitory of the Prague Technical College between student representatives and the editors of the youth daily *Mlada Fronta*. The students wanted publicity for their complaints about the deficiencies of the heating and lighting systems in their quarters and about the repeated failure of school and other authorities to heed the students' protests. In the middle of this meeting, the lights suddenly went out. Infuriated by this new proof of their grievances, the students came together in an angry assembly. Shortly thereafter, about 1,500 of them began a protest march toward Hradcany Castle, the President's residence. Many of the students carried lighted candles and shouted, "We want lights! We want to study!" The police moved to disperse the students, liberally using tear gas and clubs. According to some reports, the police even invaded the campus and beat students in their rooms— including students who had not been involved in the demonstration.

The police brutality angered the students. So did the distorted reports of the affair in the Prague newspapers. Very quickly student demands escalated far beyond the initial complaints about dormitory deficiencies and assumed a political character. These young people had felt on their own skins what the Prague police conceived of as "socialist legality." Their anger was contagious and spread swiftly to other universities.

On November 8, a large number of students of the Philosophical Faculty of the Charles University held a five-hour protest meeting and drew up a comprehensive petition. They demanded that academic immunity be guaranteed, that the police responsible for the beatings be identified and punished, that in the future the police be required to wear badges with numbers that would permit individual officers to be identified, that the police be prohibited from using chemicals,

that the National Assembly consider the events at the demonstration and take appropriate action, that the results of a
thorough investigation be published, and that the press
report all developments in this matter accurately and exten-
sively.

By mid-November, the regime was showing its alarm in
several ways. The rector of the Prague Technical University,
while admitting the justice of the students' initial complaints, accused them of letting themselves be used for political purposes against the Government. So did the editor of
the Party cultural newspaper, who charged student spokesmen with referring to the speeches of dissident writers at the
Writers' Congress of the previous June, and of showing
themselves to have a "perfect knowledge of current anti-
Communist Western propaganda." But the students had
supporters, also. Faculty members belonging to the Czechoslovak Youth League held two meetings to protest police in-
trusion into the campus. The University Committee of the
Communist Party demanded a genuine investigation of the
police brutality, though it rejected the use of demonstrations
as a means of solving problems.

On November 20, a mass meeting at the Philosophical
Faculty turned into a nine-hour sit-in, during which students voiced angry protests at police brutality and press mis-
representation. They accused the newspapers of trying to
turn the workers against the students and considered proposals, ranging from another street demonstration to visits to
the factories to win over the workers, to put more pressure
on the authorities. Many speakers went further, asking pointed
questions about the nature of Czechoslovak society and about
the blatant contradictions they now saw between theory and
practice. What kind of society did they live in, they asked,
when supposedly constitutional guarantees of freedom could
be so cavalierly overridden by the police without any reaction from higher authority? A remarkable feature of the

meeting was that Rector Oldrich Stary and Deputy Rector Eduard Goldstuecker engaged in a sympathetic and meaningful dialogue with the students, agreeing with them sometimes and disagreeing at others and giving advice for the students' consideration and decision. The outcome was what amounted to an ultimatum to the Government: Either the student demands would be granted by December 15, or all Prague's university students would take action.

On December 15, just before the deadline expired, the report of the Government commission investigating the events of October 31 was published. This was a partial victory for the students. The legitimate grievances about deficiencies in the dormitory were acknowledged, and various officials responsible lost their jobs or received other punishment. The report accused the students of encouraging police brutality by insulting the police and even attacking them physically. But it also admitted that "unduly harsh means" had been used by the police, for whom extenuation was, nevertheless, found in the form of a reference to the "confused situation." A decision had been reached not to press criminal charges against either the students or the police, but the police would receive better training as well as technical equipment, such as loud-speakers, that might help them better deal with future demonstrations.

It was a typical Novotny compromise solution to the problem, satisfying neither the angry students nor those who saw the students as counterrevolutionary agitators and wanted them handled with maximum severity. Probably not accidentally, the report appeared on the eve of the resumption of the Central Committee meeting that had adjourned the previous October. Novotny must have realized that the student agitation and the publicity attending it at home and abroad had further damaged his image and given new arguments to his opponents in the political struggle still under way.

While the public followed the student unrest, maneuvers went on behind the scenes. Some reports claim Novotny attempted unsuccessfully to have Dubcek removed as Slovak Party chief. That same month, Dubcek himself published an article that was almost openly defiant of Novotny. In it, he dared equate the Slovak contribution to the Communist victory in 1948 with the Czech contribution, though at that time Communist strength in the Czech lands had been far greater than in Slovakia. He harked back approvingly to the original agreements on Slovak-Czech cooperation reached in the mid-1940's, agreements that promised the Slovaks far greater autonomy than they actually enjoyed. He bluntly asserted that it was necessary to assess the past critically in order "to broaden the scope of future progressive development . . . to evoke a healthy and constructive dissatisfaction . . . with the existing state of affairs, to seek and find new roads of progress." Readers with knowledge of what was going on could view Dubcek's article only as a pledge of continued war against Novotny and his followers.

The next crisis came early in December, when the Presidium—including Dubcek and Novotny—met to formulate a resolution to submit to the Central Committee meeting scheduled to take place before the middle of the month. According to some reports, the original vote was eight to two for splitting the Party and the state organizations, an anti-Novotny decision implying that he would have to resign as Party boss. Other reports maintain that from the beginning the vote was a deadlock, five to five. Reportedly voting with Novotny were Premier Lenart, originally regarded as a progressive but a man who had disappointed the great expectations held for him; Michal Chudik, another leading Slovak; Otakar Simunek, a Vice Premier and Czechoslovakia's representative to the Soviet bloc's Comecon economic organization; and Bohuslav Lastovicka, Chairman of the National Assembly. Against Novotny were Dubcek, Jiri Hendrych, the ideological chief who had apparently quarreled with Novotny about the best tactics for handling the intellectuals; Drahomir Kolder, a moderate reformer who headed the Central Committee's Economic Commission; Jaromir Dolansky, at 72, a well-respected veteran of Czechoslovak Communism; and Oldrich Cernik, a Vice Premier, technocrat, and head of the State Planning Commission.

Whatever the vote, things were sufficiently unfavorable for Novotny in the first days of December that he appealed through Soviet Ambassador Stepan V. Chervonenko for help from Moscow. Chervonenko, ironically, had been Soviet ambassador to China from 1959 through the early 1960's. Originally a protégé of Khrushchev, in Peking Chervonenko had seen at first hand the complex sequence of events that destroyed the Sino-Soviet alliance and made the two nations open, bitter enemies by 1963. In December, 1967, it can be assumed, Chervonenko was anxious not to have a similar blot on his record in Czechoslovakia. It seems likely he forwarded Novotny's appeal with a fervent endorsement.

The result, on December 8, was a flying visit to Prague by Soviet Communist Party chief Leonid I. Brezhnev, who spoke to representatives of both factions and saw nothing in the situation to disturb Soviet interests. This was, after all, not a liberal-conservative split threatening to make Czechoslovakia a maverick like Yugoslavia if the wrong side won. Among Novotny's opponents were such reliable and well-known conservatives as Hendrych and Dolansky. Some reports suggest that Brezhnev's urging shifted the Presidium vote from eight to two, to five to five, with Chudik, Lenart, and Lastovicka coming over to Novotny's side. Other reports held that Brezhnev refrained from exerting any pressure once he had concluded that the squabble was purely internal. In any case, Brezhnev departed knowing that Novotny might be ousted as Czechoslovak Party chief but leaving as his parting words to the feuding factions, "This is your affair." Novotny is said to have bitterly declared afterward that he would have been better off if he had not invited Brezhnev. In any case, a Soviet hands-off policy had been proclaimed. Brezhnev and the Soviet Politburo he headed had made a historic mistake.

As the Presidium deadlock continued, tension built up in Prague. The Central Committee meeting was postponed, producing angry grumbling among many committee members who had arrived in Prague and then had to return home. Word began to seep to the outside world that a political crisis was erupting in once solid, stable, dependable Czechoslovakia.

When the Central Committee finally met on December 19, it was faced with an unprecedented situation. A deadlocked Presidium had no resolution to propose to resolve the crisis, and there was no prearranged list of speakers to dutifully approve the leaders' proposal. The result was a decision to have free debate. This set off a three-day verbal cyclone. All the bitterness accumulated over the years erupted as speaker after speaker gave vent to his passions. Supporters and opponents of Novotny exchanged personal insults and political charges. Novotny tried at the beginning to ease the tension by admitting some faults and promising concessions to the Slovaks. But matters had gone too far. Chudik, speaking for the President's supporters, threatened that the workers would never let Novotny be ousted. Hendrych asserted he had acted against the intellectuals "under the pressure of Comrade Novotny." A rank and file Central Committee member, Frantisek Vodslon, protested that the official announcement saying that Brezhnev had been invited to Prague by the Central Committee was a lie.

The most remarkable and most passionate speech was made by Ota Sik, the long frustrated and often disappointed advocate of economic reform and political liberalization. He asserted that the entire policy of the ruling Presidium was bankrupt and that a new body should be elected. He called for an end to the old Leninist ban on organized factions in a Communist country. Instead, he urged the legalization of organized opposition groups. The economic situation of the country was catastrophic, he declared, and only drastic action could meet the nation's and the people's needs. He proposed the formation of committees of economic experts to direct the economy and to have the power to make decisions binding on Party officials at all levels.

So many members of the Central Committee wanted to speak that, after three days, fewer than half of the would-be orators had had their say. With the anti-Novotny tide running swiftly, the President's supporters fought for time, arguing that it was almost Christmas and it would be wise to adjourn the meeting until early January. The proposal was accepted, along with another one that the daily direction of the Czechoslovak Communist Party be entrusted during the interim to an enlarged Presidium, the members of the original group plus the eleven regional Communist Party secretaries.

The last days of 1967 and the first days of 1968 were a period of intensive politicking. Novotny's foes sought to mobilize Party members' support at meetings throughout the country. Novotny's friends also did some proselytizing among Party members, but they turned their main efforts in other directions. They informed the Soviet ambassador that the trend of the Central Committee meeting had indicated that, if Novotny was ousted, he would be replaced by a far more liberal regime, one that would endanger Soviet interests. Chervonenko began lobbying assiduously for Novotny, paying particular attention to General Bohumir Lomsky, the Minister of Defense. Soon word was circulating that the Soviet Union would intervene if the Party followed the "revisionist" course of liberal extremists like Sik. An attempt was made to mobilize the armed forces for political pressure on behalf of Novotny. Apparently, the director of this effort was the mysterious Miroslav Mamula, head of the Central Committee's eighth department, the Party's watchdog for security in the entire Party and state and military apparatus. A subordinate of Mamula, Major General Jan Sejna, drew up a letter supporting Novotny and got an impressive list of high-ranking officers to sign it. More ominously, plans were being made for a possible military coup, using troops that had earlier been scheduled to go on maneuvers. Steps were taken to neutralize high-ranking Slovak officers so they could not interfere with the coup, but it was in vain. General Vaclav Prchlik got wind of what was planned and informed Dubcek. At a dramatic and secret Presidium meeting, Novotny was faced with evidence of the plans for a military coup. He protested he knew nothing about it and gave the orders that made a coup impossible.

In this feverish atmosphere, the expanded Presidium met in the first days of January to consider plans for the resumed Central Committee meeting. Drahomir Kolder, an opponent of Novotny, immediately proposed that Party Secretary Lubomir Strougal succeed Novotny as First Secretary. Strougal declined and nominated Vice Premier Oldrich Cernik, but he declined, too. Novotny then proposed his ally Premier Lenart. Lenart declined. Novotny, apparently expecting the declinations to continue, nominated Dubcek, and Dubcek accepted. Hence, Dubcek was the nominee the Presidium recommended to the Central Committee when it reconvened on January 3.

But Novotny had not given up. In his New Year's broadcast to the nation, he, in effect, offered major concessions to his opponents, particularly to the Slovaks. In words that echoed Dubcek's earlier demands, he called for "priority" economic development of Slovakia and its still unused resources. Novotny appeared as the great advocate of "socialist democracy," which, he now asserted, "must be increasingly applied in all spheres of life." He praised "progressive culture and art," whether born in capitalistic or socialistic countries. Plans were made during these last days of desperate effort to have Novotny nominated from the floor by a member of the Central Committee. Their backs to the wall, Novotny's followers were willing to gamble that the expanded Presidium's recommendation of Dubcek could be overridden. Evidently, the calculation was that, even at the last minute, Dubcék might be defeated in the Central Committee because he was a Slovak and the majority of those voting were, like Novotny, Czechs. Novotny may well have consoled himself with the thought that a Slovak had never headed the Communist Party of Czechoslovakia.

But all efforts were in vain. After three days of furious oratory, the announcement came: Novotny had "resigned" as First Secretary, although he retained the presidency—in the circumstances, a purely ceremonial post. Dubcek was First Secretary, and four additional members were elected to the Party Presidium: Jan Piller, Deputy Minister for Heavy Industry; Josef Spacek, Party chief of the Brno region, who had protected the liberal magazine *Host do Domu;* Emil Rigo, of gypsy origin and head of the Communist Party organization at the huge East Slovak Iron Works; and Josef Boruvka, a collective farm chairman known for his plain speaking on the country's agricultural problems. The revolution had succeeded. A new era had begun.

II

1968:
THE 200 DAYS

The Silence
of January

The Soviet Union knows how to take defeat gracefully, when and if it must. The last-minute effort to save Antonin Novotny's dominance in Prague had failed, but the superficial reader of *Pravda*'s first page on January 6, 1968, would find no obvious sign of displeasure. There was the official Czechoslovak news agency (*Ceteka*) statement on the Central Committee meeting that had accepted Novotny's "resignation" and elected Dubcek. There was the *Ceteka* biography of Dubcek, written in proper, laudatory spirit and ending with assurance of Dubcek's "faithfulness to the principles of proletarian internationalism." And there was the text of Brezhnev's protocol telegram to Dubcek, extending "hearty congratulations," wishing him "successes" in his work, and assuring him that the Central Committee of the Soviet Communist Party was "firmly confident" that the existing "brotherly, sincere friendship" between the Soviet and Czechoslovak peoples "will further strengthen and develop."

There were nuances, of course, for the sharp-eyed. For example, the picture of Dubcek on *Pravda*'s front page was a poorly reproduced one-column cut about the size of a passport picture. Some readers must have wondered why the news of this major change in Prague was placed in the bottom half of the page, directly under the text of a Soviet note protesting American bombing of a Soviet freighter in Haiphong harbor. Even more curious was the position of Brezhnev's congratulatory telegram: near the very bottom of the page, under a much longer and warmer Central Committee message marking the fiftieth anniversary of the minuscule Communist Party of Argentina. Some readers must have wondered why, since Dubcek's biography said he had spent many years in the Soviet Union, there was no effort to strike a personal note by printing an interview with some Soviet citizen or citizens who had known him.

Yet even Soviet citizens troubled by such reflections must have been reassured, for the moment, by Dubcek's biography. He was, that document reported, the son of a progressive worker who, after a few years as an immigrant in the United States during World War I, had returned home and joined the Communist Party of Czechoslovakia "immediately after its formation." In 1925, when young Alexander was only 3 to 4 years old, his family, along with three hundred other Czechoslovak Communists, had gone to the Soviet Union to live and work in an industrial cooperative. After receiving primary and secondary education in Soviet schools, the 17-year old Dubcek returned to Czechoslovakia with his family and the very next year joined the illegal Communist Party. During World War II, he, his older brother, and his father fought with the Communist partisans against the Nazis; his older brother was killed, and Alexander himself was wounded twice. After the war, the biography noted, young Dubcek worked in a distillery in the town of Trencin, while climbing the ladder of Party office to leadership of the local Communist Party unit. Then, in the early 1950's, he was selected to attend Moscow's Higher Party School, the elite international school for rising Communist Party officials, from which he graduated with honors in 1958. This was an impeccable background, roughly akin to that of a promising British junior executive from Eton and Oxford sent by I.B.M. or General Motors to the Harvard Business School. Little wonder that a decade after graduating from the Moscow institution Dubcek was the leader of the Czechoslovak Communist Party.

But even in all this, the eagle-eyed Muscovite might have seen some opportunities for questions. At 46, wasn't Dubcek a trifle young for such responsibility, especially when all the chief Soviet and other Eastern European leaders were in their fifties, sixties, and seventies? And why did the Dubcek family leave the Soviet Union in 1938? Were they victims of the Stalinist terror? Had they become disillusioned with Soviet Communism in practice as opposed to Communism in theory?

The Moscow Politburo, of course, had far more information on Dubcek. As foreigners in Stalinist Russia in the 1930's, the Dubcek family must have been kept under close surveillance. In Czechoslovakia after 1948, too, the "teachers" from Moscow worked particularly closely with Prague's secret police and sent files on rising political figures back to Beria's headquarters as a matter of course. If there had been anything really damaging, however, Dubcek would never have gotten to Moscow's Higher Party School, let alone become First Secretary of the Slovak Communist Party. That he was a Slovak nationalist was clear, but from Moscow's point of view that may well have seemed an asset. In predominantly Czech Czechoslovakia, it hardly seemed likely that a Slovak leader could build a personal power position that would let him stray far onto dangerous paths. Moreover, so far as one could then see, Dubcek lacked all elements of political charisma. Seeing Dubcek must have reinforced Moscow's feeling that he could hardly be dangerous. Tall but rather slender and ungainly, homely of face, not very elegantly dressed, he looked more like a clerk than a political leader. Such considerations must have weighed heavily in his favor when balanced against disturbing indications that he was moving toward a position perceptibly different from Moscow's. In February, 1967, he had written that "the chief method of Party guidance is, and must be, persuasion. . . . Administrative methods are alien to the mission of our Party." In December, 1967, he had written: "The Party does not live outside, nor above society, but is society's integral part. . . . We must challenge any elements of superiority or subjectivism and we must resist attempts to assert the influence of the Party in society by means of methods which society might regard as authoritative or as forceful." Brezhnev and his colleagues may have consoled themselves with the thought that such expressions of "rotten liberalism" were mere demagoguery, efforts to curry favor with restive intellectuals. But the Moscow policy-makers knew that in any case they would have to keep a close eye on a Czechoslovakia suddenly become quarrelsome and potentially troublesome. What would count was not what Dubcek had said or had written in the past but what he would do in his new job.

Finally, one other, perhaps decisive, factor must be mentioned in any explanation of why the leaders in Moscow let the momentous power shift in Prague take place, despite last minute misgivings and strivings to retain Novotny. The year 1967 had not been a good one for them, despite the enormous propaganda effort mounted for the celebration of the fiftieth anniversary of the Bolshevik Revolution. It had been the year of Svetlana Stalin's successful escape and of the tragic death of astronaut Vladimir Komarov. It had been a year of foreign-policy defeats, notably the Middle East debacle and the galling defiance of Rumania, which had recognized West Germany and had refused to follow Moscow's anti-Israel lead. Domestically, 1967 had been a year of steady battle against precisely the kind of unrest among intellectuals, young people, and nationalist minorities that had helped topple Novotny. The day Dubcek was elected in Prague, Moscow was preparing for the trial later that same month of several young writers. That trial, the Kremlin hierarchs knew, would bring more unpleasant publicity abroad. As Dubcek was being elected, much high-level Kremlin attention was also going to the last preparations for a world meeting of Communist parties in Budapest at the end of February, a meeting aimed at reconsolidating Soviet leadership of the Communist world outside China. A public quarrel with Czechoslovakia at that time would have been most inconvenient. In short, the men in the Kremlin already had many troubles on their hands when the change of leadership was taking place in Prague. It is not surprising that, divided and harassed by the other difficulties and issues, they preferred to move cautiously in relation to Czechoslovakia and to hope for the best while beginning to consider what they might do if the worst occurred.

* * *

In Czechoslovakia itself, of course, Dubcek's elevation produced a wave of speculation and puzzlement. The major part of the population knew nothing of what had happened at the October, December, and January Central Committee meetings, and for a time an effort was even made to keep the details of the bitter struggle from the rank-and-file Party members. Central Committee members journeyed throughout the country to inform the Party bureaucracy, but most of the population had to depend on rumors—some accurate, others not—or on Western broadcasting stations, though the latter at first were not fully informed. Alarm was the reaction of many in the upper and middle layers of bureaucracy;

their automatic fear was that Dubcek would institute wholesale purges of those who had risen under Novotny. That Dubcek was a Slovak was the most obvious fact to the ordinary
man in the street. Soon Czechs were grumbling about a "Slovak
dictatorship," pointing out that both the Party First Secretary and Premier Lenart were Slovaks. Had they known the
phrase, no doubt, many would have complained that "Slovak
Power" had won. In Slovakia, conversely, the change produced glee along with bewilderment. Perhaps now, many
reflected, Slovakia might begin to get a fair deal. Those
hopes were raised further a few days after Dubcek's election,
when the National Assembly met and adopted a budget
that not only increased funds allocated to the region's development but put them at the direct disposal of the Slovak
authorities.

As January wore on, the entire nation looked daily to
Prague for some word from Dubcek. But the days and weeks
passed, and there was only silence from the new leader. Not
only was he silent: There were no purges. Everyday life
continued in its normal channels, and in factories, offices,
universities, research institutes, and Party bureaus, there
were the same bosses as before. Perhaps Dubcek was merely
a figurehead and nothing had changed? Misgivings increased
at the end of the month when, still not having spoken to the
people, Dubcek suddenly flew to Moscow for a "friendship
visit." The usual uninformative communiqué issued at the
end of two days spoke of a "complete unity of views" reached
in an atmosphere of "cordial friendship, sincerity, and
friendly understanding which corresponds to the character
of fraternal relations between the two Parties." Only seven
months later, two days after more than half a million troops
had invaded Czechoslovakia, did the Kremlin add more information. At the January meeting, *Pravda* reported on
August 22, 1968, the Soviet leaders had warned that the situation developing in Czechoslovakia "may lead to a weaken-

ing of the Party of the Czechoslovak Communists and to the growth of attitudes dangerous to socialism in definite circles of Czechoslovak society subject to the influence of the bourgeois point of view and of imperialist propaganda." The Soviet leaders had warned also, *Pravda* continued, that Czechoslovakia even then was witnessing the "revival of the activities of right, revisionist elements which were trying to use the complex situation that had developed in the country for goals far from the interests of socialism." *Pravda* added that Dubcek and his colleagues had said merely that "they were conscious of the tension in the country's political situation and that they would take the necessary measures for stabilizing the atmosphere." There is no reason to doubt *Pravda*'s veracity on this, but of Moscow's fears, Dubcek told his people nothing at the time. A pattern was being set by a leader who preferred to keep his cards concealed from friend and foe alike.

So great did the criticism of Dubcek's silence and apparent inaction become in these early weeks that one of his supporters, Ondrej Klokoc, editor of the Bratislava *Pravda*, was moved to respond. He summarized the questions people were asking: "Is not everything that is now happening in this country merely something to impress the observer; won't everything finally go on as before? Isn't it high time that something should have moved since the last meeting of the Central Committee? The First Secretary . . . has been replaced—but everything else has remained unchanged." Why weren't the Novotnyites being purged, people were asking, and wouldn't the many remaining conservatives sabotage Dubcek to prove they were right? Klokoc's answer was to chide the critics for not understanding democracy, for wanting to apply the same old rotten purge tactics the other side had employed in the bad old days. Didn't others have the right of free speech without being punished for exercising it? Dubcek's abstention from purging his opponents was proof he was abiding by the noblest Leninist norms, Klokoc assured his audience.

The truth was probably more prosaic and less flattering to Dubcek's democratic and Leninist image. For one thing, as a Slovak, Dubcek must have been very conscious of the suspicion or worse with which he was regarded by many in the nation's Czech majority. For Dubcek to have begun talking and purging immediately might have reinforced the suspicions of the backward and strengthened his opponents. Moreover, Dubcek did not have very much power in his new post. He had been elected by a coalition that included conservatives as well as liberals, whose members differed among themselves about what should be done. Novotny himself still sat in the Presidium, and so did the four who had supported him in the showdown in December. The army, the secret police, and almost all other key institutions of Czechoslovak society were in the hands of Novotnyites. Moscow, acting through Ambassador Chervonenko and others, must have been exerting pressure, too. Far from being free to do as he pleased, Dubcek in those early weeks must have felt almost bound in a strait jacket. The fact that Moscow kept Dubcek waiting three and a half weeks for a meeting with Kremlin leaders suggests that the latter wanted to make their coolness to the new man in Prague very apparent. Finally, there is persuasive evidence that when the bitter battle in the Central Committee of the Czechoslovak Communist Party ended, the two sides agreed on at least a temporary mutual amnesty. They would hide the bitterness of the struggle and the identity of those leading the battle on each side, lest publication of this information divide the country as well and lead to bloody purges.

Dubcek's long January silence undoubtedly reflected the fact that he had no real program for Czechoslovakia. Fate and politics had played a cruel trick on him. Within a matter of weeks he had been transformed from chief spokesman and lobbyist for a minority group into the effective political head of the nation. All domestic issues other than Slovak grievances had been secondary in his activity, though he had placed himself more or less cautiously on the side of moderate liberals and moderate reformers on such issues as freedom for writers and changes in the national economy. It may be questioned how much he knew of foreign policy; certainly, it had never been one of his major preoccupations. At best, therefore, it can be said that when Dubcek took power, he knew the direction in which he wanted to take Czechoslovakia but had no ready blueprint or road map. A week after Dubcek's elevation, one of his followers, looking for a public statement by the new First Secretary that could be cited as a short, concise program of "Dubcekism," could find nothing more illuminating than the following:

> The period just ended was marked by an appraisal of the values established in the past, and was a test of our ability to support and extend them for the present and the future. What we are now experiencing is a historic turn, a transition to a new quality of socialist society; this has characterized our work and makes enormous claims on us.

Dubcek's silence and his seeming lack of any immediate, coherent political program at a time when the old regime had obviously been repudiated had two immediate effects. First, it threw the entire apparatus of control over public information and discussion into utter confusion. No censor and no Party bureaucrat knew what was currently right or wrong, what was allowed, and what was prohibited. Their confusion, uncertainty, and fear paralyzed them, making them extremely reluctant to ban anything short of an outright attack on the Soviet Union or on Dubcek. Second, the new leader's silence created a political vacuum into which the bold and the ambitious were tempted to move. We may suspect that some who took advantage of what quickly became the new freedom for discussion were prompted behind the scenes by Dubcek himself, who was anxious to have certain ideas advanced in public but reluctant to take personal responsibility for them. Once the lead had been given, others quickly jumped on the band wagon from either honest conviction or simple opportunism.

In the weeks of Dubcek's silence, therefore, three formerly secondary figures, a Slovak, a Czech, and a Jew, suddenly thrust themselves—or were thrust by unseen hands behind the scenes—to the center of the Czechoslovak political stage. All three were veteran Communists who had been framed in the early 1950's and had served years in Novotny's prisons. All three quickly became major spokesmen for new democratic trends in the nation's life, as authors of widely printed articles and frequent guests on the nation's radio and television programs.

Gustav Husak, the Slovak, was the first to appear on center stage. As noted earlier, he had been head of Slovakia's government from 1946 to 1950, then imprisoned and convicted as a bourgeois nationalist, and finally freed but restricted to working as a historical researcher. A week after Dubcek's election, Husak's article in the Slovak periodical *Kulturny Zivot* set the tone for much that was to follow.

Czechoslovakia's people, he complained, had been treated like kindergarten tots during the Novotny regime, with its attitude of "hold onto the line, children, so you don't get lost; don't ask questions, you won't understand until you're bigger; do as you're told or you'll be punished." But the people of Czechoslovakia were really mature, cultured adults who, like other Europeans, wanted to know what was going on and to understand their nation's policies, to have a voice in key decisions and in electing leaders, and then to praise or criticize or replace those leaders on the basis of their performance. Husak phrased his call for the needed changes in these words:

> The citizen wants to see in his national and state representatives his own civic and national self-realization. He wants guarantees that he can exercise his right of choice, control, and responsibility freely. This is a problem of the progressive democratization of the social order and involves the liberation and development of all the people's creative forces, its physical and intellectual potential, and its commitment to act. It is a problem of institutionally expressing and guaranteeing the cooperation of millions of hands and brains.

Husak had published, in short, a plea for genuine democracy in a Marxist state.

More surprising to many was the sudden emergence of Josef Smrkovsky as a spokesman for the new liberal trend. He had been a leading Czech Communist in Prague at the end of World War II, helping direct the uprising there in the closing days of the war. He too had been purged, but he had been politically as well as judicially rehabilitated afterward. When Novotny stepped down, Smrkovsky was already a member of the Party Central Committee and Minister of Forestry and Water Economy in Premier Lenart's cabinet. In the mid-1960's, Smrkovsky was widely regarded as an opportunist who had toadied to Novotny. But in mid-1967, Smrkovsky had given some reason to think he was a more complex character. He did this by personally exploding a favorite regime myth: the idea that the Americans had not been interested in liberating Prague at the end of World War II and had therefore callously permitted many Czechs to die needlessly. On the contrary, Smrkovsky reported in mid-1967, the Americans had been willing to liberate Prague, and some of them had arrived in the city at the height of the uprising. Smrkovsky revealed that he himself had refused American help for fear that liberation of

Prague by the United States would hamper the Communist Party's plans for the future. And, of course, Smrkovsky's breath-taking political career in the Dubcek era indicates that he must have distinguished himself in the Central Committee debates that preceded Novotny's ouster. In any case, he moved quickly early in 1968 to seize the limelight and build up personal popularity. In the process, he won the reputation of a "publicity hound" among some of the cynical foreign correspondents in Prague.

Nevertheless, Smrkovsky's article in the trade-union paper *Prace* on January 21 must be regarded as a major and useful statement of what the victorious reformers had in mind. He began by emphasizing that more than personalities had been involved in the Central Committee struggle and that "everything which interests and troubles every Communist and every citizen has been at issue." The basic goal "is the elimination of bureaucratic manners and remnants of the past from our Party and from the state apparatus." Decisions must be made on a democratic basis; the rule of individuals or administrative bodies over the people must be made impossible. "The administration must be the assistant and the executor of the political will of the people, of the nation, of the Party—and not the other way around!"

He then went on to call for realistic attitudes, for the avoidance of promises that could not be fulfilled, for a policy of telling "the truth to the nation, whether it is palatable or not, and then we must settle everything through a common effort with the nation." He called for reconciliation of the workers, the farmers, the intellectuals, and the young people, all based on "mutual trust." Finally, he outlined what was, in effect, the basic essence of Dubcekism:

> We must determinedly correct, repair, and rectify the deformations of socialism which occurred in the past, and we must not permit new ones to arise. Conflicting opinions about the solutions of problems must be settled in a democratic man-

ner, as is stipulated in the Party statutes. They must not be settled by means of an authoritative pronouncement. High posts of office must not be regarded as held for life. Conditions must be established which permit an honorable discharge from, and a return to, high and even the highest positions. . . . An honorable and socially dignified retirement of older officials must be facilitated for those who deserve it. . . . In the economic sphere, the economic reform must be resolutely continued and developed as a whole and its principles must be "pushed through" to every place of work. In the social sphere, the democratic spirit must be restored and an atmosphere for the exchange, and contest, of opinions must be created, permitting the most valuable and progressive ideas to prevail over conservative and outdated opinions. . . .

The issue is that the whole nation should again rally to bring about an upsurge of all creative forces, to bring about the reconstruction, development, and creation of its socialist people's state, of our Czechoslovak Socialist Republic.

They were brave, inspiring words. They and their equivalent repeated by Smrkovsky and then by a multitude of lesser political figures—journalists, radio and television commentators, and the like—sparked the dreams and hopes that soared so high in Czechoslovakia until August 20, 1968. However, experience was to show that not all these pledges would be kept, not even by those, like Smrkovsky, who made them.

Eduard Goldstuecker, a Jew, had been an envoy to Israel before being arrested, made to "confess" that he was a "Zionist spy and traitor," and convicted and sentenced in the early 1950's. Like Smrkovsky, he had been rehabilitated; he became a professor of German literature at the Charles University, a deputy rector, and the successful leader of the fight to readmit Franz Kafka's writings into his native land. At the age of 55, he had the reputation of a cautious liberal, one who wanted more freedom but accepted the fact that the Communist Party would remain the leading force in Czechoslovakia. Some considered him an opportunist who put survival above all and who had taken care to cultivate the friendship of Party ideologist Jiri Hendrych. But, at the Writers Congress in June, 1967, Goldstuecker had denounced censorship, and in November, 1967, during the crisis at Charles University, he had shown more ability to communicate meaningfully with the angry students than had any other administrator. At the end of 1967, he had declined the chairmanship of the Writers Union, although he would probably have been the one man acceptable to both the dissident writers and the old Party hierarchy.

Goldstuecker appeared on center stage on January 24, when the old leadership crisis of the Writers Union—going back to its stormy June 1967, meeting—was finally resolved by his election as Chairman. Chosen to serve as Vice Chairman were the dismissed Central Committee alternate member Jan Prochazka and the Slovak writer Miroslav Valek, who, as head of the Slovak Writers Union, had more than once shown his sympathy with the advocates of greater literary freedom. These choices would have been enough to show that quite a different wind was blowing among the intellectuals than had blown in previous months. But an even stronger blast was the announcement that the former editors of *Literarni Noviny,* the weekly taken away from the Writers Union the previous September, had been authorized to establish and publish *Literarni Listy,* a new weekly organ of the Writers Union, which would begin appearing in March.

All this was sensation enough, but soon Goldstuecker was to add to it as he began his career as a radio and television star. In one of his first interviews after being named Chairman of the Writers Union, Goldstuecker announced that the Union would appeal for clemency for Jan Benes. Benes, a young writer, had been sentenced to five years in jail for "disrupting the Republic and attempting fraud," but his trial the previous July had been seen, correctly, as the first response of an angry regime to the June revolt at the Writers Congress.

In the weeks that followed, Goldstuecker was to use his new platform at the head of the Writers Union to become one of the great preachers for the new humanistic socialist democracy, for the marriage of Marxism in economics with democracy in politics. Early in 1968, at the height of his public career, he would become so intoxicated with the perspectives ahead that he would call for making Czechoslovakia a land "with more freedom than any bourgeois country."

At that time, few knew what a historic role *Literarni Listy* was to play in the months ahead. But the announcement of its publication and the other Writers Union developments at the same time must have come like an electric shock to Czechoslovak liberals and progressives. At last there was meaningful action, and persons who had suffered because of their devotion to liberty were being pushed to the fore. It promised much for the future—though Dubcek was still publicly silent as January ended.

But it was not only new liberal voices that were coming into prominence in January; conservatives—or at least moderate reformers who, alarmed by developments, were becoming conservative—were also advancing. The case of Vasil Bilak is particularly important. Late in January, he was elected First Secretary of the Slovak Communist Party to succeed Alexander Dubcek. It is almost inconceivable that Bilak could have gotten this post without Dubcek's enthusiastic endorsement; yet in the months that followed, Bilak turned out to be one of the most conservative members of Czechoslovakia's ruling group. Here, for example, is what Bilak had to say in April about press freedom:

> The Communists employed in radio and television must realize that radio and television are instruments of state policies, that they have not ceased to be instruments of the ideology and

policies of the socialist state, and that for this reason they cannot serve anything else than the interests of the socialist state.

I think that it is a shortcoming in the work of the mass communications media not to have properly reflected all the wealth of ideas and suggestions contained in the many documents of the Central Committee, in comrade Dubcek's speeches. . . . Every thesis deserves to be thoroughly explained and commented upon in order that the views and the minds of the people be united toward positive work.

Naturally, it is more comfortable to collect sensational reports, to reprint articles from the bourgeois press, to publish all sorts of unilateral statements, but it is of little social value. Those who work in this fashion probably do not realize that they are ignoring the progressive role of their own Party and that they do injustice to many honest people.

There was not a word of this with which the men in the Kremlin would have disagreed, but it completely contradicted the philosophy of free speech and free press, which was to become central to the "Dubcek revolution" in Czechoslovakia in 1968. Bilak was not alone, of course, in such thinking. Drahomir Kolder, a Czech member of the Presidium, also increased his importance under Dubcek. His views were so agreeable to Moscow that, as the months went by, when Leonid I. Brezhnev phoned Dubcek about one problem or another, he would also ask, "And what does Comrade Kolder think?" The point is that in January, 1968, a broadly based coalition united behind Dubcek to oust Novotny. But, the ouster accomplished, the months that followed showed how very different were the views represented in this coalition and how inevitable was the resultant conflict among factions supporting such incompatible philosophies.

5

The Speeches
of February

Religion, according to Marx, is the opiate of the masses in a
capitalist society. Committed to atheism, Communist regimes
have had to find a substitute for religion to distract people
from discontent that otherwise would be easily generated by
monotonous work, dreary and overcrowded housing, and low
wages. The substitute is sports, which drain excess energy
from millions of participants and give vicarious thrills to
millions of spectators. In Czechoslovakia, sports are a national
mania. When this ordinarily harmless madness suddenly be-
comes entangled with sensitive matters, powerful psychological and political effects can result.

So it was on February 15, 1968, when the Olympic hockey
teams of Czechoslovakia and the Soviet Union met in Gre-
noble, France. The Soviet team was undefeated and was
favored to win the championship. On the previous day,
Czechoslovakia had lost its first game to Canada. Every
Czechoslovak who could do so was watching or listening to

the game, hoping against hope for a victory over the Soviets. Czechoslovakia won by a score of five to four, and an explosion of joy engulfed the nation. Thousands of people took to the streets to celebrate the event.

When I visited Prague two weeks later, the glow from victory was still perceptible. To the ordinary man in the street this defeat of Big Brother was proof that, with the advent of Dubcek something at last had changed. Time and again, I was assured by waiters, cab drivers, and similar proletarians that "Novotny would never have let us win." All of a sudden, the vague hopes that things might improve suddenly took on a concreteness they had not had before. National pride and a newly reinforced sense of national worth were suddenly and unexpectedly joined to the movement for domestic reform.

How much and what kind of domestic reform should there be? How rapidly should changes take place and in what directions? Who should lead the state, the Party, and the key social institutions during the reform? About these and related questions, there were bitter struggles all through February. An amazed population, accustomed to public unanimity among Communists, watched in disbelief as the debate and struggle unfolded in the newspapers and other media. The pro-Dubcek liberals—Communists and non-Communists alike—controlled the press, radio, and television almost completely and were using these media to educate the population in the ideas of democratic Communism. This activity required dramatic reversals of position by some of the individuals who had climbed on the liberal band wagon rather late. But if Jiri Hendrych was trying to appear as an apostle of tolerance and democracy, why couldn't lesser folk? There were still conservative die-hards even in the press and many more of them in high and intermediate places elsewhere. Denied what they considered an adequate forum in the mass media, these individuals could still use the power of their position to impede change; they could make speeches and spread rumors; and they could try to organize underground opposition to the dominant Dubcek faction.

Since the battle front was everywhere, the struggles in individual factories, Communist Party organizations, and administrative hierarchies were extremely varied. A few examples will illustrate what was going on. The Writers Union had received formal permission to reestablish its own weekly publication, to be named *Literarni Listy*. Since no one doubted that, once begun, this periodical would be an eloquent and powerful voice for reform, conservative officials sought to delay publication and to minimize the periodical's influence. What better way than to restrict the circulation and size of *Literarni Listy*? When the editors asked for a paper allocation sufficient for printing 150,000 copies of a sixteen-page weekly, they were offered only enough paper for 50,000 copies of a ten-page weekly. The Writers Union finally got enough paper, but, for a time, resistance was fierce. Victory came only when the dispute was publicized and public opinion had made its pressure felt.

In many of the nation's factories and mines, the conservatives fared well during the early weeks after the Dubcek take over. To the mass of workers, talk of democracy and other abstract freedoms meant little. On the contrary, many were fearful of reform, apprehensive that the new regime would shake up the economy and end the old comfortable ways. The conservatives began to exploit the workers' fears and prejudices. Czechoslovakia had been taken over by a group of counterrevolutionary intellectuals, so the rumors went, and the workers would have to pay for this disaster. There would be mass unemployment, large wage reductions, and a forced speed-up of the pace of work, the alarmists told their receptive audience. No less a dignitary than President Novotny joined in this campaign. He not only went to factories to make speeches but he began to develop the common touch. He would suddenly appear at a workers' restaurant, buy beer for everyone, and explain how glad he was that at last he could talk directly to the workers. When asked why he had not mingled with the proletariat earlier, he would explain that while he was both President and Party First Secretary he simply could not escape from the pile of essential work always on his desk. The idea was spread that the workers' only hope against liberal reforms lay in the armed workers' militia, the group that had played such a key role in the February, 1948, seizure of power. In February, 1968, the conservatives had already begun whispering: The workers' militia should take up its guns to preserve the gains made two decades earlier.

In part, the conservative tactics were born of desperation. To the astonishment of many, Dubcek could be a most effective politician when he entered the fray publicly. On the first day of February, the new Party First Secretary ended his long silence by addressing the Seventh Congress of Agricultural Cooperatives in Prague. He was a simple but effective speaker, who projected warmth and friendliness. He did not—as his predecessors had done—berate the farmers or tell them how to raise their crops and livestock. Rather, he made plain that the new regime trusted the peasants as well as the workers and wanted and needed genuine support and cooperation. He emphasized the importance of democracy along with discipline, to which priority had been given in the past. "Democracy," he told his audience, "is not only the right and chance to pronounce one's own views, but also the way in which people's views are handled, whether they have a real feeling of co-responsibility, co-decision, whether they really feel they are participating in making decisions and solving important problems." Government organs, he declared, have the obligation to create the best conditions in which farmers can apply their skills and initiative, not to give orders on when and how to reap and sow. He defined his objective as helping agriculture to "achieve full and equal rights."

His speech completely transformed the meeting from the earlier, stereotyped congresses where strict Communist Party control had determined who should speak, what should be said, and what the final resolutions should contain. A storm of free debate and fiery criticism broke out. The delegates had interpreted Dubcek's words as an invitation to speak their minds and voice their many grievances. In this unprecedented situation, the final resolution of the Congress—prepared in advance by Ministry of Agriculture officials in accordance with tradition and precedent—had to be completely rewritten during a frantic drafting session. Into that resolution went a demand for a national farmers' organization that could lobby and exert pressure for the peasants' economic and other interests. Into it also went calls for full democracy on the collective farms, for giving collective farms the same legal and economic rights as other socialist organizations, for an end to monopolies in the machinery, chemical, building-materials, and other industries that served agriculture poorly, and for extending to collective farmers the same social insurance and other benefits enjoyed by industrial workers.

Nothing like this public demonstration of democracy in action had ever been seen in Communist Czechoslovakia. Clearly, if this meeting set a pattern for the future, there would be many changes in all areas of the country's life. That the farmers' meeting was intended to set such a pattern was strongly hinted a few days later with the announcement that an Action Program was being prepared, which would define the Party line in all major areas of the nation's life, spotlighting mistakes of the past and prescribing what must be done in the future. A few days after this announcement, Josef Smrkovsky—emerging prominently as a regime spokesman in the press and over the air waves—wrote in *Rude Pravo*, "It lies on us, on Czechs and on Slovaks to enter courageously into unexplored terrain and in it to look for *our Czechoslovak socialist road. This is in the last analysis our duty* [to ourselves] *and to the whole international socialist movement*" (emphasis in original).

However, the most intense struggle during this period probably raged behind the scenes. Whatever their earlier promises to their defeated opponents, Dubcek and his supporters knew that to survive they would have to break the old guard's tight hold on many key positions in the country. The prime target, of course, was Novotny, still occupying the President's office and home in Hradcany Castle on the hill overlooking Prague. Hints began to appear in the press and other media that it was getting to be time for him to resign, but he remained deaf to them. Rumors soon began to spread that he was frequently seeing the Soviet ambassador and that he had hopes of a political comeback.

By mid-February, it had finally become possible to remove lesser, though important, conservatives. Thus, on February 16, Frantisek Havlicek was dismissed as head of the Central Committee's ideological department. In that post since March, 1967, Havlicek had played a key role in carrying out the harsh ideological controls of the previous year. But Havlicek's superior, the "reformed" Jiri Hendrych, remained, while Havlicek's successor, Jaroslav Kozel, was on record as opposing any leniency in ideological matters. But perhaps Kozel had also reformed.

Even more important changes came three days later. Lieutenant General Vaclav Prchlik, age 50, was promoted from chief of the Army Political Administration to head of the Central Committee department for state administration— the feared "eighth department," which was the Party's watchdog over the entire security, judicial, and military apparatus. Though few knew it at the time, Prchlik was being rewarded for having tipped off Dubcek about the planned military coup at the height of the struggle for power. The man Prchlik succeeded, Miroslav Mamula, had played an important role in the Novotnyites' machinations two months earlier. This was a key change because Mamula had been Novotny's Beria, the former ruler's eyes and ears. The issue of Novotny's survival was fully joined, though few realized the importance of the change.

Four days after this shift, an article by Major General Egyd Pepych—General Prchlik's former deputy, who had succeeded him as head of the Army Political Administration—appeared in the army weekly *Obrana Lidu*. General Pepych wrote about "disturbing phenomena, which were meant to influence the deliberations of the Party Central Committee" during the power struggle earlier. He accused "certain functionaries" of the main Party committee at the Ministry of Defense of having given "one-sided information" about Central Committee proceedings to the top officers of the Defense Ministry. It was quickly recognized that General Pepych was hinting broadly that a military coup had been considered to save Novotny. Behind the scenes, even more sensational involvement of military-political figures was being prepared. The struggle to destroy Novotny politically was moving into high gear; General Pepych was preparing the stage for what was to come.

*   *   *

Dubcek and his colleagues were primarily concerned with domestic reforms, but from the beginning they were aware of the foreign-policy implications of their democratization and of the dangers that might come from abroad. The Hungarian Revolution had taught a lesson that was not forgotten. From the beginning, Dubcek was determined to avoid offense to the Soviet Union and to his Communist neighbors. Thus, he was careful in the speech to the collec-

tive farmers' congress—as well as in all later speeches—to
reiterate Czechoslovakia's loyalty to the Soviet Union, to
denounce West German "Neo-Nazism," and to support
Walter Ulbricht's East German regime. His trip to Moscow
at the end of January obviously had been intended to reassure the Soviet leaders. On February 4, he met with
Hungary's Janos Kadar at a town on the Hungarian border.
Three days later, he met with Poland's Wladyslaw Gomulka
at Ostrava. Both meetings ended with similar protocol declarations and with statements about full unity of views, but
observers noted that the communiqué issued after the
Gomulka meeting did not mention the usual "cordiality" in
describing the atmosphere. Then more days passed, and there
was no Dubcek meeting with the leader of the third of
Czechoslovakia's Communist neighbors, East German Walter
Ulbricht.

There were important differences in the situations of each
of Dubcek's three Communist neighbors, and these would
color their views of the beginnings being made in Czechoslovakia. Dubcek had every reason to suppose that, of the three,
Hungary would be the most sympathetic. Janos Kadar had
been installed in power in Budapest by Soviet bayonets in
1956, but he had done much in the intervening years to try
to create substantial popular support for himself. Under the
slogan "He who is not against us is with us," Kadar had
sought, with some success, to enlist the energies and enthusiasm of large numbers of non-Communists in his country's internal development. Many of the intellectuals who
had played prominent roles in creating the atmosphere for
the Hungarian Revolution of 1956 had been permitted to
resume work in safety and comfort. George Lukacs, the
brilliant Marxist philosopher who had served in Imre Nagy's
revolutionary cabinet in 1956 and had been arrested at the
same time as Nagy, had been fully reinstated, readmitted to
the Communist Party, and given a large, comfortable, airy

Budapest apartment overlooking the Danube. Early in 1968, Hungary was in the throes of a major economic reform that was very much influenced by Ota Sik's doctrines in Czechoslovakia and was going further in some respects than the Prague reform had. It was reasonable to expect Kadar to look with some sympathy and understanding on what Dubcek hoped to do. But Dubcek knew too that there were potential points of friction with the Hungarians. Slovakia had once been part of Hungary, and a Slovak like Dubcek would be the last to assume that ambitions to restore that former suzerainty had died out entirely in Budapest, although on this issue Kadar has been noticeably moderate and internationalist. Dubcek knew there were over 500,000 Hungarians in Czechoslovakia—most of them in Slovakia—and that many of them resented what they considered Slovak domination and cultural pressure as much as many Slovaks detested earlier Czech dominance and cultural pressure.

Even if the word cordiality had not been omitted from the communiqué after the Gomulka-Dubcek meeting on February 7, there would have been little reason to suppose that encounter was as pleasant as the Dubcek-Kadar talks. There was irony, of course, in the fact that Gomulka, like Kadar, had once been a prisoner of the Stalinists and had been accused of Titoist treachery. Unlike Kadar, Gomulka had come to power in defiance of Soviet wishes, but over the years, Gomulka had become as completely devoted to Moscow as Novotny was, and the atmosphere in Poland at the beginning of 1968 was far more tense than in Hungary. Gomulka had based his entire policy on his belief that Poland required Soviet assurance against any future German effort to get back the German territory incorporated into Poland in 1945. Under Novotny, a common fear of West Germany had brought Czechoslovakia, Poland, and East Germany into what foreign observers had come to call the "hard northern tier" or the "iron triangle" of Soviet-dominated Eastern Europe. To Gomulka, therefore, the fall of Novotny must have raised the awful possibility that Czechoslovakia might leave the "iron triangle" and open the door for West German influence. Nor could Gomulka have been happy, when he met with Dubcek on February 7, about the evidence of increasing democracy in Czechoslovakia. In Poland, Gomulka had tightened the reins, purging dissident intellectuals and making plain that he would stand for no trouble from the students. Gomulka must have feared the changes in Prague as a source of new encouragement and support for the trouble-making elements in his own country. To add to Gomulka's worries, his own position was being challenged by very powerful forces craftily assembled by Poland's security chief, General Mieczyslaw Moczar, whose "partisan" faction preached a brand of intensely nationalistic and anti-Semitic Polish Communism. Behind Gomulka's insecurity, too, was the continued and unique power in Poland of the Roman Catholic church, a rival living in troubled coexistence with the ruling Communists. It would be surprising if Gomulka, at the meeting on February 7, did not point out to Dubcek the dangers that Czechoslovakia's new road posed for Poland.

That Dubcek and Ulbricht did not meet during the first month and a half after the former's elevation is a hint that friction and mutual suspicion were deep. For Ulbricht, who had managed to keep much of his population only by building the Berlin Wall in 1961, the new Prague talk of democracy was anathema from the beginning. He, like Gomulka, worried about political infection from Czechoslovakia. This fear expressed itself quickly in an East German ban on the import of the German weekly published in Prague for Czechoslovakia's small German population. Even more, Ulbricht worried about the impact of the Prague changes on his effort to keep West Germany isolated from as much of Eastern Europe as possible. He saw the Kiesinger-Brandt "Grand

Coalition" in Bonn to be engaged in a policy of winning over the Eastern European states and thus isolating East Germany. Ulbricht had good reason to associate Eastern European deviation from the Moscow line about West Germany with betrayal of East Germany. Had not Rumania, with its strident nationalism, resumed diplomatic relations with Bonn in 1967? Tito was doing the same thing in the first weeks of Dubcek's rule. Prague's position must have seemed questionable to Ulbricht, who had not been completely satisfied even with Novotny's policy. The 1967 West German–Czechoslovak agreement to exchange trade delegations had had more of a political tinge and had suggested much more improvement of Prague-Bonn relations than Ulbricht had liked. Ulbricht must have sensed that as Dubcek wrestled with his difficult economic problems he would be tempted to turn to Bonn for loans and other aid—help that was unlikely to be given without political concessions of some sort.

For the moment, in early and mid-February, neither Czechoslovakia nor its neighbors were interested in publicly exposing any of their mutual points of friction. All planned to be represented later that month at the world Communist conference in Budapest, which Moscow had struggled so long to arrange. Dubcek, understandably, was also anxious to have the Prague celebration of the twentieth anniversary of the February, 1948, Communist take over proceed smoothly, with no international complications.

But if the press, radio, and television were to be free to report and comment, then inevitably they would begin to report the independent ideas on foreign policy, as well as the independent ideas about domestic arrangements, that were circulating in Czechoslovakia. In an article in early February, Smrkovsky put new emphasis on the need for equality among socialist states and argued that industrialized, developed Czechoslovakia needed "to create a type of socialism which would have something to say even to the industrial countries of Europe with their mature revolutionary workers movements." The heretical implication, of course, was that the Soviet Union had not done so. Smrkovsky suggested that the Czechoslovak Communist Party should be interested mainly in Western Europe—a far cry from its previous role of trying to win underdeveloped countries by extending economic and military assistance. A stronger indication of independent foreign-policy thinking in Czechoslovakia was given by an article in the Prague *Army Review,* which defended the Yugoslavs from past criticisms by the international Communist movement and praised them for not bowing down to the Soviet model. On Radio Prague on February 20, Eugen Loebl, Slovak economist and rehabilitated purge victim, asked publicly how long it would take Czechoslovakia to revise the "unequal relations with the Soviet Union" in the economic field.

Against this background, the leaders of Eastern Europe gathered in Prague on February 21–23 to mark the twentieth anniversary of Communist rule in Czechoslovakia. The Soviet leadership sent a very strong delegation. Accompanying Brezhnev was Peter Shelest, Politburo member and Party boss of the Ukraine (where serious nationalist discontent had come to the surface in recent years), and two important regional Party leaders, K. F. Katushev and L. S. Kulichenko. Gomulka came from Poland, Ulbricht from East Germany, Kadar from Hungary, Nicolae Ceausescu—the Rumanian Party chief—from Rumania, and Velko Vlahovic—one of Tito's leading deputies—from Yugoslavia.

On the afternoon of February 22, during the main observance of the anniversary, both Alexander Dubcek and Leonid I. Brezhnev made speeches. The Soviet leader used the old clichés about the eternal friendship of the Soviet and Czechoslovak peoples. Concealed in the rhetoric, however, were two warnings: first, that the Communist Party must be the ruler of Czechoslovakia; second, that Czechoslovakia must beware of falling victim to nationalism as China—and other states Brezhnev did not name, though it was not hard to guess he had Rumania in mind—had done. Brezhnev completely ignored the change that had just occurred in the Prague leadership.

Dubcek's speech was the comprehensive statement of his democratic reform Czechoslovakia had awaited for a month and a half. Dubcek tried to make his program as palatable as possible for Brezhnev and his other guests, claiming he was going back to 1948 and the teachings of Klement Gottwald for inspiration. But in Moscow, the editors of *Pravda*— and their chiefs—were not fooled. From Moscow's point of view, so much in Dubcek's speech was ideologically wrong that *Pravda* simply omitted over two-thirds of it. Such massive censorship suggests that Brezhnev and Shelest must have been infuriated by Dubcek's speech, perhaps believing that the Czechoslovak leader had deliberately defied and mocked them by enunciating this "revisionist" program in their presence. The character of the speech is best suggested by a few of the key paragraphs *Pravda* omitted:

In the early 1950's our peoples lived through one of the great dramas in all their history. Never before had it been possible to effect, within such a short historical period, such profound transformations in the socio-economic, political, and ideological life of the country. Unfortunately, the magnitude of the errors and shortcomings which the then leadership of the Party, regrettably, failed to avoid corresponded to the scale of those truly gigantic processes. There were many setbacks also in inner-Party life, the consequences of some of which are still felt by us. In the atmosphere of false suspicion these problems and equally serious socio-political problems were compounded by such negative phenomena as violations of socialist legality from which not only Communists suffered. I think that the task of true rehabilitation of the dignity of all those who during the first and especially the second world wars honestly served the republic, the cause of its progressive development and of the victory of socialism in our country is an integral part of our present-day efforts for the all-round democratization of the entire society and the Party. We must remove, along both state and Party lines, all the injustices done to people, and we must do so consistently and without reservations.

Science and culture are probably the most complex and delicate branch of Party activity. For here we are dealing with educated people whose work requires deep understanding and appreciation and does not tolerate stagnation, set formulas, impatience, or haste. Neither cultural nor scientific creation is free of difficulties, setbacks, and errors. It is influenced not only by shortcomings and defects in our work, which lead to disenchantment and disillusionment. We do not always correctly appraise the significance, impact and, more important, the causes. As a result, in this field we have had more frequent undesirable conflict situations that tend to aggravate relations between Party bodies and scientists and artists. However, these minor shortcomings, which occur in every field, cannot and should not prompt us to base our policy toward scientists, writers, cinema workers, artists, and other cultural workers on distrust of their public activity, its content and direction. On the contrary, our policy must be based on trust and fruitful constructive cooperation. We must eliminate everything that tends to hamstring scientific and artistic creation, everything likely to breed tensions. . . . However, the Party cannot relinquish its right and duty to see to it that artistic creation helps to form socialist man.

I do not think we can win over the youth by reproaching it or by telling it that everything it enjoys had to be won by hard effort. For young people all this is a workaday reality, something they take for granted. They do not regard it as something that had to be fought for. However, that is not the central point. The enthusiasm of the youth cannot be restricted to constantly praising our achievements. Our young people want to have achievements of their own, bring to reality their dreams and ideas, just as older people did in their young days, when the revolution gave them the opportunity. The youth must not be given gifts, things won for it by others. It must be afforded the conditions necessary to develop its own initiative, work for its own goals, that will enable our young citizens to perform their duty as a generation.

Latterly, the old view of the Party as a force which, instead of giving political leadership, decides minor issues in an authoritarian way has again gained dominance. . . . No one is likely to deny that this understanding of leadership was largely responsible for the fact that the work of many of our administrative, economic, and public institutions was largely deprived of meaningful content and responsibility, that public initiative was not encouraged, and many of our undertakings bore the stamp of formality.

For the Party to carry through its leading role in the present situation means first and foremost to create the necessary preconditions for the growth of creative initiative, to provide greater scope for confrontation and exchanges of opinion, to make it possible for every Communist to be informed thoroughly, objectively, and in good time about events in his own country and abroad, so that he should possess a point of view with regard to the Party's policy and. particularly, that he should participate not only in effecting, but also in framing the Party's political policy and in its actions, especially in the sphere in which he is employed. In brief, it means that at present, while retaining the essential centralism, we should lay the greatest accent on developing more, and above all deeper, democratic forms, and this not only in the upper Party echelons, but especially "lower down," in the organizations and among the membership.

These and similar passages were not the words of a Jeffersonian democrat. Dubcek carefully reserved the Communist Party's supreme power to assure that artistic creation "helps to form socialist man." His call for thorough, objective, and timely information was to make sure that Communist Party members were well informed, without any consideration of the rights of non-Communists. The speech had other such flaws, from a Western point of view. But to Leonid I.

Brezhnev and his comrades, coming from a Soviet Union then rapidly sinking back into neo-Stalinist barbarism, the Dubcek speech must have sounded like the most arrant and dangerous radical revisionism. They must have returned to Moscow deeply disturbed, pondering how long they could permit such dangerous heresy to be propagated next door to the Soviet Union, in the very heartland of their Eastern European empire.

6

The Scandals of March

On March 1, 1968, Czechoslovak news media reported that a hitherto obscure military officer, Major General Jan Sejna, had fled the country while under investigation for the alleged theft of about $20,000 worth of grass seeds. He had driven across the border into Hungary with his 18-year-old son and his 21-year-old mistress, the reports added. Czechoslovak authorities had asked Hungarian officials to detain and return the general. On subsequent days came word that the fleeing general had traveled successfully from Hungary into Yugoslavia and then into Italy. On March 5, news arrived that Sejna and his companions had defected to the United States and were in Washington. A stunned and incredulous nation asked who was General Sejna, what did a general have to do with grass seeds, and how could he leave the country while under investigation. Still more questions were raised when it became known that he had departed with a diplomatic passport, escaping—obviously after having been warned

—while the legal authorities were lackadaisically seeking to have his immunity as a member of the National Assembly lifted so that they could arrest him. When the answers to these and other questions came, they set off a political earthquake that sent much of the remaining Novotny power structure crashing in ruin.

With censorship practically gone—the censors were still reporting to their offices daily but occupied themselves by reading novels, doing crossword puzzles, and other harmless activities—Czechoslovakia's journalists had a chance to show they could dig deeply and effectively. A few months earlier, under Novotny, an incident such as the Sejna case might never have been mentioned publicly or might have been reported in a brief paragraph and never referred to again. But in early March, 1968, Czechoslovakia had a free press and this was the first major scandal since the January liberation from the censors. Prague's reporters seized the opportunity enthusiastically. Each day's newspaper brought a new sensation. Rumors then embroidered and elaborated on the press revelations. Here is the picture that emerged from these sources.

General Sejna was a former farm laborer with very little formal education. He had, however, a knack for making powerful friends who were willing and able to help him. The most powerful of these friends was Antonin Novotny, Jr., son of the President and former Party First Secretary. In earlier years, when young Novotny had been with the Foreign Trade Ministry, he and Sejna had engaged in mutually profitable business deals. One example that received wide attention was of the time the two men allegedly received authority to test foreign cars, theoretically in order to discover features of the automobiles that might be added to Czechoslovak cars. Using government funds, according to the stories, Novotny, Jr., and Sejna bought Mercedes-Benzes, Porsches, Jaguars, and the like, drove them for a few months, and then sold them to rich friends and pocketed the proceeds. Sejna, the accounts held, made and kept friends by giving the best parties in Czechoslovakia—elaborate and expensive affairs lubricated by limitless amounts of liquor and graced by numerous beautiful and cooperative women. He was said to be a very generous man, always willing to make soldiers and military supplies available whenever a friend wanted to build a house in the country or obtain some other amenity. He also prided himself, it was said, on his reputation as a ladies' man, but his charm reportedly boomeranged on him in 1966, when his nomination for the Central Committee roused such indignation among the men he had cuckolded that it was turned down. He had had another setback a few years earlier, when he had applied for admission to Czechoslovakia's leading higher military academy but had been refused because he lacked the necessary educational requirements. His proposed promotion to major general in the mid-1960's had drawn stiff opposition. That resistance collapsed, however, when the order to promote him was signed by President Novotny and Minister of Defense Bohumir Lomsky.

On and on went stories of blackmail, embezzlement, drunken orgies and theft of Government property. Within a few days, in short, Sejna and his friend, young Novotny, became the embodiment of the corruption everyone knew had pervaded the Novotny regime and of *la dolce vita* that corruption had permitted for a select few at or near the pinnacle of power.

It quickly became apparent, too, that the Sejna affair had a political side. When Sejna fled, it was revealed, he was head of the Main Party Committee of the Ministry of Defense, the very body that Major General Pepych had accused in late February of having tried to influence the Central Committee at the height of the struggle to remove Novotny. As the furor about Sejna's escape was at its height, General Prchlik—the man who had warned Dubcek of an impending coup attempt—

revealed publicly that a tank division had been mobilized at a key moment in Novotny's struggle to retain power. Even the dullest reader of Prague's newspapers could understand that Sejna was being charged with having been a key figure in the effort to save Novotny by a military coup. As a Government commission began investigating the reported plot, a high military leader, Colonel General Vladimir Janko, a Deputy Defense Minister, shot himself to death shortly before he was scheduled to testify at the inquiry. To many it seemed that suicide was confession. Five months later, Sejna, in the United States, denied many of the charges against him, but by then his denial was of interest to historians only.

At the end of February, just before the Sejna case became public knowledge, the Novotny faction was at the height of its counterattack. The President himself, speaking at the twentieth-anniversary celebration, had admitted that some mistakes had been made but asserted, in effect, that only relatively minor reforms were needed, not the tidal wave of change the Dubcek era promised. Novotnyites controlled major sections of the Party apparatus, most of the mass organizations, the secret police, the army, the Party organizations in the largest factories and in other numerous strategic points. They enjoyed substantial worker sympathy. Some of the reform leaders, such as Eduard Goldstuecker, had been uncomfortable in meetings with workers who charged the intellectuals and the communications media with treachery. Pro-Novotny pamphlets were circulating and finding believers among many who were bewildered and disturbed by the new ideas and the new ferment. Among the most conservative members of the Central Committee, which had brought Dubcek into power, the events of January and February had caused deep disquiet because they brought fears that the Communist system in Czechoslovakia, as these conservatives understood it, might be destroyed. As March began, Novotny had good reason to suppose he had a fighting chance to make a political comeback from his post as President.

All these hopes died in the wake of the national indignation and anger provoked by the scandals. The nation felt betrayed and besmirched, and it noted that although the newspapers, radio, and television provided new sensational details every day, there was no refutation from the Novotnyites. Neither Novotny nor his son made any denials or any effort to state their case. General Bohumir Lomsky, the Defense Minister, did appear on television to read an unconvincing statement denying that he knew anything about the plot to use the military for political cases. Of the other charges against Sejna he said nothing.

The public verdict of guilty rolled in on a giant tide of petitions and resolutions from the grass roots, demanding that every aspect of the Sejna case be investigated and explained to the public and demanding the ouster of those who had fouled themselves in this political cesspool. In the atmosphere thus created, every charge that had been raised against the old regime in the past—the complaints of the students against the police, of the writers and artists against the censors, and the like—immediately gained acceptance and support. The Novotnyite position collapsed under this national assault.

The completeness and rapidity of the Novotnyite debacle is best indicated by mentioning some of the high points of the March collapse. On March 5, the day it became known Sejna was in Washington, the Presidium of the Communist Party dismissed Jiri Hendrych as Central Committee Secretary responsible for ideological affairs and replaced him with Josef Spacek, the liberal head of the Brno Party organization. Hendrych had voted against Novotny in the December confrontation, but he was too closely identified with the President in the public mind to survive as overseer of the nation's culture and thought.

On March 12, the Minister of Interior, Josef Kudrna, apologized to Prague's university students and condemned the unnecessary brutality of individual policemen in the clash of the previous October 30. He announced that seven policemen had been disciplined and that all students hurt by the police would be indemnified. To permit better public control of the police in the future, Kudrna revealed, all policemen would begin wearing badges with numbers on them so they could be easily identified. It was perfectly predictable that the student leaders would regard this major retreat by the security authorities as utterly inadequate.

Also on March 12, the three top leaders of the Czechoslovak trade unions resigned. (One of them, Secretary Bedrich Kozelka, was the Communist who, in February, 1948, had gone to Hradcany Castle with the delegation that forced the sick President Benes to approve Klement Gottwald's Communist government.) That same day, an employee of the Czechoslovak Radio spoke over Radio Prague denouncing the continued jamming of Radio Free Europe's programs in Czech and Slovak. He demanded that individual citizens be allowed to hear the broadcasts they wanted to without any outside interference.

On March 13, the Communist Party cell at the Ministry of Foreign Affairs publicly criticized the work of the Ministry and, in a thinly veiled attack on Foreign Minister Vaclav David, called for punishment of those responsible for "deformations." Czechoslovak foreign policy must acquire its own independent features even while being based on the Soviet alliance, the Ministry's Communists asserted.

On March 14, Politburo member Michal Chudik, who had voted against Dubcek and for Novotny in the December struggle, resigned as chairman of the Slovak National Council. That same day, the National Assembly passed a motion of no confidence against Interior Minister Kudrna and Prosecutor General Jan Bartuska.

On March 15, President Novotny, under pressure of the preceding day's National Assembly vote, dismissed Prosecutor General Bartuska and Interior Minister Kudrna. That same day, the Central Publication Board—the Communist Party cell in the censorship organization—issued a statement demanding the end of political censorship. Never before had the existence of secret police control over publications been publicly admitted in Czechoslovakia.

The flood mounted day after day, drowning more and more of the politicians and bureaucrats who had risen with Novotny. The head of the Czechoslovak Youth Federation, the chairman of the journalists union, top regional political bosses, conservative editors of newspapers and magazines— these and others were dismissed or resigned rapidly in the days that followed. Once the top figures fell, the purge of conservatives worked its way deeper into the manifold bureaucracies of Czechoslovakia, ousting more and more of the lesser figures who had been identified with Novotnyite repression and had not switched sides in time.

The chief target of this purge campaign, inevitably, was President Novotny. As long as he remained head of state and a member of the Communist Party Presidium, the possibility that he might regain power remained very real. Even in early March, some of his more perceptive supporters saw that to preserve his position Novotny would have to counter the liberals by entering the public debate and using television and radio as Dubcek and Smrkovsky were doing so effectively. But Novotny eschewed any such direct and open efforts to state his case, and his silence only increased the growing national conviction that the charges against him, his son, and his clique were true. As March progressed, resolutions from an increasing number of Party and other conferences poured into Prague demanding Novotny's resignation. Large mass rallies, often attended by thousands of students and workers, became common, and many of them were dominated by demands that Novotny resign. Finally, on March 22, Prague Radio announced that Antonin Novotny had resigned as President for what were termed reasons of health. Shortly thereafter, Antonin Novotny, Jr., resigned as the director of Artia, the Czechoslovak state organization engaged in the export and import of books and other cultural goods. In less than three months after Dubcek's initial victory, the Novotny machine had disintegrated, thanks largely to General Sejna, his decision to save himself in the United States, and the existence of a free press, radio, and television that could and did spread the whole unsavory story before a shocked and angry nation.

But more than a purge of members of one Communist faction by the members of another Communist faction was taking place in those tumultuous days. To a large extent, the whole system of organizational control and discipline through which the Communist Party had exercised its dictatorship was disintegrating. Encouraged by Dubcek, Smrkovsky, and others, Czechoslovak citizens began exercising their initiative, and soon each day's news brought reports of unexpected and spontaneous developments. Student groups, for example, began leaving the Czechoslovak Youth Federation to form their own organizations, an action they had wanted to take for a long time. Newspapers and magazines began declaring themselves independent of their nominal publishers and even attacked them on occasion. On March 12, for example, the editors of the Prague evening newspaper *Vecerni Praha* denounced the paper's publisher, the Prague Committee of the Communist Party. They accused the Committee of having forced the newspaper a few days earlier to print a statement that sought "to disorient the public" and with which the editors disagreed. The Young Pioneers, the Communist organization for children, announced its independence of the over-all youth organization and began enrolling adults as well as youngsters. *Svazarm,* the organization that gave civilians military training, began to break up into many parts; its youth organization announced that it was turning itself into the Czechoslovak Boy Scout movement, though two decades earlier the Boy Scout movement had been suppressed as a tool of imperialism and its key leaders had been sent to jail. Special interest groups began forming their own separate organizations. The hop growers organized to protect their own interests. The railroad engineers announced plans to set up a separate union of railroad engineers. To a visitor in Prague in those days, it seemed as if society was coming apart and reforming in a quite different pattern.

To many Czechoslovaks, the most moving events of these March days were the tributes—unprecedented under Communist rule—paid to the Masaryks, to Thomas on his birthday on March 7, and to his son Jan on March 10, the twentieth anniversary of the former Foreign Minister's suicide or murder. Overnight, all efforts to turn these major figures of the Czechoslovak Republic's history into nonentities and to blacken their reputations were undone. Numerous articles and radio and television programs acquainted the younger generation with these two men and their major contributions to the nation's life and tradition. A thrill of patriotic pride ran through the country now that the truth about the past could be told again. Pictures of Thomas Masaryk, long banned, began to appear spontaneously in store windows and on shop walls. Most impressive was the demonstration that took place on Sunday, March 10, at the Masaryk family grave in the cemetery of the village of Lany, twenty-five miles from Prague.

It was a cold day, with intermittent freezing rain and snow. When I got to the grave site at about 3 o'clock in the afternoon, dozens of warmly dressed people were standing near the graves, on which many flowers and wreaths had been placed. Hundreds of people had already been there to pay their respects. Talking to some of the visitors, it was apparent to me that they had a sense of having been liberated. "I would never have dared come here in the old days," was a frequent comment. Then, about 4 o'clock in the afternoon, a crowd of about three thousand students marched down Lany's main street to the grave. They had come by special train to the Lany station and had walked the mile or two to the cemetery. Two banners were unfurled briefly: On March 10, this action was still a sign of bravery, with possibly serious consequences. One banner declared "Truth Will Prevail—Even Here?" and the other, "Jan—We Shall Never Forget You." Then a young bearded student climbed on a nearby gravestone and delivered the following short speech:

> We stand at the grave of a man who died an unusual death twenty years ago, a great son of a great father. He was a cosmopolitan in the best sense of the word. He said in February, 1948, "I have always gone with the people and I shall always go with the people." Let us remember this man at this crucial time in which we hope people of the quality of Jan Masaryk will lead our nation.

Then, after singing some patriotic hymns, the students left to march back to their train. All through that afternoon, all through the ceremony, not a policeman was seen. The contrast with the clubbing and tear-gassing of the student demonstrators five months earlier could not have been greater.

These and other signs of the breakdown of the old order and of the reappearance of spontaneity in the population alarmed the most conservative members of the original Dubcek coalition. They, as well as the Novotnyites, saw the danger that the forces set in motion might go further than the reformers had intended, that non-Communist and even anti-Communist trends might become uncomfortably powerful. The result was a curious coalition between men like

Drahomir Kolder, a Politburo member who had supported Dubcek, and Martin Vaculik (no relation of Ludvik Vaculik the dissident writer), the Prague Communist Party chief who had backed Novotny. Their cry now became that the press and the radio were going too far, and they hinted not very subtly that the reins had to be pulled tighter. A number of district Communist Party conferences took up the cry. So, too, did Dubcek, though characteristically he tried to straddle the issue. Speaking at Brno on March 16, he first praised the press, radio, and television for having "accomplished much meritorious work" in spreading "interest in what is happening at present among the widest strata of the population. It has been a long time since the citizens' interest in our domestic political events was so great." At the time Dubcek spoke, it was normal for all newspapers to be sold out at 6 A.M., while millions tuned in daily, with great expectations, to the most daring radio commentators, such as Milan Weiner and Jiri Dienstbier, and to the popular 7 o'clock television news program in the evening. But, Dubcek continued, the journalists' activities "have sometimes manifested an imprudent character." Then, showing he was still basically a Communist Party *apparatchik,* he proceeded to tell the journalists what the Party expected of them: "To aid the enforcement of the basic trend," and to influence "the active attitude of the wide strata of citizens toward the Party policy." He warned that it was a "demand" upon those in charge of mass communications media "that the rate of presentation of the main problems is not too precipitate, mainly so that our entire society may really be able to master the problems set forth." His message was clear: Slow down!

A week earlier, however, Smrkovsky had spoken in a quite different vein over Radio Prague, saying: "At the present time we are bothered by other much worse things which are a thousand times more serious than that some journalist says a few words more than he ought to have said." What had happened in the week between the Smrkovsky and Dubcek statements to make them adopt such different emphases?

The answer was that Eastern European Communism found itself, in mid-March, 1968, in the most serious crisis since October–November, 1956. To the accelerating chain reaction of freedom and reform in Czechoslovakia there had suddenly and unexpectedly been added the element of mass student near-revolutionary violence in Poland. Gomulka's earlier presentiment about the potential contagion of Prague events had proved correct. One of the main cries of the student demonstrators in Warsaw was "Long Live Czechoslovakia!" All the leaders of Eastern Europe and the Soviet Union remembered very clearly that in 1956 a peaceful revolution in Poland had helped trigger violent and disastrous revolution in Hungary. Was 1968 to be a replay of 1956, with Czechoslovakia doing for Poland what twelve years earlier Poland had done for Hungary? The wires between Moscow and Prague must have been busy with Brezhnev's demands for slowing the Czechoslovak pace. In Poland, Interior Minister Moczar decided to meet the student protestors with maximum force, and for a few days major riots pitted thousands of students against hundreds or thousands of policemen swinging clubs, throwing tear gas, and using water cannon, in virtually all of Poland's large cities.

The Polish troubles had begun the previous January with the Warsaw presentation of the classic patriotic play *Dziady*, by Poland's Shakespeare, Adam Mickiewicz. Written in 1832, the play portrayed the sufferings of Poland's people at the brutal hands of the Russian Czar. Audiences in January, 1968, were turning a 130-year-old play into nightly anti-Russian demonstrations by thunderously applauding such lines as "Polish history is conducted in a prison cell," "Everyone sent here from Moscow is either a jackass, a fool, or a spy," and "We Poles have sold our souls to Moscow for silver rubles." Angered, Gomulka's regime closed the play, raising a storm of protest from intellectuals and students.

This anger culminated early in March with student demonstrations in Warsaw that were met with police violence. The police brutality precipitated bigger and angrier demonstrations, which developed into bloody and dangerous riots. From Warsaw the student unrest spread to virtually every other major university. So fearful was the Polish Government of the Czechoslovak example that at the height of the disturbances it expelled two Czechoslovak correspondents who had come to cover the story. Moczar, a notorious anti-Semite, then used the riots as a pretext for beginning a major anti-Jewish campaign. The Polish press was filled with accusations that the riots were really a Zionist plot. The newspapers printed lists of the alleged ringleaders of the riots, almost all identified as Jews. The press then went on to point out that the fathers of many of these Jewish students were prominent Communists, important officials, or leading intellectuals. Soon a major anti-Semitic witch hunt was in progress. Every day brought reports of new dismissals and forced resignations of Jews in important positions. This propaganda pictured Poland, a nation of more than 30 million people, as being in deadly danger from the plotting of the twenty-five thousand Jews who remained in Poland, a large fraction of them elderly invalids in old people's homes. In part, this campaign was Moczar's effort to strike at Gomulka and force him out of power by depicting him as a protector of the Zionists. But the anti-Zionist campaign was also a highly effective and shrewd effort to appeal to the worst prejudices and most irrational fears of the masses of Polish workers and peasants. It sought to assure that the student rebellion would not spread and become a national revolution. The strategy worked, although Moczar did not succeed in toppling Gomulka.

It is tempting to speculate on what might have happened if, at the height of the Polish violence, Czechoslovakia had similarly erupted. The virus of revolt might then have spread to Hungary and even to East Germany, and Russia would have been faced with its greatest crisis since Stalin founded the Soviet empire at the end of World War II. This did not happen because the Czechs and the Slovaks saw no point in revolting against the reformer, Dubcek. Moreover, historically there has never been much love lost between Poles and Czechs. The Dubcek regime made sure that the full importance, fury, and drama of the Polish events were obscured and underplayed in the Czechoslovak press while the riots were at their height. This cautious approach in early March reflected the influence of old habits and the fear of antagonizing the Polish and Soviet governments. The result of this caution was that the Polish situation was stabilized, potential allies were lost, and five months later Polish troops and tanks were among the invaders who captured Czechoslovakia at the Kremlin's order. Later in the spring, when Czechoslovak media did speak out candidly on the Polish situation, it was too late to influence Warsaw events positively.

Even as Czechoslovakia, absorbed in its own internal upheaval, watched passively the victory of Communist reaction in Poland, there were already signs of trouble ahead with the Soviet Union and other neighbors. In late February and early and mid-March, an ominous silence about Czechoslovak events enveloped the Soviet, East German, Polish, Bulgarian, and Hungarian press. In Moscow's *Pravda*, for example, on most days there was no news about Czechoslovakia, and the occasional article that did appear was brief and uninformative. Thus, on March 17, *Pravda*'s correspondent in Prague, V. Zhuravsky, had an article of less than one hundred words informing his readers that district and regional Communist Party conferences were taking place in Czechoslovakia and that Dubcek had spoken in Brno. Of the fiery debates, of the resignations, dismissals, and other signs of convulsion, and of the sensational revelations of the Sejna case, there was no word. Since a similar technique had been used in Czechoslovakia in the Novotny era, Prague's leaders and journalists must have known that this silence was ominous, signifying deep disapproval and fear of having the Soviet people know what was going on. But the Soviet Union had not yet interfered vigorously and directly with the developments in Prague. Apparently, there was no serious trouble when Dubcek and the rest of the Czechoslovak delegation met with the other Soviet-bloc leaders on March 5–8 at the Warsaw Pact meeting in Sofia. Then, Rumania's refusal to endorse the nuclear nonproliferation treaty had provided the main visible excitement. Moscow seemed also to have taken very calmly the timid deviations from its line contained in the speech of the Czechoslovak delegate to the Budapest consultative meeting of Communist parties at the end of February. The most important of those deviations was the suggestion that anti-Yugoslav theses of the 1957 and 1960 international Communist declarations be repudiated.

Thus, many Czechoslovaks were somewhat shocked when they woke on the morning of March 23, the day after Novotny's resignation, to learn that Dubcek and other Prague leaders had gone to Dresden in East Germany to meet with leaders of other socialist states. It turned out to be a one-day meeting of all the Warsaw Pact members except Rumania. Czechoslovakia was the main topic of discussion. The uninformative *Tass* communiqué blandly reported the next day:

> Representatives of the Communist Party of Czechoslovakia and of the Government of the Czechoslovak Socialist Republic reported on the course of the realization of the decisions of the January plenum of the Czechoslovak Communist Party which was directed at effectuating the line of the Czechoslovak Communist Party's 13th Congress. Confidence was expressed that

the working class and all workers of the Czechoslovak Socialist Republic, under the leadership of the Czechoslovak Socialist Party, will guarantee the further development of socialist construction in the country.

It was clear even then that an alarm had been sounded. The Dresden meeting had obviously been convened hurriedly, twenty-four hours after Novotny's resignation, and many suspected that Soviet concern about that event had been the precipitating factor. In any case, what business did an international Communist meeting have concerning itself with Czechoslovakia's internal affairs? Pressed by a flood of anxious questions about what had really happened at Dresden, Dubcek admitted to the press that fears had been expressed about anti-socialist elements taking advantage of Czechoslovakia's democratization. Dubcek added reassuringly that he had supplied the information the others needed and that the meeting had ended with general assurance of support for Czechoslovakia's course.

Five months later, *Pravda* supplied a fuller and probably more accurate account of what had happened at that meeting:

At the Dresden meeting, the Czechoslovak comrades did not deny that some negative processes were developing in the country, that the radio, television and press had slipped out from under the control of the Party and were actually in the hands of anti-socialist elements, that the rightist forces were consolidating. Instead, the Czechoslovak representatives asserted that the Party controlled the situation as a whole and that there was no basis for serious concern.

The Soviet representatives and the delegations of all the other brotherly parties openly noted that in their opinion the picture appeared in a different light. They showed the reality of the danger which hid in the complexities of the situation. From all the facts, they reached the conclusion that they were in the presence of events that could lead to a counterrevolutionary overturn. The Soviet, Bulgarian, Hungarian, Polish and East German Communist Party delegations said that they supported the leadership of the Czechoslovak Communist Party, support the positive content of the decisions of the January plenum, and that all of their positions were directed to help the Czechoslovak comrades rebuff the increasingly brazen anti-socialist elements and strengthen the position of socialism in Czechoslovakia.

It must have been a stormy meeting, indeed. With hindsight, one may suspect that after this meeting, planning for a possible invasion of Czechoslovakia began in Moscow and the other capitals concerned. Most fateful of all, perhaps, Dubcek had explicitly conceded that an international Communist meeting had authority to intervene, even by such a discussion, in the internal affairs of Czechoslovakia. The Rumanians were wiser. They refused to attend the meeting, apparently on the grounds that no international meeting had the right to discuss the internal affairs of a socialist country. It did not take much imagination, after all, to perceive that what was done in the case of Czechoslovakia might also be done in the case of Rumania. But Dubcek preferred to hide from his people the full gravity of what had happened, putting the emphasis on reassurance rather than speaking frankly and preparing for any possible attack.

The Soviet people, too, were curious about what had happened at Dresden. On March 28, *Pravda* printed a summary of Dubcek's interview, mentioning the disquiet of some of those who had gathered in Dresden. Underneath this dispatch, *Pravda* printed an attack on the "slanderers" in the Western press who, it said, were trying to stir up trouble among the socialist countries. These "slanderers," *Pravda* continued, were presenting "the relations between the Communist parties of the Soviet Union and Czechoslovakia in a false light, using the old formula about 'Soviet interference.'" But such efforts were futile, *Pravda* assured its readers, for, "in actuality the relations among socialist countries have been and are being built on the basis of hearty friendship, equality and confidence, mutual support and noninterference in each other's affairs." The intention of the article was to reassure Prague, and it did.

But two days later, even in Prague, some perceptive people who read Brezhnev's speech of March 29 to Moscow's Communists were disquieted. They saw that Brezhnev was expounding a doctrine far different from Dubcek's; the Soviet leader was emphasizing the monopoly of the Communist Party's "guidance and directing influence" and was making no mention of grass-roots political initiative or spontaneity. He was calling for still tighter control of intellectuals. They noted that Brezhnev asserted that "the ideological struggle in our times is the sharpest front of the class struggle" and warned that capitalism banked on "nationalist and revisionist elements" in the socialist countries.

In Czechoslovakia itself, in the week after the Dresden meeting attention focused on one key question: Who would succeed Novotny as President? Three leading candidates soon emerged: Ludvik Svoboda, age 72, the retired general and former Defense Minister who had led the Czechoslovak troops fighting alongside the Red Army in World War II; Josef Smrkovsky, age 57; and Cestmir Cisar, age 47. The latter had earned a reputation as a liberal in his attitude toward intellectuals and, particularly, students, when he held Party and Government offices earlier in the 1960's. But Cisar had been banished to Bucharest as ambassador to Rumania—some said as punishment for excessive liberalism; others claimed Novotny was jealous because Cisar had such an impressive television personality. The story was also told that when Novotny told Cisar of his ambassadorial assignment, he said he understood Cisar had wanted to go to Paris, so he was sending him to the Paris of Eastern Europe—Bucharest.

The campaign for President of Czechoslovakia was probably in many respects the freest in modern times in a Soviet-

bloc nation. Organizations adopted resolutions and sent
letters nominating and supporting different individuals. War
veterans' organizations proposed Svoboda, and the Soviet
leaders made it more or less plain that he was their favorite.
The intellectuals favored Smrkovsky, seeing in him a strong
proponent of democratic principles and a man who, as President, would help make sure there was no turning back from
the road toward greater democracy. Youth and student organizations backed Cisar. At the height of the campaign,
Smrkovsky got an unexpected assist from East Germany in
the form of attacks on Czechoslovak democratization by an
East German ideologist, Kurt Hager. Hager contended that
trends in Czechoslovakia were really serving West Germany's
purposes, and he spotlighted Smrkovsky as the man "West
German propaganda centers" quoted most zealously. A feeling of shock swept over the country, reflected in the Czechoslovak Foreign Minister's unprecedented act of calling in the
East German ambassador to protest this interference in
Czechoslovakia's internal affairs.

In this difficult situation, Dubcek and his colleagues felt
that the Presidency had to go to Svoboda in order to ease
Moscow's fears. But concessions had to be made to public
feeling, too. The result was that important consolation prizes
went to the other two candidates, prizes available because of
Novotny's dismissal both as a member of the Party Presidium
and as a Party secretary. Smrkovsky became a member of the
Presidium and thus got a seat in the top policy-making body.
Cisar became a Party Secretary with responsibility for culture
and education.

The students who were not satisfied by the Central Committee decision made their discontent plain that very evening by parading in a demonstration for Cisar. The parade
wound up at midnight outside Communist Party headquarters, and the students shouted for Dubcek. Summoned from
his home, the First Secretary soon appeared and answered

questions put directly to him: "What are the guarantees
that the old days will not be back?" one student asked. "You,
yourselves, are the guarantee. You, the young," Dubcek replied. "Why was Cisar not nominated?" another student
asked. "Because he is going to have a lot to do here at the
Central Committee. I will need him here. . . ." When
asked about the future role of the Slovak leader Gustav
Husak, Dubcek confided "a state secret," revealing that
Husak would become a Deputy Premier. Nothing like this
impromptu confrontation had been seen in Eastern Europe
since Communist rule was established. But Dubcek's answers did not satisfy the students. Two days later, when the
National Assembly met in Hradcany Castle to approve
Svoboda as President, some students staged a sit-in demonstration that lasted long after the vote approving Svoboda.

7

The Suicides
of April

At the beginning of April, the body of Dr. Jozef Brestansky, Vice President of Czechoslovakia's Supreme Court, was found hanging from a tree in woods near Prague. He had been working on problems connected with the rehabilitation of persons unjustly convicted in the 1950's but apparently feared revelation of the fact that he himself had approved unjustified sentences of innocent people in that period. During the rest of the month, there was an average of one political suicide a day, mainly among members of the secret police who had been linked with the brutalities of the 1950's. One of the most sensational suicides was that of Dr. Josef Sommer, who hanged himself in his Prague apartment. He had been a doctor at Prague's infamous Ruzyne Prison a decade earlier and was a specialist in medical torture of prisoners. One of his victims in that period was General Josef Pavel, a prisoner in the 1950's, who, at the time of Sommer's suicide, was the newly named reformist Minister of Interior of Czechoslovakia.

The suicides symbolized the despair of many who had been linked to the old regime. In a mere three months, they had seen their comfortable world vanishing along with the premises on which thousands of Novotnyites had built careers and won good jobs. But not all who saw the foundations of their good fortune disappearing gave up. At the Central Committee meeting in late March and early April, some went over to counterattack at this first opportunity since Dubcek's election the previous January.

Central Committee member Bohus Chnoupek, for example, began his speech with a denunciation of the "rightist excesses" in the country. Not very subtly, he reminded his comrades that some workers were declaring that "If the Central Committee is unable to prevent extremes, the workers will use the same methods as the students," a patent threat of mass street demonstrations or worse. Then, with heavy sarcasm and obvious pain, Chnoupek told what he saw in Czechoslovakia at that point:

> I believe that although there are personal tragedies of officials who for decades have devoted their best efforts . . . ; although there is an arbitrary recalling of plant directors; although . . . there have cropped up demands to restore the pre-February [1948] situation, to permit private enterprises to use up to 50 employees; although the National Security Corps members are joining the People's Party, and members of the editors' offices of youth publications are joining the Socialist party; although a West German bourgeois journalist was [unprecedentedly] admitted to a Party conference; although—and I confess that this fact staggered me most—blood revenge and vendetta are coming to the fore, and the skull hunters are bringing down some functionaries as on a hunt; although the Czechoslovak Youth Federation has disintegrated; although the editorial offices are "making themselves independent" and judges are hanging themselves; although . . . a slogan is circulating in

the rural areas to operate the "national committees without the Communists" . . . perhaps it is still possible to agree with Comrade Smrkovsky that up to now we have not had any striking attempt at overthrowing socialism.

Chnoupek illustrated the poisonous atmosphere in the debate by charging:

> Unfortunately, among the main initiators of the current process of revival, one often finds people who violated the norms of Party life and socialist legality and who now teach others about renaissance and democratization. Quite frequently they again put in the public pillory even those who once were their victims. . . . Today they point fingers at each other, and many of them proclaim Leninist norms of socialist democracy and even sit on the platforms of mass meetings where they reply to questions about the democratization process, questions posed by the young who do not remember and therefore do not know.

A week later, when *Pravda* in Moscow belatedly got around to reporting the Czechoslovak Central Committee meeting, Chnoupek was the first of the rank and file speakers that *Pravda* quoted and mentioned by name.

At the other extreme of the Communist Party political spectrum, also, there was concern about this pivotal Central Committee meeting. True, victory after victory had been scored, and the many political corpses of defeated and dismissed Novotnyites littered the political landscape. But some 40 of the 110 Central Committee members were still unreconstructed reactionaries, aching for a chance to make a political comeback and even scores with their adversaries. The triumph of the previous January could still be reversed —and by only a relatively small swing of Central Committee votes. The political imperative demanded a complete purge of the Novotnyites, but they had been elected at the 1966 Party Congress, however, and unless they resigned—which most of them refused to do—they could only be replaced at another Congress. In the normal course of events, the next —the fourteenth—Congress would not take place until 1970. Thus, the liberal faction pressed for the convening of an extraordinary Party Congress immediately, or as soon as possible, to carry out the needed purge.

The liberals fought for their goal outside, as well as inside, Party meetings. This new spring of Czechoslovak politics was a time of public meetings everywhere—mass rallies at which students, workers, and even farmers heard speeches and asked questions, often impertinent ones. The most important of these meetings were even broadcast on radio and television so that the whole nation could, in effect, participate in the debate. The most effective speakers at these open meetings—Smrkovsky, Goldstuecker, Sik, and Prochazka— were now major public figures. Moreover, television was making it a regular practice to go to the people, to interview ordinary citizens—housewives, clerks, factory workers, postmen—in the streets, soliciting their opinions and broadcasting them nationally. Sometimes they got surprising answers, as in the case of a man who said that Novotny had had his opportunity and failed and now Dubcek was getting his chance. But, this extraordinary man in the street added, if Dubcek did not deliver on his promises then he, too, should go and let someone else try.

Even more ominous, from the traditional Communist point of view, was the rising clamor for genuine opposition parties and for an end to the Communist Party's political monopoly. Even the traditionally tame and subservient non-Communist parties—the Peoples and Socialist parties in the Czech lands and two smaller groups in Slovakia—were speaking up in new accents, removing their servile leaders of the past, and cautiously arguing that they were entitled to more independent roles than their past functions of merely approving what the Communist Party decided.

New groups were appearing on the scene, and few doubted that these new organizations had great political potential. On March 31, for example, some three thousand former political prisoners met on an island in the Vltava River, which bisects Prague, to form Club 231, a name chosen to mark the article of the penal code under which those attending had been arrested and convicted. Hour after hour, former convicts mounted the stage to recite their stories of political persecution, torture, imprisonment, loss of rights, forced abandonment of professions and homes, and denial of education and job opportunities to their children. Many had been active in non-Communist political parties before 1948, and it was for this "crime" that they had suffered, although their indictments charged treason and espionage. "Never Let It Happen Again," a white banner with red letters declared from the stage. The meeting was conducted with full permission of the authorities, but no Communist leader attended. Eduard Goldstuecker sent a letter recalling his past comradeship in jail with these other innocent victims of the old order. The prime demand at the meeting was for full rehabilitation of, and compensation to, all who had borne the burden of punishment without guilt.

Elsewhere, in publications like *Student* and *Literarni Listy* and in public speeches, writers such as Vaclav Havel were demanding the legalization of genuine opposition parties. The philosopher Ivan Svitak created a sensation by pooh-poohing the progress made to date as "an improvisation arising from extraordinary circumstances of a personal power struggle in the Presidium." The Stalinist apparatus remained, he warned, and "we must liquidate it or it will liquidate us."

Amid growing babel of voices and sharpening conflict of political forces, Dubcek sought to hew to a middle line. In his report to the Central Committee meeting that began at the end of March and continued into early April, he emphasized that "the Communist Party of Czechoslovakia continues to be, with even greater justification today, the decisive organized progressive force of our society. We shall solve and rectify the injustices and mistakes of the past, but this does not entail belittling and abusing the past." He warned against efforts to "implement basic changes hastily, in improvised fashion at the pace shown over the past few weeks—which neither we nor the general public can keep up forever." He reminded the nation that "we are concerned not just with any democracy but with Socialist democracy. We are concerned not with weakening the role of the Party but with its full implementation under new conditions." He aligned himself, at least partially, with those condemning the "excesses" of the past weeks, arguing that "Old wrongs cannot be replaced by new ones. The wave of criticism has been one-sided—almost a monologue, without opponents." The goal, he said, was "to establish a type of Socialist democracy corresponding to the conditions of Czechoslovakia." He was trying to set limits on the spontaneous revolution that had been set in motion and to curb it. No doubt he hoped to honor the promises he had given at Dresden that he would impose order on what more and more conservative Communists were calling "anarchy."

The consolidation of the situation that Dubcek aimed for was illustrated by the compromise composition of the new Presidium elected at the Central Committee meeting. All those who had supported Novotny at the time of the five to five deadlock the previous December were removed; so, too, were the compromised Jiri Hendrych and the aged Jaromir Dolansky, who had asked for retirement. To compensate for those removals, the "extreme liberal" Ota Sik was denied a place in the Presidium, and the liberal collective farm chairman, Josef Boruvka, who had won a place in the Presidium the previous January was not re-elected. Of the eleven who had been elected, only three—Josef Smrkovsky, age 57; Josef

Spacek, age 40; and Frantisek Kriegel, age 60, a Jew from Galicia, a physician by profession, and the head of the National Assembly's Foreign Affairs Committee—could be classified as hard-core liberals. Dubcek and Deputy Premier Oldrich Cernik were centrists. Those who tended to be to the right of center and who were increasingly worried about the weakening of the Party included six members: Frantisek Barbirek, age 41, the acting chairman of the Slovak National Council; Vasil Bilak, age 50, who had been elected the previous January to succeed Dubcek as Slovak Communist Party chief; Drahomir Kolder, age 42, a Central Committee Secretary; Jan Piller, age 45, the Deputy Minister of Heavy Engineering; Emil Rigo, age 42, the Slovak gypsy who headed the Party organization in the East Slovak Iron Works; and Oldrich Svestka, age 48, the editor of *Rude Pravo*. There was an even more conservative cast to the three candidate members of the Presidium—factory manager Antonin Kapek, age 46; Premier Jozef Lenart, age 45; and Prague Party chief Martin Vaculik, age 45.

Premier Lenart's government had to be radically changed, too. He, like Dubcek, was a Slovak, and much Czech discontent had built up during the three months that Slovaks had headed both the Party and the state. The new regime under Premier Oldrich Cernik, a Czech, showed the effects of a thorough purge of key Novotny figures, as well as an effort to avoid disturbing the Russians. Ota Sik, the economic reformer, was made a Deputy Premier, but without direct operational responsibility or power. The liberals won three key posts: Josef Boruvka was Minister of Agriculture; General Josef Pavel, a Spanish Civil War veteran and former political prisoner during the Novotny period, became Minister of Interior; and Miroslav Galuska, former journalist, movie writer, and organizer of the Czechoslovak Pavilion at Expo '67, took over the Ministry of Culture and Information. Other key places tended to go to technicians and to people without any sharp political profile. Thus Lieutenant General Martin Dzur became Minister of Defense in place of the discredited Bohumir Lomsky, who had finally admitted to the Central Committee that there had been a military plot the previous December. Dr. Jiri Hajek, former ambassador to London and former chief delegate to the United Nations, became Minister of Foreign Affairs in place of Vaclav David, whose only claim to fame was the fidelity with which he followed the Soviet foreign-policy line.

One liberal did get a major Government post, guaranteed to keep him in the public eye: Presidium member Josef Smrkovsky became Chairman of the National Assembly and hastened to assure the nation that he intended to make that body a genuine parliament, despite long years of rubber stamp behavior. Smrkovsky's job, like that of Premier Cernik, emphasized that the Communist Party Presidium was keeping the highest Government executive and legislative posts in its control. There were limits to the implementation of the principle of separation of Communist Party and state, which had precipitated and then apparently triumphed in the convulsion of late 1967.

The key Dubcek move toward consolidation in the first days of April was the publication, at last, of the Action Program of the Communist Party of Czechoslovakia, subtitled "The Czechoslovak Road to Socialism." This was the new Party line, the document around which Dubcek wanted all Party members and all Czechoslovaks to close ranks. Inevitably, it was a compromise platform, bearing clear imprints of the contending arguments of liberals and conservatives. Nevertheless, it was a remarkable contribution, the most liberal, comprehensive statement of policy ever issued by a ruling Communist Party allied with Moscow. At the time, Moscow's distaste for the document was evidenced *sotto voce,* by the grossly inadequate coverage *Pravda* gave its contents. Late in August, after the invasion, *Pravda* was to complain that the Action Program provided Czechoslovakia's rightists "with a sort of legal platform for further attacks on the Communist Party, on the foundations of socialism, on the friendship of the Czechoslovak and Soviet peoples." Seen from Moscow, the Action Program was a revolutionary contradiction of many of the fundamental principles regarded as inviolable by the Communist Party of the Soviet Union.

In essence, the Action Program embodied many of the ideas already mentioned. It assailed the past "suppression of democratic rights and freedom of the people, violation of laws, licentiousness and misuse of power" while hailing the "great historic successes" that had been achieved. It denounced the old system of managing the economy by "directives from the center," which had resulted in "slow increase in wages . . . stagnation of the living standard . . . the catastrophic state of housing . . . the precarious state of the transport system, poor quality goods and public services," with the consequence that "apprehensions arose about socialism, about its human mission, about its human features. Some people became demoralized; others lost perspective."

The Action Program explicitly assumed that all groups in the nation "agree with the fundamental interests and aims of socialism," but it warned "there can be no overlooking the various needs and interests of individual people and social groups." Socialism can flourish, it asserted, only "if scope is given for the assertion of the various interests of the people" so that "the unity of all workers will be brought about democratically." The Program stressed that the foundation of Czechoslovak statehood "is the voluntary and equal coexistence of Czechs and Slovaks" and added that "the overlooking of the interests of a smaller nation by the larger is incompatible with socialist relations between nations." The goal was "a new model of socialist democracy" and such a state and social order "as will correspond to the

actual layout of interests of the various strata and groups of
this society, as will give them the possibility of expressing
their interests in their organizations and of voicing their
views in public life." It denounced egalitarianism in living
standards because "it puts careless workers, idlers, and ir-
responsible people to advantage as compared with the dedi-
cated and diligent workers, the unqualified compared with
the qualified, the technically and expertly backward people
as compared with the talented and those with initiative."
Such leveling, the Program declared, "has spread to an un-
heard of extent and this became one of the impediments to
an intensive development of the economy and to raising the
living standard."

In perhaps the most direct challenge to Soviet views and
practice, the Program denounced the idea of the leading
position of the Communist Party "as a monopolistic concen-
tration of power in the hands of Party bodies" or as a
"universal 'caretaker' of society" or as "the instrument of the
dictatorship of the proletariat." Instead, the Program phrased
its conception of the leading role of the Communist Party
in these terms:

> The Communist Party enjoys the voluntary support of the
> people; it does not practice its leading role by ruling the society
> but by most devotedly serving its free, progressive socialist de-
> velopment. The Party cannot enforce its authority, but this
> must be won again and again by Party activity. It cannot force
> its line through directives but by the work of its members, by
> the veracity of its ideals.

Party members are seen as the most active workers in each
sphere of the nation's life and therefore are entitled to hold
leading positions in different organizations. But this "must
not lead to the practice of appointing Party members to
functions, without regard to the principle that leading representatives of institutions of the whole society are chosen by

society itself . . . and that functionaries of these compo-
nents are responsible to all citizens or to all members of
social organizations."

Inside the Party, the Program called for "confrontation of
views," asserting:

> Each member of the Party and Party bodies has not only the
> right, but the duty to act according to his conscience, with ini-
> tiative, criticism, with different views on the matter in ques-
> tion, to oppose any functionary. . . . It is impermissible to
> restrict Communists in these rights, to create an atmosphere of
> distrust and suspicion of those who voice different opinions, to
> persecute the minority under any pretext—as has happened in
> the past. The Party, however, cannot abandon the principle of
> requiring the fulfilling of resolutions once they are approved.

Similarly for the society as a whole, the Program demanded,
"Our democracy must provide more room for the activity of
every individual, every collective. . . . People must have
more opportunity to think for themselves and to express
their opinions."

Perhaps the peak of the libertarian dreams of the Program
came in this passage:

> Socialism cannot mean only liberation of the working people
> from the domination of exploiting class relations, but must
> make more provisions for a fuller life of the personality than
> any bourgeois democracy. The working people . . . can no
> longer be prescribed by any arbitrary interpretation from a
> position of power, what information they may or may not be
> given, which of their opinions can or cannot be expressed
> publicly, where public opinion may play a role and where not.
> Public opinion polls must be systematically used in preparing
> important decisions and the main results of the research are to
> be published. Any restriction may be imposed only on the basis
> of a law stipulating what is anti-social—which in our country
> is mainly the criminal law. The Central Committee of the
> Communist Party of Czechoslovakia considers it necessary to

define more exactly than hitherto . . . when a state body can forbid the propagation of certain information [in the press, radio, television, etc.] and exclude the possibility of preliminary factual censorship. It is necessary to overcome the holding up, distortion, and incompleteness of information, to remove any unwarranted secrecy of political and economic facts, to publish the annual balance sheets of enterprise, to publish even alternatives to various suggestions and measures, to extend the import and sale of foreign press. Leading representatives of state, social, and cultural organizations are obliged to organize regular press conferences and give their views on topical issues on television, radio, and in the press. . . .

The Party realizes that ideological antagonists of socialism may try to abuse the process of democratization. At the present stage of development and under the conditions of our country, we insist on the principle that bourgeois ideology can be challenged only in open ideological struggle before all of the people. . . .

The constitutional freedom of movement, particularly the traveling of our citizens abroad, must be precisely guaranteed by law; in particular, this means that a citizen should have the legal right to long-term or permanent sojourn abroad and that people should not be groundlessly placed in the position of emigrants; at the same time it is necessary to protect by law the interests of the state, for example, as regards the drain of some categories of specialists, etc.

Referring to the secret police, the Action Program declared:

The State Security Service must have such a status, organizational structure, numerical state, equipment, methods of work, and qualifications which are in keeping with its work of defending the state from the activities of enemy centers abroad. Every citizen who has not been culpable in this respect must know with certainty that his political convictions and opinions, his personal beliefs and activities, cannot be the object of attention of the bodies of the State Security Service. The Party declares clearly that this apparatus should not be directed and used to solve internal political questions and controversies in socialist society.

The section on foreign policy, predictably, emphasized such old themes as "alliance and cooperation" with the Soviet Union, struggle "against the aggressive attempts of world imperialism," and approval of Ulbricht's East German regime "as an important peace element in Europe." But it also contained nuances suggesting some possible changes in foreign policy. Thus, in the past, Czechoslovak foreign policy "did not make use of all the opportunities for active work, it did not take the initiative in advancing its own views on many important international problems." The stereotyped reference to "neo-Nazi and revanchist tendencies" in West Germany was accompanied by a call for "giving support to the realistic forces" in that country. The reference to the Middle East said nothing about supporting the Arabs but briefly called for "a political settlement of the Middle East crisis."

There was much more to the Action Program, but the excerpts presented above show that it represented a radical change in Party line. There were loopholes in many sections, of course, but a sincere and successful effort to realize this Program would have made Czechoslovakia at least the rival of Yugoslavia as the most open and nearly democratic Communist-ruled country in the world. The biggest omission, from the point of view of a genuinely democratic program, was the lack of any mention of an opposition party or parties and the concurrent acceptance of the possibility of a Communist Party loss of power by legal and constitutional means.

Moscow was not reassured by the new leadership in Prague under Dubcek. And it most emphatically disliked the Action Program. Both of these facts became very evident in mid-

April. On April 9 and 10, the Soviet Central Committee met in Moscow and heard a Brezhnev speech entitled "On the Pressing Problems of the International Situation and the Struggle of the Communist Party of the Soviet Union for Unity of the World Communist Movement." The speech was not published, indicating the delicacy of the issues Brezhnev had discussed. Czechoslovakia was certainly one of the main topics. The Central Committee communiqué at the end of the meeting took pains to "specially emphasize the significance of the Dresden meeting" and then added—in words whose full significance was to become evident in August—that the Central Committee "confirmed anew the readiness of our Party to do all that is necessary for the steady political, economic, and defensive strengthening of the Socialist commonwealth." The Central Committee made plain that it was worried about the weakening of ideological commitment in the Soviet Union, ordering an "irreconcilable struggle against hostile ideology" and declaring that the "strengthening of all the ideological activities of our Party assumes special significance." On April 12, *Pravda* belatedly provided some news of the Prague Central Committee meeting, choosing its quotations carefully so as to emphasize the fears conservatives had expressed about "excesses" and about the dangers to Communism.

Several days later, a week after publication of the Action Program in Prague, *Pravda* finally got around to telling its readers about it. Here, too, Moscow's fears were vividly evident. The *Pravda* summary grossly denatured the original document. It omitted key features and tried to portray the Prague line as being more or less consonant with that of the Soviet leaders. But *Pravda*'s more perceptive readers must have grasped that this was not true because in the same issue of *Pravda* was a long article, stretching over two pages, aimed at refuting the Action Program's conception of the Communist Party and its role. Czechoslovakia was not mentioned, of course, but it was not hard to penetrate the thin veil of Aesopian language as *Pravda* emphasized that the Communist Party must be the "directing force of socialist society," the "real political leader and organizer of the working class" with the concomitant monopoly of power. *Pravda* stressed that only "enemies of socialism relying chiefly on nationalistic and revisionist elements" could oppose this conception. The warning to Prague could hardly have been more pointed.

By mid-April, the lines between Moscow and Prague—between Brezhnev and Dubcek—were drawn firmly and even publicly. That which the Czechoslovak leaders hailed as the "revival" and "renaissance" of their country was attacked by *Pravda* as the essence of bourgeois subversion of socialism. The Action Program had opted for greater democracy, the Soviet Central Committee for a return to tight Stalinist controls. How long could two such different conceptions of Communism exist peacefully side by side, especially when one side—Moscow—was so evidently fearful of contagion from the other?

Simultaneously, another source of Prague-Moscow tension was building up rapidly, taking the shape of what the Moscow *Pravda* on August 22 called "a clearly inspired wave of anti-Soviet propaganda in the press, radio, and television." Understandably, *Pravda* did not think it wise to tell its readers the real point at issue—the Czechoslovak demand for a frank and complete explanation of what lay behind the injustices and judicial murders of the 1948–54 period of Communist rule in Prague.

One of the first to raise the issue was a military prosecutor, Lieutenant Colonel Milan Richter, who wrote in the Ministry of Defense weekly, "It must be said frankly that the most flagrant illegalities did not originate in our country, but were a direct result of Beria's 'long arm.' After the 20th Congress of the Soviet Communist Party, the chief [Soviet] advisers of the former Czechoslovak Minister of Defense, Generals Markov and Likhachev, were sentenced to death in Moscow."

However, the real storm began on April 2, when the Prague weekly *Student* published philosopher Ivan Svitak's article demanding an investigation to ascertain whether Jan Masaryk had committed suicide in 1948, as officially claimed, or had been murdered. Svitak cited evidence throwing doubt on the suicide claim and noted that material had been found connecting a Major Franz Schramm with the case. Major Schramm, Svitak noted, later became the liaison officer between the Soviet and Czechoslovak security forces. Svitak had touched an extremely sensitive nerve. The very next day, the Czechoslovak State Prosecutor announced he would start an investigation. Old wounds were opened as contradictory evidence was weighed. Inevitably, in the atmosphere of the time, suspicions turned immediately to Soviet involvement. The pressure of public speculation on this point became unmistakable on April 16, when *Rude Pravo* not only printed cautious support of the thesis that Masaryk had been murdered but raised the question of what role "Beria's gorillas" had played in the case. *Rude Pravo* then asked "our Soviet friends" to provide assistance in determining the circumstances of Masaryk's death. Rumors circulating in Prague held that Stalin had personally ordered the murder of Masaryk and that it had been carried out by a squad of Soviet agents who had dragged the Foreign Minister out of his bed and thrown him out the window. These rumors were reported in the foreign press, and still Moscow remained silent.

As April neared its end, there came an even more sensational development. Karol Bacilek, former Minister of National Security and former First Secretary of the Slovak Communist Party, declared that the whole falsified Slansky trial had been ordered by Stalin. Anastas Mikoyan had come from Moscow to order a reluctant Klement Gottwald to stage the show trial in whose arrangement the twenty-six Soviet advisers in the secret police ministry had played a significant role.

This was a far more explosive revelation than the earlier talk about Beria. Beria had been executed in the Soviet Union in 1953 as a spy and a traitor, and many Soviet injustices had been blamed on him. Mikoyan was alive and was a respected elder statesman in Moscow. Implicitly linking Mikoyan to the Prague frame-ups was a charge that the Soviet Union still had a long way to go before it would completely come to terms with the crimes of the Stalin era. Since Brezhnev, Premier Aleksei Kosygin, and others in the 1968 Soviet Politburo had played prominent roles under Stalin, Mikoyan's involvement also raised the question of whether these survivors of the Stalin era did not bear a share of responsibility for other judicial murders still unrevealed.

As April neared its close, Moscow could conclude that any hopes Brezhnev might have entertained at Dresden a month earlier that Czechoslovakia would calm down had proven illusory. From the Soviet point of view, the situation was becoming worse daily. Every day, the news brought more discomforting intelligence. On one day, Prague announced that Ladislav Mnacko, who had fled the previous summer in protest against the Soviet bloc's anti-Israel policy, was being rehabilitated and that his banned novel *The Taste of Power* would be published in both Czech and Slovak. On another day, Prague students offered apologies to the U.S. embassy because North Vietnamese students there had stolen the embassy's American flag. *Rude Pravo* printed an editorial demanding that the international Communist conference being planned for Moscow late in 1968 abandon "the practices of classical diplomacy and behind-the-scenes talks" and substitute instead "the principles of openness and comradeship." Czechoslovak sources leaked to the foreign press the news that Moscow was applying economic pressure on Prague, reducing essential wheat shipments while simultaneously offering a 400–500-million-ruble hard-currency loan, presumably on the condition that the Dubcek leadership mend its ways. Czechoslovak newspapers openly criticized the Soviet Union for hiding the real nature of changes in Czechoslovakia from the Soviet people. Jan Prochazka gave an interview to the French press agency, condemning the Soviet persecution of "our brother" Alexander Solzhenitsyn and declaring that in the past Czechoslovakia had had no foreign policy, behaving merely as a "branch office of the Soviet Union."

By the end of April, at the latest, influential voices must already have been demanding stern action to stem Czechoslovakia's increasing departure from Moscow's line and Moscow's practices. Peter Shelest, the Ukrainian Party boss, must have been one of the earliest hawks because his territory, already suffering from an epidemic of revived Ukrainian nationalist sentiment, was the one most vulnerable to contagion from Czechoslovakia. Alexander Shelepin, the former chief of the secret police, was probably also an early hawk (although some reports dispute this). He had been humiliated and demoted earlier by the Brezhnev-Kosygin leadership, and Czechoslovakia offered an invaluable opportunity to charge Brezhnev with the serious error of failing to save Novotny in December, 1967. Premier Kosygin, on the other hand, probably led the doves. He had staked his political future on a *détente* with the United States and more rapid improvement of Soviet living standards. Both goals would be threatened by any explosion in Central Europe. Dmitry Polyansky, attempting to build a political future as the spokesman for the interests of the Soviet peasants, also probably looked unfavorably on any adventure with Czechoslovakia that would divert resources from internal needs. The Soviet marshals, no doubt, warned about the danger of

Czechoslovakia's falling into the hands of NATO and argued that events in Prague proved that the military budget should be increased. But of these arguments no word appeared in the Soviet press.

While Soviet suspicion and fear of Czechoslovak developments deepened, Washington remained silent for more than three months after Dubcek's coming to power. In part, the changes in Prague came too rapidly to be quickly appreciated by the Johnson Administration, whose energies were fully engaged in the Vietnam War. In part, some responsible Washington officials feared that any undue suggestion of American interest in, or help for, the Dubcek regime might backfire by increasing Soviet anxiety and leading to Soviet action against Prague. Saddest of all, the State Department apparently felt it could not take the one concrete action the Czechoslovaks wanted from Washington: It could not prevail over the private interests whose property claims against Czechoslovakia had caused the United States to veto the return of $20 million in Czechoslovak gold that had been seized by the German and then by the Western allies during World War II. Congress, which had earlier killed President Johnson's proposals for liberalizing trade with the Communist nations, seemed in no mood to do anything to help Czechoslovakia. Finally, in April, the State Department broke its official silence. A spokesman declared that the Department was "watching with interest and sympathy recent developments in Czechoslovakia, which seem to represent the wishes and needs of the Czechoslovak people." It was a minimal gesture and hardly even began to represent the great tide of real interest and sympathy for Czechoslovakia then flowing through all informed sections of the American people.

8

The Signals
of May

Shock waves engulfed the foreign ministries and military headquarters of the world on May 9, 1968. Insistent reports from Poland and East Germany told of massive Soviet troop movements toward the Czechoslovak border. Alarm heightened when correspondents in Warsaw flashed bulletins that Western diplomats and reporters seeking to visit the area of military activity had been turned back by Polish roadblocks. Over Radio Prague, commentator Peter Pithard publicly implored Czechoslovakia's friends not to force his nation into a "fatal choice" and not to permit "a repetition of the tragic history of the reckoning of Yugoslavia or perhaps even that of Budapest of 1956." Had a Soviet invasion of Czechoslovakia already begun, or was it only imminent? Had the decision to invade been made the previous day at the mysterious and unexpected Moscow conference of the Soviet leaders with Poland's Gomulka, East Germany's Ulbricht, Hungary's Kadar, and Bulgaria's Zhivkov? Was it to hide the invasion decision that the conference's communiqué had been so uninformative and vague? An anxious world waited far into the night for answers to these questions.

The first invasion scare proved a false alarm. The very next day, the Czechoslovak Government, which had remained silent at the height of world anxiety twenty-four hours earlier, tried to minimize the significance of the troop movements near its borders. There had merely been some routine maneuvers about which the Czechoslovak authorities had been fully apprised in advance, Prague insisted. Nobody was fooled, of course. Moscow had given a public signal, the most threatening of the many warnings it had been issuing that week. The men in the Kremlin wanted the Czechs and Slovaks to know that Soviet patience was wearing thin and that the Soviet Army was available as a weapon of last resort if all lesser methods failed to end the heresies rampant in Prague.

Ironically enough, the immediate sequence of events that had sent the apprehensions of Soviet and other Eastern European leaders rocketing to new peaks had begun on May Day, the traditional international workers' holiday. Even under Novotny, hippies and students in Prague had made May Day unique in the Communist world, an occasion better known for bizarre happenings and clashes with the police than for the usual Communist rededication to international proletarian solidarity. It was predictable that in the spring of Dubcek's rise to power an unprecedented May Day would take place.

Gay, spontaneous, informal, and relaxed were the words foreign correspondents used to describe the vast outpouring of merry Prague citizens. There were Boy Scouts, in uniforms that had been banned only a few weeks earlier, and hippies. There was the traditional People's Military—the factory workers' strong-arm squads that had played so large a role in the Communist take over in February, 1948—and athletes from the Sokol, Czechoslovakia's historic physical culture movement that was then just reemerging after two decades of prohibition. There was a group carrying the American flag and another proudly bearing the Israeli flag. A little boy who was perched on his marching father's shoulders carried a placard saying, "Tell me the truth now so that I won't have to search for it when I grow up." Other posters and placards proclaimed, "Make Love, Not War," "Fewer Monuments, More Thoughts," "Stop Jamming Foreign Radio Stations," "Democracy At All Costs," "Let Israel Live," "Truth Prevails [Czechoslovakia's national slogan] But It Takes Some Doing," "I would like to increase our population, but I have no apartment."

An indignant Bulgarian ambassador stalked off the reviewing stand when a passing contingent carried a placard proclaiming that Macedonia—often claimed by Bulgaria—really belongs to Yugoslavia. At one point, the happy throng simply engulfed Dubcek, as hundreds sought to shake his hand and get his autograph. In this emergency, the police were called to free the Party chief, and Prague's Party Secretary, Bohumil Simon, took the microphone to apologize. He recalled that he had promised there would be no use of police (such as had provoked violence in previous years) but said, "it is necessary to restore order," a fact the crowd good-naturedly took as self-evident. Nothing like this fantastic May Day parade had ever been seen in a nation allied to the Soviet Union. That evening, three hundred demonstrators appeared before the Polish embassy in Prague, protesting loudly against anti-student violence and anti-Semitic expulsions in Warsaw.

The worst was yet to come. On May 3, thousands of students and adults gathered at the statue of Jan Hus in Old Town Square for an authorized meeting that quickly turned into a massive anti-Communist demonstration.

Using a sound truck provided by the municipal radio network, speaker after speaker rose to denounce Communism. Two former political prisoners told how they had been tortured and imprisoned for crimes they did not commit. Another speaker read excerpts from Karel Capek's essay of the 1920's, "Why I Am Not a Communist." The document assails the Communist Party as a power-hungry organization that ignores the needs of the workers while it rules in their name. Other speakers denounced Polish anti-Semitism and called for resumption of Czechoslovakia's diplomatic relations with Israel, a motion that the crowd fully supported. One student speaker read the program of KAN, the Club of Committed Non-Party Members, a new political movement that already had thousands of members and was actively proselytizing, though its activities were still not legally approved. Another speaker called for democracy and opposition parties, declaring "We have been rabbits long enough." He then went on: "We hear we should be grateful to the Communist Party. Yes, we are grateful for the present shortages in housing and transport, grateful for bad worker morale, grateful for legal insecurity, for a currency without value, for a low economic standard." The crowd cheered.

Late that night, near midnight, Party First Secretary Dubcek, Premier Cernik, National Assembly Chairman Smrkovsky, and Slovak Party chief Bilak flew off to Moscow.

Apprehensive and puzzled by this sudden and unexpected trip, few in Czechoslovakia were satisfied by the early hints that the leaders had gone to Moscow to negotiate for the long-rumored Soviet hard currency credit of 400–500 million rubles. Nor was concern diminished when the visit proved a one-day affair and a customarily uninformative communiqué was issued—one that the most perceptive noted said nothing about "complete agreement," which was a standard diplomatic phrase during high-level talks with the Russians in the Novotny era. With more and more critical voices being raised about the lack of information, Dubcek apparently

felt compelled to give reassurance. This took the form of a
"newspaper interview." Later, it became known that the
questions and answers had all been prepared by Dubcek and
his colleagues and merely transmitted to the news media:
Yes, there had been economic discussions and the Russians
were examining Czechoslovak proposals, Dubcek told his
people. But he reached the core of his nation's anxieties in
this passage, which he made as soothing as possible:

> Our Soviet friends received with understanding our explanation
> on our endeavors aimed at the further development of socialist
> democracy and at the strengthening of the Communist Party
> as its leading force. They expressed the conviction that the
> Czechoslovak Communist Party, which enjoys the support of the
> overwhelming majority of Czechoslovak people, will be able to
> successfully implement its aims. It is customary among good
> friends not to hide behind diplomatic politeness but to speak
> openly as equals. It was in this spirit that our Soviet comrades
> expressed their anxiety lest the process of democratization in
> our country be abused against socialism. It must be said that
> our Party has frequently, since the January plenum, emphasized
> its fundamental disagreement with anti-socialist excesses, and
> considers it an inseparable part of its policy to oppose these
> excesses with determination.

Even from this cautious statement, it was plain that Moscow felt that the demonstrations of May 1 and May 3 in
Prague were intolerable. A few days after Dubcek spoke,
however, insistent and probably reliable Prague rumor reported that the meeting had been much rougher than Dubcek had been willing to let his people know. Apparently, the
Soviet leaders had insisted that Czechoslovakia was more and
more coming to resemble Hungary just before the anti-
Soviet revolution of 1956. They demanded fast and vigorous
action to halt the rot in the Communist Party position.

Later, on August 22, 1968, after the invasion, *Pravda* gave
a more open discussion of the Soviet view of the May 4

meeting: Moscow had asked for the meeting because of concern over the deterioration of the situation in Czechoslovakia. *Pravda*'s version of the Dubcek delegation's position at this meeting is most intriguing:

At the May 4 Moscow meeting, the Czechoslovak Communist Party leaders themselves spoke about the seriousness of the situation in the country. More than that, they said that the negative features of the internal political development in the country "go beyond the limits of our purely internal affairs and affect the brotherly countries, for example, the Soviet Union, Poland." And it was impossible to disagree with this.

The Czechoslovak leaders said also that they were prepared to take the necessary measures in order to master the situation. They said then literally the following: "The enemy acts. He wants to turn events in the interests of counterrevolution."

They recognized that the enemy was trying first of all to discredit the Communist Party, weaken its influence on the masses, that there was a growing demand to create a legal political opposition to the Communist Party of Czechoslovakia, which could by its nature become only an anti-Socialist opposition, and that "if firm steps are not employed, this may degenerate into a counterrevolutionary situation." They said that they know the persons specifically guilty of this and affirmed they possess evidence of these persons' connection with imperialist circles and that an end will be put to this.

No doubt Dubcek and his colleagues, as Communists, were concerned about the growth of anti-Communist sentiment that was being expressed publicly in Czechoslovakia. But it seems unlikely that the Soviet account is fully accurate. If this had been the Dubcek attitude, later history would have been very different. What seems more likely is that the Soviet version of the Czechoslovak position is distorted and omits much of a different character. If accurate—which is by no means certain—the most extreme statements quoted by *Pravda* may have come from the most conservative member of the Czechoslovak quartet, Vasil Bilak, whose views differed from those of his colleagues. But Dubcek failed to act on his obligations as a political leader when he returned. He neither warned his people of the seriousness of the Moscow suspicion, nor did he take steps to make possible any resistance to Soviet pressure, should it escalate. Most serious of all, he failed to indicate clearly enough that the Soviet Union was pressing to have its troops enter Czechoslovakia. True, he spoke vaguely about military cooperation in the Warsaw Pact and the importance of military maneuvers for that cooperation. But he did not reveal that—as seems certain in view of subsequent developments—he had surrendered to Soviet pressure for large-scale Warsaw Pact maneuvers in Czechoslovakia in the near future—maneuvers that would permit tens of thousands of Soviet, Polish, and other foreign troops to enter the country. He said nothing about another topic on the Moscow agenda: the Soviet demand for permanent stationing of its troops in Czechoslovakia, allegedly to guard the country's frontier with West Germany. This lack of candor was to provoke a crisis and unity-weakening suspicion when the facts became known.

In Moscow, Warsaw, and East Berlin, the Dubcek "newspaper interview," with its emphasis on reassurance rather than on Moscow's demand for quick, energetic action, must have stirred fury. The Kremlin's displeasure became evident when the *Tass* version of the interview appeared in *Pravda*. That version simply omitted any reference to Dubcek's claim of Soviet understanding for efforts to build a socialist democracy. But it reproduced faithfully his acknowledgement of Soviet disquiet and his vague reference to military maneuvers.

The Dubcek interview appeared on the evening of May 6. Only two days later, a turn toward harshness was evident in the Soviet press. It was a measured set of angry signals. On the one hand, various Soviet newspapers did print articles by Premier Cernik, President Svoboda, and others marking the twenty-third anniversary of Czechoslovakia's liberation, mainly by Soviet troops, and swearing friendship to the Soviet Union. But simultaneously, new, angry notes appeared. Thus, a *Tass* statement published in *Pravda* angrily denied the accusations, published weeks earlier in Prague, about possible Soviet responsibility for Jan Masaryk's death. *Tass* labeled these accusations "lying from beginning to end" and charged directly that the Czechoslovak newspapers printing them were deliberately fomenting "anti-Soviet attitudes among politically unstable people." *Literaturnaya Gazeta,* the most widely read newspaper of Soviet intellectuals, carried a slashing attack on Jan Prochazka, accusing him of anti-Marxism and anti-Sovietism. The message undoubtedly was aimed at Soviet intellectuals, warning them against believing there was any reality to Dubcek's claim of Kremlin "understanding" for attempts to build a socialist democracy.

Even more serious, Brezhnev and Kosygin met on May 8 with Ulbricht, Gomulka, Kadar, and Zhivkov in another of the now increasingly usual one-day conferences. At its end, another uninformative communiqué appeared. But soon the customary "reliable sources" reported that Ulbricht and Gomulka had pushed for hard and speedy action against Czechoslovakia, while Kadar had pleaded that Dubcek be given a chance. To placate these angry vassals, Brezhnev had a trump card—Dubcek's major concession on the Warsaw Pact maneuvers in Czechoslovakia in June. Even so, the decision must have been taken that day to stage the elaborate troop movements of May 9 as a warning to Dubcek of what might happen if he did not deliver. Gomulka must have been particularly angry at Prague during the Moscow meeting, which may explain why so much of the publicized troop movement took place in Poland. Early in May, Prague's liberals were concentrating a heavy propaganda fire on the repressive measures in Poland, employing newspaper articles, radio broadcasts, and petitions to denounce the violence against students and the purging of Jews. The Charles University in Prague was probably most offensive from Warsaw's point of view: It publicly offered to receive and give professorial chairs to four of the most eminent scholars who had been fired in Poland. Needless to say, the scholars were not permitted to accept the proffered posts. Instead, Warsaw tightened its restrictions on entrance into Poland of potentially subversive Czechoslovak university students.

Literaturnaya Gazeta's attack on Jan Prochazka was only the first of a series of Soviet denunciations. The second, on May 14, in *Sovetskaya Rossiya*, was far more serious, a direct blow at the new post-Novotny nationalism in Czechoslovakia. In the crudest possible fashion, *Sovetskaya Rossiya* defamed Thomas Masaryk, father of the Czechoslovak Republic. Masaryk, the newspaper assured its readers, was an "absolute scoundrel," who had paid 200,000 rubles in 1918 to have an anti-Bolshevik terrorist try to murder Lenin. *Sovetskaya Rossiya* sneered at the notion of Masaryk as the "liberator" of his country or an "enlightened President." To make sure that no one missed the significance of the signal it was giving, *Sovetskaya Rossiya* added: "We would not raise this issue now except for the fact that some people in fraternal Czechoslovakia, with a clear purpose in view or as a result of misguidance, have raised their voices with the slogan 'Back to Masaryk!' and are echoing long-forgotten reactionary legends about the 'President-democrat.'"

In the atmosphere of the time, Moscow's propagandists could have picked no surer way to alienate and insult the majority of Czechoslovakia's people. Only a short time earlier, President Svoboda had laid a wreath on Masaryk's grave. On the day that the attack appeared, officials announced that one of Prague's main streets would be renamed for the first President. If Moscow had planned to increase anti-Soviet feeling, it could not have proceeded more effectively, as was obvious from the spate of newspaper, radio, and television answers to the slanders. Now it was the turn of the Prague media to charge that "an anti-Czechoslovak campaign" was going on in Moscow. They raised the question of the Soviet annexation of Czechoslovakia's Carpatho-Ukraine area in 1945 and of the effects on Czechoslovakia of the 1939 Stalin-Hitler Pact. They also printed new details about the role of Soviet secret agents in stage-managing the purge trials of the early 1950's.

An already poisonous atmosphere became daily more venomous. Once again, a *deus ex machina* appeared on the scene. On May 17, three days after the offending article about Masaryk, Soviet Premier Aleksei Kosygin suddenly arrived in Prague. A few hours after his arrival, an eight-man Soviet military mission headed by the Soviet Defense Minister, Marshal Andrei A. Grechko, also flew into Prague, with almost no advance warning. Only three days earlier, Premier Cernik had revealed that an invitation had been extended to Kosygin but had added the Soviet Premier would *not* come soon. Prague was suddenly host to the Soviet state's highest political and military leaders.

It is probably significant that the official Soviet attempt to justify the August invasion and present Moscow's view of the background, in *Pravda* on August 22, 1968, does not mention the Kosygin visit, yet when he arrived for what proved to be an eight-day stay, *Pravda* announced he had gone to Czechoslovakia "for a short-term rest and cure" and for "a continuation of the exchange of views on problems of mutual interest." Moreover, Premier Kosygin arrived in Prague at a time of very high Soviet-Czechoslovak tension. He conferred several times with Dubcek and with other top Prague leaders. What was he up to, and why was his visit not recalled by *Pravda* on the day after the invasion?

One clue is provided by Kosygin's public behavior. He

spent most of his time at Karlovy Vary, the famous spa, taking the baths twice a day. He mingled with German tourists, took walks holding his granddaughter's hand, and happily let television camera men photograph him walking around the town as he talked pleasantly to a young lady reporter. Kosygin's behavior was designed to reassure Czechoslovakia and the world, to project an image of normality and friendship toward Prague, and to counteract the fears and anger aroused both by the Soviet troop movements of May 9 and by the May 14 attack on Masaryk. It is significant that shortly after Kosygin's arrival in Prague, the Czechoslovak news agency quoted "authorized sources" as saying the talks with Kosygin had shown "understanding" for Czechoslovakia's policies. This time, Prague informants insisted, the claim was true, not just *pro forma*.

It is likely, however, that Kosygin went to Czechoslovakia not as the spokesman for the entire leadership, but for a fraction of that leadership. His projection of a public image of good will suggests that he came, in effect, as the envoy of the Moscow doves, hoping that quiet negotiations with Prague leaders would ease the tensions significantly. As Premier of the Soviet Union, he could discuss authoritatively the possibility of a large Soviet hard currency loan, while probing for political concessions in return. There are signs that he made some gains. During the time he was in Czechoslovakia, Dubcek and his colleagues made plain they would not allow the formation of opposition parties. They also put pressure on the press to stop polemics against other Communist nations. During this same period, too, the Czechoslovak Defense Ministry finally announced publicly that there would be joint Warsaw Pact maneuvers in the country during June. However, Kosygin could not reach full agreement with Prague, and the easier atmosphere proved only temporary. When Kosygin finally left Prague, his departure was as sudden and unexpected as his arrival. His abrupt exit suggested that in the end he had failed to attain his full objectives. Little wonder *Pravda* "forgot" to mention his visit when trying to justify the invasion.

Even while Kosygin took the waters at Karlovy Vary, internal struggle continued in Czechoslovakia. As before, Dubcek and his middle-of-the-road comrades found themselves under attack from the right and from the left. The dissonance from the right was evident in Prague on May 18, the first full day of Kosygin's visit. For hours that day some ten thousand students marched, shouting anti-Communist, anti-Soviet and pro-democratic slogans. They drank beer en route, exploded firecrackers, and had a very good time. The carnival spirit of the student parade was well summarized by some of the signs they carried: "With the Soviet Union Forever—But Not a Day Longer" and "Long Live the Soviet Union, But at Its Own Expense." Not a single policeman interfered with them. That same evening, KAN held a meeting of five thousand persons in a restaurant on an island in Prague's Vltava River. One speaker declared, "The Communist Party has opened a door by its liberalization program, and we are going through that door. We have no objection to being part of an orchestra, but in that orchestra we want to hear not only the drum, but all the other instruments." The chairman of the meeting asserted that KAN wanted political liberty and social justice, that it hoped to represent non-Communists and work together with the Communist Party for a "socialist republic based on humanistic and democratic socialism." But the potential for an opposition political party was plain.

Less than a week later, the Ministry of Interior moved to implement the ban on opposition political parties. The Ministry announced that "organized activity purporting to be that of a political party" would not be permitted. Its excuse was that existing law did not envisage the formation of new political parties, and therefore the Ministry had no authority to license them. The legalistic excuse was an example of totalitarian mentality, which assumes that if an action is not specifically authorized it must *ipso facto* be forbidden.

From the left, the attacks on Dubcek's policies emphasized that the new leaders were endangering Communist rule. Anonymous leaflets carrying the conservatives' message particularly to factory workers were distributed in many parts of Czechoslovakia during May. The writers of the leaflets sought to take advantage of the workers' fear of unemployment and worsening economic conditions and of the workers' distrust of the intellectuals. "Workers, be vigilant. We must not permit the destruction of socialism and the restoration of capitalism," one declared. By May 17, the campaign had reached such proportions the *Rude Pravo* reprinted the text of one leaflet, which, it said, was being read to workers at "improvised sessions" held in Prague plants. The propaganda sheet declared: "The inventors of the new model of Socialism—Goldstuecker, Sik, Kriegel and Cisar—try to deceive us for their mercenary interests. Under the slogan of 'liberalization' they fight their way into the leadership and try to take over power. Actually, they want to restore the first bourgeois republic by revisionist means." The anti-Semitic appeal here was clear; Goldstuecker—the Writers Union head—and Kriegel—a member of the Presidium—were known to be Jews, and Sik was of Jewish origin.

More serious than the anonymous writings was the emergence of a conservative faction in the new leadership. More and more, rumors in Prague began to point at Communist Party Secretary Alois Indra, a former Minister of Transportation, and Presidium member Drahomir Kolder as the men Moscow and Warsaw wanted to see replace Dubcek and Cernik. The sympathy of Slovak Communist Party First Secretary Vasil Bilak and Communist Party Presidium member Frantisek Barbirek with the conservatives was plainly revealed in mid-May. They met openly with the East German ambassador, Peter Florin, who toured Slovakia on a barely disguised proselytizing mission to drum up opposition to Dubcek. Inevitably, the conservative agitation brought a liberal counterattack. Near the end of May, Premier Cernik, Goldstuecker, and others went on speaking trips to the provinces to explain the Dubcek policies to ordinary citizens and to win more grass-roots support.

Neither the anxieties about Soviet policy nor the internal Communist Party struggle prevented progress in formulating and applying, at least initially, the reform policies of the Dubcek leadership. Religious groups benefitted because the tight limits on their activities were eased and their publications began to share in the general greater press freedom. The story of the past era of religious persecution and of the mistreatment of priests and ministers emerged. The commissars who had formerly supervised church activities were withdrawn, and the puppet movement of "peace priests" was dissolved. The acting leader of the Czechoslovak Catholics, Bishop Frantisek Tomasek, was allowed to travel to Rome, where he consulted with the exiled Josef, Cardinal Beran, who had been freed from jail in 1963 on condition that he leave the country and never return. Lesser Catholic bishops, barred in 1950 from occupying their diocesan posts, were permitted to resume their ecclesiastical work, as were other priests and ministers who had earlier been compelled to turn to secular pursuits. It became possible for Roman Catholics faithful to Rome to form the Movement for Conciliatory Resurgence, under Tomasek's leadership.

Former political prisoners gained when the Party Presidium announced that persons who had served sentences for political offenses could resume their former occupations, rather than, as earlier, being restricted to manual labor. But legislation for rehabilitation being considered in the National Assembly did not grant blanket amnesty to all who had been sentenced under the security laws. Instead, it provided for the examination of each case of alleged conviction of an innocent person. Those found to have been unjustly imprisoned would be paid 20,000 crowns for each year spent in jail, 25 per cent of the amount to be paid immediately, the rest in ten years. Work was proceeding, too, on plans to restructure Czechoslovakia into a federal union of Czechs and Slovaks. Under the most favored plan, there would be parallel Communist Party and Government units in Slovakia and in the Czech lands, under national leadership in Prague. Some Slovaks were pressing for an even looser relationship.

Economic reform was also very much on the leaders' minds during May. They understood that if the Dubcek policies were to survive, the post-Novotny rulers had to provide a better standard of living. The flood of demands that had accompanied the spread of democratization emphasized this. Utilizing the newly approved free speech, workers were insisting on higher wages, and local groups were calling for more investment funds to meet their areas' pressing needs. The nation, however, did not have the resources to meet all these demands, justified and understandable as many of them were. These pressures made the Dubcek group eager for foreign-currency loans that would permit the purchase of Western technology needed to make Czechoslovak production fully competitive on world markets in both quality and quantity.

At a press conference with Premier Cernik on May 14, Deputy Premier Ota Sik summarized the regime's thinking on needed economic changes: Czechoslovakia would welcome Western capital investments, which would make possible "joint ventures" with domestic enterprises. He set as the ultimate goal full convertibility of the nation's currency unit, the crown, into foreign currencies, but recognized that this would be a difficult objective to reach. Sik outlined a far more drastic domestic economic reform than had ever taken place in the country. He envisaged a central economic policy-making body presiding over a completely decentralized industry, in which enterprise managers would have full autonomy and would have to compete for credits and markets. Free enterprise, Sik announced, would be permitted in the service industries where private individuals could set up enterprises in which they worked with their families and perhaps "one or two apprentices." Later that month, Premier Cernik revealed a major reduction in Czechoslovakia's formerly ambitious plans for expanding heavy-industry output; the 1980 steel production goal had been cut from 24 million to 13 million tons, and the 1980 electric power production target had been reduced from 154 billion kilowatt-hours to 90 billion.

In May, too, Czechoslovakia sought to improve its relations with other countries and with foreign Communist parties that might help to moderate the hostile pressures being exerted by the Soviet Union and its allies. Italian Communist Party leader Luigi Longo was received in Prague with utmost hospitality, which he repaid by publicly expressing approval of the Czechoslovak reforms. Longo was anxious to identify his Party with the Prague evolution because Italy was on the eve of an election in which it was important to convince voters that a vote for the Communist Party was not a vote for dictatorship and subjection to Moscow. Yugoslavia's Foreign Minister, Marko Nikezic, visited Prague in mid-May and made plain Belgrade's approval of the Czechoslovak development, as well as Yugoslavia's hope that the Czechoslovak evolution would similarly influence other Communist nations. As a gesture toward the United States, Pan American Airlines was allowed to open a modern office in Prague, not far from the site where construction had begun on a tourist hotel to be built and operated with American participation. West German business and cultural contacts were growing, aided by the increasing activity of the new West German trade mission in Prague. Later events were to show that Moscow was paying particularly close attention to these last developments. A hint of this came in May, when the *Pravda* correspondent in Bonn accused the West German press of trying to encourage anti-socialist forces in Czechoslovakia.

The "2,000 Words"
of June

If an armed, violent, and bloody anti-Communist revolt had
broken out in Czechoslovakia, it could hardly have caused
more panic among the top leaders in Prague than was actually observable there on June 27 and 28, 1968. An extraordinary session of the Communist Party Presidium, called
suddenly, adopted a strong resolution of condemnation.
Party Secretary Alois Indra sent telegrams to all local Party
organizations warning against "counterrevolutionary incite-
ment." Alexander Dubcek interpolated an expression of
"great concern" into the text of a previously prepared
speech. Premier Oldrich Cernik appealed to the National
Assembly for, and received, unanimous approval of his denunciation of those who, he said, would create "a climate of
nervousness, apprehension, and legal uncertainty."

Since nothing even faintly resembling an armed revolution had occurred, the reason for the obvious panic among
the usually stolid leaders in Prague was a mystery at the

time. The avowed cause hardly seemed commensurate with the violence of the reaction. The cause was a statement by author Ludvik Vaculik, signed by seventy people—some famous, some obscure—and published in four newspapers on the morning of June 27 under the title "2,000 Words." Not until two months later did it become clear that the panic observed in Prague was less the result of the statement itself than of the immediate reaction to it in Moscow. *Pravda,* in its August 22, 1968, history of Soviet-Czechoslovak relations, called "2,000 Words" an "open call to struggle against the Communist Party of Czechoslovakia, against the constitutional power." *Pravda* then revealed that, apparently on the same day that the statement appeared, the "leadership of our Party called A. Dubcek's attention to the danger of this document as a platform for further activization of counterrevolutionary actions. He replied that the Central Committee Presidium is considering the problem, that the appeal will be given the sharpest evaluation, and that the most decisive measures will be taken." Judging by what Dubcek and Cernik actually did on June 27 and 28, the telephoned warnings and threats from Moscow must have been scorching. Perhaps it was to prevent a Soviet military take over of Czechoslovakia right then and there that Dubcek and Cernik took their frantic moves to establish their opposition to "2,000 Words."

It is hard to believe that "2,000 Words" was more than a convenient pretext for Soviet leaders looking for any excuse to exert more pressure on Prague. The contents of the document are mild to an American accustomed to George Wallace's election speeches, Black Panther manifestoes, and some of the oratory on American campuses during various college riots. Only by taking words out of context or by even more unscrupulous distortion can this document be represented as a "platform" for counterrevolution. On the contrary, as its contents make plain, the statement was written because of fear that the peaceful revolution begun in January, 1968, was slowing down and being lost in a morass of bureaucratic resistance at the grass roots. It was an attempt by liberals, moved by the desperate fear that the ground was dissolving beneath their feet, to intensify the struggle against the conservative forces that sought to sabotage the gains of the previous months. Here is the essence of the manifesto that aroused such a storm in June:

> The central political organs have done all they can up to this point. It is up to us to make new inroads in the districts and communities. Let us demand the resignation of those who have abused their power, who have harmed public property, who have acted dishonestly or cruelly. We must find ways to induce them to leave. Such steps include public criticism, resolutions, demonstrations, collecting funds for their retirement, strikes and boycotts. . . . But we must reject methods which are illegitimate, indecent or gross, since they might prejudice Alexander Dubcek. We must decry the writing of insulting letters, since they can be exploited by those who receive them. . . .
>
> Let us change the district and local press, which has degenerated into a mouthpiece for official views. Let us demand the establishment of editorial councils composed of representatives of the National Front or let us start new newspapers. Let us establish committees for the defense of free speech. Let us have marshals to maintain order at our meetings. . . .
>
> Let us support the security organs when they prosecute genuine criminal activity. We do not want to cause anarchy and a state of general insecurity. Let us avoid disputes among neighbors and renounce spitefulness in political affairs. Let us unmask informers. . . .
>
> Recently there has been great apprehension that foreign forces may interfere with our internal development. Faced with their superior strength, the only thing we can do is humbly hold our own and not start trouble. We assure the government that we will back it, if necessary even with weapons, as long as

the government does what we mandate and assures our allies that we will observe our alliance, friendship, and trade agreements.

Excited reproaches and unfounded suspicions make the government's position more difficult, without being of any help to us. We can insure a new balance in our system only by improving internal conditions to such an extent that the revival can be carried to a point where we can elect statesmen who will have sufficient courage, honor, and political wisdom to defend such conditions. This, by the way, is the problem of governments in all the small countries of the world.

As at the end of the war, we have been given a great chance once again. We have the opportunity to take up a common cause, which for all practical purposes we call socialism, and mold it so that it will correspond to the good reputation we once had and the high esteem in which we held ourselves.

It was the simplest sort of demagoguery to misrepresent this document. Taken out of context, its references to "strikes," "demonstrations" and "weapons" could be, and were, represented as calls to armed "counterrevolution." Vaculik and his cosigners had made themselves vulnerable on another count. They had warned that a federal government with more autonomy for the Slovaks would not by itself solve more fundamental problems or bring better living conditions. They had written that "the rule of the Party-state bureaucracy may still survive, especially in Slovakia because, in its victorious fight, 'it has gained greater freedom.'" This was obviously a slap at the conservative primacy in Bratislava under Bilak and Barbirek, but such words could be, and were, misrepresented as a chauvinist Czech attack on Slovak demands for greater autonomy.

The liberals had blundered by giving their enemies such weapons, yet even in the first days after publication of "2,000 Words" it became evident that the proclamation had touched a deep national chord. Along with the bureaucrats' denun-

ciations came a flood of endorsements from many elements
of the population. The note of desperation and fear in the
appeal turned out to be shared by many in Czechoslovakia.
By late June, there was a crisis of confidence in the country,
a terrible apprehension that the dreams of earlier months
had been betrayed. At the time, no great political sophistica-
tion was required to see that Czechoslovakia was almost an
occupied nation and that a mobilization of the internal
forces opposing democracy had taken place.

It had all begun in the last days of May when two events
occurred almost simultaneously. One was the beginning of
the Communist Party Central Committee meeting. The
other, startling and unexpected to many, was the arrival of
the first units of Soviet, Polish, and other Warsaw Pact troops
for the "maneuvers." At first, the Central Committee meeting, which extended to early June, seemed to have been a
victory for the liberals. On the opening day, the Central
Committee expelled Antonin Novotny from its ranks and
suspended his Party membership. Also suspended were six
men who had played key roles in the Stalinist trials of the
early 1950's, notably former Premier Viliam Siroky and
former Chief Prosecutor Josef Ulvalek. Several conservatives
—most prominently the former Defense Minister, General
Bohumir Lomsky—resigned from the Central Committee.
Apparently, the long liberal campaign for an early convening of the Fourteenth Communist Party Congress had won.
That Congress, the Central Committee decided, would meet
on September 9, 1968.

A closer scrutiny induced dismaying reflections among the
liberals. They noted, for example, that Dubcek had significantly modified his position and was obviously seeking
above all to quiet Soviet fears. Thus, his speech to the Central Committee singled out "anti-Socialist tendencies" as the
main danger to Czechoslovak democratization. He stressed
"the leading role of the Communist Party" much more

firmly than before and in accents closer to Moscow's. He reminded the communications media that, even with the lifting of censorship, they would be expected to be careful of what they wrote and said and showed, implying self-censorship with an eye to the interests of the Party. He attacked would-be opposition groups, centering his fire on Club 231, composed of former political prisoners, which, Dubcek charged, had members "who have been condemned for anti-state activities." In discussing the decision to move the Fourteenth Congress up to September, 1968, Dubcek made no reference to the liberals' main objective: purging the Central Committee of its conservative members. Instead, he talked about the importance of the coming Congress for strengthening the role of the Communist Party in the country. Dubcek had reproaches for conservatives as well and pledged the implementation of the Action Program. On balance, many liberals decided he had pussyfooted at the Central Committee, avoided a direct confrontation with the remaining conservatives, and had his eye fixed more on re-assuring Moscow than on meeting the nation's need for rapid democratization.

Even more alarming was the growing evidence, as June progressed, that the people of Czechoslovakia had been the victims of a gigantic deception. They had been given no inkling of the fact that tens of thousands of Soviet, Polish, East German, Hungarian, and even some Bulgarian troops, with numerous tanks and airplanes would enter the country for "maneuvers." The bitterness this aroused and the course of the subterfuge were well described as June ended by the Bratislava weekly, *Kulturny Zivot:*

> The play has developed according to the strict rules of drama. In the spring it was said there would be no maneuvers and no maneuvers were contemplated. In the second stage it was tentatively admitted that a tiny and ordinary exercise of staffs was being prepared. People not well acquainted with military mat-

ters visualized staff officers over maps shifting small tanks in a sand table game.

The true play started when the press secretary of the Ministry of Defense reminded us that staff exercises needed signal troops, estimated at about one battalion. Then in rapid succession so-called security units and marking units were added, then tanks and aircraft and the whole glittering cast was on the stage.

With heavy irony the periodical reported the reaction of an "innocent citizen"—obviously a representation of the average man—"who did not grasp the intentions of the play's director and who telephoned Radio Prague in some alarm to report that Soviet troops and tanks had been marching through his town for four hours."

The Soviet purpose in practicing this deceit was plain. By sending several tens of thousands of troops and hundreds of tanks into Czechoslovakia, Moscow hoped to frighten the democratic Communists and the non-Communists in the country. It was a crude exercise in pressure and power politics. But why did Dubcek and his colleagues accede to this scheme and damage their political credibility with their own people? Presumably, Dubcek felt that he had no alternative, that if he did not admit Soviet troops on the pretext of maneuvers, they would come as invaders. Here, as throughout this period, neither Dubcek nor Smrkovsky nor Cisar nor Kriegel nor any of the other prominent reform Communists ever gave the slightest public hint that there was any need or possibility for Czechoslovakia to defend itself by force of arms. Instead, they relied desperately upon unwearying recital of their friendship for the Soviet Union and of their devotion to the Warsaw Pact and proletarian internationalism.

Then, to fill the liberals' cup of bitterness to overflowing, the People's Militia held a nationwide mobilization on June 19 at the Prague-Ruzyne airport. Ten thousand armed workers gathered from all parts of the country to be addressed by

Dubcek. In previous months, it was from this group that some of the most vocal objections to the democratization had come. In reaction, some non-Communists had begun agitating for the dissolution of this Communist Party private army. Dubcek, still maneuvering between the different factions, apparently had consented to a public demonstration with the idea of winning this important group over to the reform program. The consequences were quite different, for the meeting was turned into a pro-Soviet and anti-liberal demonstration. The assembled militiamen adopted a resolution pledging themselves to be the guarantors of Czechoslovak loyalty to the Soviet Union. The resolution said:

> We shall not permit anyone to blacken or threaten the principles of the construction of socialism and Communism which were formulated by V. I. Lenin and for whose realization we laid the foundation in February, 1948. We do not agree with, and divorce ourselves from, the irresponsible actions of some journalists who try to break our friendship by spreading different distortions from the bourgeois press.

Whether or not all the militiamen wanted the resolution to be used for this purpose, it was promptly delivered to the Soviet embassy in Prague on June 20 and was printed prominently in *Pravda* in Moscow the following day. A few days later, there was a barrage of answering messages from workers in plants all over the Soviet Union, all pledging solidarity with the People's Militia of Czechoslovakia. The Soviet propagandists could not have manufactured better "evidence" that the working class of Czechoslovakia was against the most radical reformers. From Dubcek's point of view, the whole affair brought one advantage: He had been presented positively in the Soviet press and associated in it with the people's militia. The liberals, understandably, saw the incident in quite a different light.

Dubcek had reason to be worried. Even the unopposed admission of thousands of Soviet and allied troops to Czechoslovakia had not satisfied Moscow. This was evident from several events. Moscow delivered a formal and stiff diplomatic protest when a Prague newspaper reprinted a *New York Times* story telling of Prague reports that General Sejna had been able to escape because he had a passport secured for him by a Soviet general. A Czechoslovak parliamentary delegation to the Soviet Union, headed by Smrkovsky, had been coolly received. Smrkovsky himself had felt under pressure to deliver speeches to Soviet audiences, assuring them of Prague's loyalty and denouncing journalistic "extremists" in Czechoslovakia. True, when the delegation met with Brezhnev, the Soviet leader reportedly had tears in his eyes as he vehemently denied that the Soviet Union wanted to stop Prague's democratization. But two days after those tears, *Pravda* published a vitriolic attack on one of Dubcek's closest associates, Party Secretary Cestmir Cisar, accusing him of heresy and ideological association with earlier deviationists who, according to *Pravda*, had finally betrayed the cause of Marxism. The attack by an old Stalinist propagandist, Fedor Konstantinov, charged Cisar with attacking Leninism as an ideological monopoly applicable only to Russian conditions.

This was a serious warning of future trouble. There had been no earlier comparable public attack on a high Czechoslovak Communist Party figure. The nature of the charges explicitly drove home the point that Moscow believed the Leninist variety of Marxism was as valid for Czechoslovakia as for the Soviet Union. Finally, and in some ways most worrisome, after months of negotiation, there was no sign of progress in the effort to get a large Soviet hard currency loan. Even a visit to Moscow by a Czechoslovak economic delegation brought no visible gains.

Dubcek did not confine his fence-mending to the Soviet Union. In May, he had received Bulgaria's Todor Zhivkov and renewed a 20-year friendship agreement with Bulgaria. In June, he went to Budapest to renew a similar treaty with

Hungary and to confer with Kadar. There was every external indication on that visit that Czechoslovakia's relations with Hungary were relatively good, even though the Hungarians made plain they wanted better treatment of the more than half a million Hungarians living in Czechoslovakia. Foreign Minister Jiri Hajek went to East Germany to try to reassure Ulbricht and his ruling group that their apprehensions about Czechoslovakia were without foundation. That same month, Czechoslovakia dutifully promised to provide more aid to North Vietnam, listing among the goods it would send "machine tools, diesel engines, automobiles, tractors, medical supplies and means necessary for strengthening the defense capacity" of the Hanoi forces.

These and other efforts could not satisfy Moscow because they did not touch what the Kremlin thought were the essentials. When Dubcek had denounced anti-Socialist forces at the Central Committee meeting in late May, the Russians had thought he was finally going to act, to reimpose censorship, purge the Communist Party of "revisionists," and generally restore discipline. But nothing of the sort happened. The press, the radio, and television continued to ventilate heretical ideas, and liberals were not purged. On the contrary, all available information suggested that liberal ideas were gaining strength. On June 27, for example, *Rude Pravo* reported that in its recent poll the creation of opposition parties had been favored by 90 per cent of its non-Communist readers and by more than half of the Communist Party members responding. On June 26, the National Assembly had passed a bill ending prepublication censorship but making the chief editors of publications responsible for any disclosures of state secrets. Even the vote on this measure showed the new spirit in the country. Thirty of the deputies voted against the bill, and seventeen abstained, a far cry from the old unanimity.

But it was the free-wheeling Czechoslovak communications media that daily rubbed salt into raw Soviet wounds by taking their freedom seriously and refusing to heed the injunctions to be discreet. One of the chief offenders was the magazine *Student*. In June, it published defense testimony, given at the Moscow trial the previous January, of several young Soviet intellectuals, testimony that had not been made available to Soviet readers. *Student* pointed out that poems praising Stalin had been printed in Moscow while the novels of Russia's greatest living writer, Alexander Solzhenitsyn, were barred from Soviet bookstores. When *Pravda* attacked Cestmir Cisar, Prague's *Svobodne Slovo* categorically denied that Cisar was an anti-Communist, and the trade union newspaper *Prace* recalled the Stalinist past of *Pravda*'s author. *Prace* sarcastically called the article "a distinctive way of enriching our discussion before the Party Congress." *Rude Pravo* struck a blow at the conservatives' anti-Semitic propaganda by reprinting an anonymous letter sent to Writers Union head Eduard Goldstuecker and the latter's reply. The letter declared that the reform program in Czechoslovakia was the work of Jews and harmed the workers. It concluded, "Don't worry, your time will come, your days are numbered, you disgusting Jew." Goldstuecker, in his reply, drew attention to the parallel between the letter's anti-Semitism and the anti-Semitism propagated by the secret police during the Slansky and related trials of the early 1950's.

One of the most effective uses of the communications media was made by Deputy Premier Ota Sik, who used a *Rude Pravo* article and a series of television lectures to hammer home the harsh facts of Czechoslovakia's economic debacle. To workers demanding ever more insistently that they get wage increases, Sik replied, "The Government is approaching the national economy like one approaching a bare cupboard," adding, "We have nothing left for a handout." Then he launched into a series of dismaying statistics to illustrate the magnitude of the catastrophe the old regime had visited upon the national economy: Nearly two-thirds of the nation's machinery was obsolete, but the old machines were often more productive than new equipment installed in new factories manned by untrained and unskilled housewives and newly-transplanted peasants. Czechoslovakia had one of the lowest ratings in Europe in housing construction; only Portugal, Spain, and Yugoslavia lagged behind. The country was losing enormous amounts by exporting heavy industry products at less than their cost of production. More than half of the country's output of steel was of low quality, and only 5 per cent was of high quality. Vast quantities of goods were being produced that could find no sale. Only one-third of Czechoslovakia's manufactured goods met world market standards of quality, with the situation most catastrophic in new goods such as semi-conductors, only 8 per cent of which met world quality standards. Czechoslovak steel had an average durability of 40 per cent less than the world norm. The countryside had been depopulated of young people, and as early as 1960 two-thirds of all workers in agriculture were over 47 years of age. Only half of the nation's output was available for general consumption, less than the amount in any developed capitalist country. A Czechoslovak worker had to work 117 hours to earn enough to buy a transistor radio, while a West German needed to work only 12 hours to buy one. On and on he went with sobering statistics and dismaying comparisons. His statements were very instructive for his domestic listeners but earned him no friends in Moscow. The policies he denounced had been borrowed from the Soviet Union, and many of the same unfavorable comparisons he drew between Czechoslovakia and the capitalist countries could be drawn even more tellingly for the Soviet Union and capitalist countries. Czechoslovakia's living standards, as everyone knew, were much higher than those of the Soviet Union.

In the midst of this confused situation, with powerful

Soviet pressures on Prague but the vitality of the Czechoslovak revival movement still high, the United States finally
decided to take a small step that would be helpful. It was not
as "big" a step as settling the long dispute over the $20 million
in Czechoslovak gold held in the West, but it was better
than nothing. On June 16, the United States Government
announced that it was willing to negotiate an agreement
with Czechoslovakia, releasing $5 million owed to residents
of that country in Social Security and other blocked annuity
payments. The negotiations did not take long. In ten days,
the agreement was signed, opening the way for negotiations
on other issues. Even in doing this, the State Department
had made sure that it could not be criticized for being "soft
on Communism." The United States terms, accepted by
Prague, required that every one of the eligible pensioners in
Czechoslovakia be personally interviewed by an American
consular official. It had taken "only" five months and three
weeks since Alexander Dubcek's coming to power for this
first step toward *rapprochement* and help.

It is doubtful if Dubcek and his colleagues ever expected
very much aid from the United States. They were well aware
that nothing would arouse Soviet suspicions faster than even
a remote sign that basic changes were taking place in Wash-
ington-Prague relations. The tireless reiterations of vows to
strengthen the Soviet bloc and the innumerable denunciations of the United States in Vietnam all suggest that relations with Washington had low priority in Prague's list of
concerns.

West Germany was quite another story. West Germany
was a next-door neighbor and already an important commer-
cial partner of Czechoslovakia. From the beginning of the
serious revival of Czechoslovakia's tourist industry in the
late 1950's, West Germans had been prominent among visitors from the capitalist world, and West Germany was rich.
Inevitably, from the very beginning, economic aid from

Bonn was in the thoughts of those who had to wrestle with Czechoslovakia's difficult and pressing economic problems. The matter can be stated simply: How could Czechoslovakia get West German economic aid without incurring danger-ous political liabilities that would endanger Czechoslovak standing with the Russians, the East Germans, and the Poles? By June, with the hoped-for Soviet loan still entangled in seemingly endless negotiations, the pressure was greater than ever for some kind of economic understanding with Bonn.

It was natural, therefore, that Foreign Minister Hajek chose his words carefully when he addressed the foreign affairs committee of the National Assembly on June 11:

> We are for a realistic view. While we are seriously studying the present rise of neo-Nazism in the German Federal Republic, we are not closing our eyes either to the expressions of a realistic appreciation of realities and prospects of development, which are making their way also in the ruling circles of the German Federal Republic.

Hajek had spoken cautiously. He had taken care to add the usual formula to protect the interests of the East Germans and to remind Bonn that Prague demanded that West Ger-many recognize the 1938 Munich Pact as invalid from its very beginning. But despite these cautions, Hajek's state-ment could hardly be read except as an expression of inter-est in Bonn's policy of building bridges to Eastern Europe. Moscow could not have liked these remarks. Hajek, in the same speech, threw cold water on the hopes for resumption of relations with Israel. But this sign of orthodoxy could hardly have made up, in Moscow's eyes, for the gesture to-ward-Bonn. Jiri Hajek, in short, was no longer in the best graces of the Kremlin.

10

The Ultimatum
of July

By the beginning of July, 1968, Moscow had made the basic decision: Czechoslovakia must be brought to heel and its dangerous heresies ended by whatever means were necessary. Three possible solutions dominated the tactical debates at Soviet Politburo meetings. Ideally, the slippery and evasive Dubcek would finally be made to deliver on the many promises he had given during the preceding half year. Such a solution was so attractive in terms of minimizing military, political, and economic complications that it was agreed that one last try should be made. Alternatively, the Politburo hoped for an internal *coup d'état* in Prague, with Kolder, Indra, Bilak, and friendly generals seizing power, disposing of Dubcek and his troublesome friends, and cleaning up the mess with a minimum of direct Soviet military involvement. But by now, the men in Moscow were ready for direct invasion of Czechoslovakia if need be. The contingency planning begun months ago had been completed. Tens of thousands of additional troops had been put into place in the great Soviet-controlled arc surrounding Czechoslovakia. The East Germans and the Poles had been ready for weeks, and by the beginning of July, Hungary's Kadar, during a state visit to Moscow, had been forced into line as well. The process of preparing Soviet public opinion for even the extreme last alternative was well under way. All over the country, Party agitators, properly briefed, were convening factory meetings to hear June's pro-Soviet resolution of the Czechoslovak People's Militia and to pass their own resolutions expressing the willingness of the Soviet people to help "defend the conquests of socialism."

The public signal, for those who could understand the Aesopian language employed, came on July 3 at the Soviet-Hungarian friendship meeting in the Kremlin's Congress Hall. Brezhnev and Kadar spoke. Both men agreed in their evaluation that the United States was convulsed by political assassination, Negro and youth revolt, the poor people's march on Washington, and dissension arising from the Vietnam War. A "rotten society," a "degrading society," a "disintegrating society"—these were the terms, Brezhnev told his audience, that even those favorably disposed toward the United States were applying to that country. Kadar chimed in that American society was in the toils of a "heavy crisis." The implication was plain: The United States was too caught up in its own troubles to do anything about Eastern Europe. Moscow and its allies could proceed as they wished in dealing with Czechoslovakia.

Brezhnev and Kadar made plain that they intended to do something. Brezhnev was particularly belligerent as he charged that "apologists for the bourgeois order are prepared to pose in any pseudo-socialist clothes" in order, under the mask of "national forms," to shatter the socialist system and "weaken the brotherly ties among socialist countries." The Soviet Union, Brezhnev emphasized, "can and will never be indifferent to the fate of socialist construction in other countries." Kadar went further, raising the specter of direct intervention. The Hungarian Communists, he declared, "express full solidarity with the Communists, with those who defend the power of the working class, the cause of socialism against the encroachments of dogmatists, revisionists, the class enemy. We understand the sense of the struggle, and we are prepared to extend international aid by all means." This was a fateful warning indeed, and delivered by the man whose own power traced back to the "international aid" Soviet troops had given in 1956 in crushing the Hungarian Revolution. Kadar had been considered by Dubcek the most sympathetic of the Kremlin's allies. In June, the Hungarians had not only signed a friendship treaty with Prague but their Central Committee had formally endorsed the Czechoslovak Action Program and its objectives. Then *Literarni Listy* had published an article praising Imre Nagy, on the tenth anniversary of his execution, for having led the 1956 Hungarian Revolution. The result was a political storm in Budapest, and not even a public apology by Dubcek had soothed a majority of Kadar's colleagues. The "2,000 Words" manifesto had produced more indignation among Budapest leaders, who were still uneasy about the loyalty of their own people.

Hard on the heels of these Moscow speeches came action. In the next few days, Dubcek received letters from Moscow and its allies. In effect, the Czechoslovaks were peremptorily ordered to attend another Communist summit meeting on the pretext that "2,000 Words" had revealed a serious threat to Communist power in Prague. This was flagrant intervention in Czechoslovakia's internal affairs. Prague stood firm. By a majority vote—there is some evidence that Kolder, Bilak, and Presidium alternate member Antonin Kapek formed a pro-Soviet minority—the Presidium turned down the invitation. Understandably, the Presidium gave a soft answer, suggesting that bilateral talks first be held between the Czechoslovak leaders and the Soviet, East German, Polish, Hungarian, and Bulgarian leaders to prepare the way for a broader meeting. However, no amount of circumlocution or courteous language could disguise the fact that, for the first time in its history, the leadership of the Czechoslovak Communist Party had turned down a Soviet order to attend a meeting. It was a major act of courage on the part of Dubcek and his comrades. All of them understood that they were igniting a crisis of the first magnitude, one that could have very dangerous consequences for each of them personally as well as for their nation. Moreover, all of them knew that, even as they defied Moscow, thousands of Soviet troops were in Czechoslovakia, while additional tens or even hundreds of thousands of Soviet and Soviet-controlled troops stood at Czechoslovakia's borders.

Ironically, these troops probably played the decisive role in moving Dubcek, Smrkovsky, Kriegel, and the rest of the Presidium majority to defy Moscow. Determined to create a system of Communist rule responsive to the people's will, Dubcek must have been acutely conscious of the severe blow the entrance of the troops had inflicted on his countrymen's confidence in him. Czechs and Slovaks alike knew they had been tricked and lied to when the "staff maneuvers" had turned out to involve tens of thousands of troops and thousands of vehicles, including tanks. In the first two weeks of July, the nation was becoming angrier as it became more obvious daily that the Soviet troops had no intention of leaving promptly, though the maneuvers had ended on June 30. As evidence mounted that Moscow hoped to keep its soldiers in Czechoslovakia indefinitely, the prestige of the nation's leaders plummeted. Dubcek found himself caught in a major crisis of confidence. He and his comrades had to show firmly that they were prepared to defend the national interests against the Soviet Union, or suffer the loss of their political capital—the trust and support of the people. Only such considerations can explain their unprecedented defiance of Moscow.

There was a tragicomic quality about July's succession of official Prague announcements on when the "allied troops" would leave and the subsequent succession of lame explanations as to why they had not left as previously promised. At first, the Soviet commanders said their equipment needed to be repaired before it could be taken out, and additional "repair troops" entered Czechoslovakia. Then it was said that there were the usual difficulties in getting needed spare parts and that the troops were tired and needed to rest before they could depart. Next the Soviet commanders developed a hitherto unknown solicitude for the normal flow of traffic along Czechoslovakia's roads and insisted their vehicles could only move at night and slowly, in order to avoid accidents. Finally, it was suggested that the bridges and roads on which Soviet heavy equipment had entered Czechoslovakia were really unsafe and had to be strengthened before the vehicles could go back over them. Such excuses were the stuff of public "explanation," but behind the scenes the talk was much more open and ugly. According to diplomatic sources in Warsaw, Soviet Marshal Ivan Yakubovsky, commander of the Warsaw Pact troops, told the Prague leaders he was dissatisfied with the performance of Czechoslovak troops and wanted more maneuvers to give them additional training. When the Czechoslovaks replied that mid-summer maneuvers were impossible because they would interfere with the harvest, Marshal Yakubovsky reportedly replied that the "allied troops" had no objection to waiting in Czechoslovakia to begin maneuvers in the fall. At this point, the diplomatic sources said, the Prague leaders took another unprecedented action: They formally demanded the exit of the Soviet troops.

The reality in mid-July was that the Soviet forces in Czechoslovakia were positioned and equipped to play key roles if the orders came to take over the country militarily. The "signal troops" among them, some authoritative sources reported, had equipment designed to jam the Czechoslovak radio and television transmissions and to substitute Soviet programs in Czech and Slovak. They had printing equipment to turn out leaflets giving the occupation authorities' instructions to the population. The Soviet troops had extensive dossiers on Czechoslovak political leaders and lists of persons to be arrested at a prearranged signal. Moscow's forces even tested at times their ability to interrupt telecommunications between Prague and the outside world, causing what at the time seemed to be inexplicable interruptions in service to Moscow and other points. These preparations did not go unnoticed by Czechoslovak authorities, and the countermeasures taken helped to explain some unpleasant surprises the Russians suffered when they did strike a month later. As rumors spread about these crude preparations to end Czechoslovak freedom, they increased popular resentment and anger.

Moscow repeated an old error: It grossly underestimated the strength of nationalistic feelings in a once pliant satellite. The crude pressure tactics forced the liberal and centrist leaders of the Czechoslovak Communist Party to straighten their backs and begin acting like the rulers of a truly sovereign, independent state. By the end of the first week of July, Dubcek and his colleagues knew that they would have the support of the nation if they acted in the courageous tradition of Jan Hus. Moreover, they must have been ashamed of the panic that had seized them on June 27 under the Soviet bullying set off by the publication of "2,000 Words." The national reaction to that manifesto had shown that its appeal reflected far more nearly the prevailing mood than did the official denunciations. The flood of resolutions sup-

porting "2,000 Words" became, in effect, a national plebi-
scite in favor of standing up to Moscow.

At this historic moment of defiance in Prague, the pressure
of hawks in Moscow, East Berlin, and Warsaw for a swift
military move against the defiant Czechoslovaks must have
been very strong, but a Politburo majority still preferred to
avoid the most drastic action. Premier Kosygin knew that a
military blow at Prague would forfeit all or most of the
progress he had made toward a *détente* with the United
States. That progress in 1968 had already brought into being
a Soviet-American Consular Agreement, completion of the
long-negotiated nuclear proliferation treaty, and, in a few
days, would result in the scheduled beginning of direct,
regular air travel between New York City and Moscow.
These advances had been made despite the strains arising
from the Vietnam War. Kosygin cannot have been enthusiastic about losing these gains because of too precipitous
action in Czechoslovakia. Mikhail Suslov, too, must have had
his misgivings. He had worked for years to bring a majority
of the world's Communist parties to a meeting now finally
set for November 25 in Moscow. An invasion of Czechoslovakia could undo all his patient effort. The result of these
competing pressures was a compromise: The quarrel would
be escalated but not to the point of a direct military take
over. The door would be left open for a Dubcek retreat or
for a coup in Prague. The Soviet Union and its four allies
would meet in Warsaw on July 14. Simultaneously, the Soviet
and allied press would step up the war of nerves.

Pravda's contribution on July 11 was a major article headlined "Attack Against the Socialist Foundations of Czechoslovakia." Here, for the first time, an explicit analogy was
publicly drawn between the events in Czechoslovakia and
the situation in Hungary in 1956. Those who backed the
"2,000 Words" manifesto, *Pravda* told its readers, were

counterrevolutionaries linked to foreign imperialism. It added that these 1968 villains were even more devious and subtle than their Hungarian predecessors. The day before, in the shot that opened the campaign, Moscow's *Literaturnaya Gazeta* had attacked by name Czechoslovak Presidium member Frantisek Kriegel for expressing some sympathy for the manifesto. In the same vein, *Pravda* warned that there were "individual leaders" in Czechoslovakia who were "trying to minimize the danger of this counterrevolutionary statement." In the context of the article's urgent warnings, this could only be read as notice that there was treachery in the highest circles of the Czechoslovak leadership. *Pravda* quoted the Hungarian Party organ as seeing many similarities between Czechoslovakia in 1968 and Hungary in 1956 and as arguing that it was necessary to use any means to fight the enemies of Socialism effectively "in the given situation."

If Moscow had thought to frighten Prague, it had miscalculated. Four days after the *Pravda* blast, the Dubcek leadership counterattacked. Its spokesman was Lieutenant General Vaclav Prchlik, head of the State Administrative Department of the Central Committee and the man who had warned Dubcek in December of the plans for a military coup. On July 15, he held a press conference and publicly demanded a reorganization of the Warsaw Pact. The Pact's members should be treated as equals, he said, and they should be protected against groupings of some members of the Pact, an obvious reference to the Soviet Union and its four partners who were meeting that very day without either Czechoslovakia or Rumania in attendance. Prchlik noted that nothing in the Warsaw Pact Treaty gives any state the right to station troops on the territory of any other state without the latter's consent; on the contrary, he pointed out, the treaty specifically calls for respecting state sovereignty and the principle of noninterference in internal affairs. The Joint Command of the Warsaw Pact, Prchlik revealed, consists only of Soviet "marshals, generals, and officers," while other states merely have liaison officers without any right of decision. This should be changed he urged. Prchlik's subordinate, Colonel Oskar Bizik, went even further. He emphasized that it was not up to the Soviet Union alone to decide when Soviet troops left Czechoslovakia, and he criticized the fact that Moscow had not respected the position of Dubcek and Premier Cernik on the issue.

In this tense situation, an amazing transformation occurred in Czechoslovakia. A country long divided along national and political lines, a country whose inhabitants had long distrusted each other and their leaders, a country well schooled at Munich and afterward in the servile necessities of bowing to superior power suddenly went on a binge of nationalism. No matter that there were Soviet troops inside the country and many more on the borders. Czechs and Slovaks were tired of being slaves and lackeys. They wanted to stand tall and be treated as equals, even by the powerful Soviet Union. An almost audible roar of applause and support came from the nation to Dubcek. A flood of resolutions and letters of support descended upon the Party leaders. Vera Stovickova expressed the national consensus well on Radio Prague when she declared Czechoslovakia could not appear before the tribunal of its "allies" because "we are being criticized for what we did not say, blamed for what we did not think, and condemned for what we ourselves are condemning." While the hubbub abroad about the "threat to socialism" mounted, the reality in Czechoslovakia was a proud, calm, and orderly country going about its business as though there were no enemy or danger for a thousand miles in any direction.

The five-power Warsaw meeting had ended on July 15 with a communiqué saying that a joint letter had been sent to the Central Committee of the Czechoslovak Communist Party. On July 18, the letter, a virtual ultimatum, was published. Not since Stalin's quarrel with Yugoslavia in 1948 had the Communist world seen such a document. Appropriately enough, the Yugoslav press printed the letter under the title "Cominform 1968."

Essentially, the letter was an expansion of the *Pravda* article of July 11. The tone was that of a sorrowful parent clucking over the errors of his not very bright 8-year-old whom he loves but regretfully has to chastise. "Don't you, comrades, see these dangers?" the letter asks at one point after a long recital of the supposedly rampant subversion, allied with imperialism, growing in Czechoslovakia. The letter does not neglect to avow its signers' "sincere friendship" and to assert stoutly that "We neither had nor have an intention to interfere in such affairs which are strictly the internal affairs of your Party and your state, to violate the principles of respect, independence, and equality in the relations among the Communist Parties and Socialist countries."

The core of the letter was the doctrine that Czechoslovakia's internal affairs were really not only her own business. "The frontiers of the socialist world have moved to the center of Europe, to the Elbe and Sumava Mountains," that is, to Czechoslovakia's western borders, the letter explained primly.

And we shall never agree to have these historical gains of socialism, independence and security of our peoples endangered. We shall never agree to have imperialism, using ways peaceful and nonpeaceful, gouge a gap from the inside or from the outside in the socialist system and alter the correlation of forces in Europe in imperialism's favor. . . . Each of our parties is responsible not only to its working class and its people, but also to the international working class and the world Communist movement, and we cannot evade the obligations following from this. . . . That is why we believe that the decisive rebuff to the anti-Communist forces and the decisive efforts for the preservation of the socialist system in Czechoslovakia are not only your but also our task.

Here was the assertion that Czechoslovakia's people were
not the sole masters of their own fate and that Czechoslovakia's sovereignty was not sufficient to prevent the intervention of other nations in its affairs. Then came the demands,
the orders that had to be followed by Czechoslovakia to
please its Communist neighbors: "A decisive and bold offensive against the right wing and anti-Socialist forces," "a halt
of the activity of all political organizations coming out against
Socialism," "the mastery by the Party of the means of mass
information—press, radio, and television," "the closing of
the ranks of the Party itself," and "the struggle against those
who help the hostile forces." Translated into simpler language, these were demands for an end to free speech and to
the free press, a halt to all political activity by forces not
under the direct control of the Communist Party, and a
purge of the Czechoslovak Communist Party to remove all
those Moscow did not trust.

At the end of this amazing document came the hint to
Moscow's allies within the Czechoslovak Communist Party—
the letter calls them the "healthy forces"—to go into action:
"The task today is to provide these healthy forces with a
clearcut perspective, to stir them to action, to mobilize their
energy for the struggle against the forces of counterrevolution." There followed the ominous assurance: "In this struggle you can count on the solidarity and all-round assistance
of the fraternal socialist countries." To make sure no one
missed the point, *Pravda* in Moscow on July 19, in a front
page editorial printed in large type, declared: "The Communists, all the workers of Czechoslovakia can be confident
that the Communist Party of the Soviet Union, the Soviet
Government, our people are ready to show them all necessary
aid in defense of the socialist conquests." In the context,
such words could only be an invitation to Dubcek's foes to
seize power in the confidence that the Soviet army would
come to their aid if need be. In Moscow's planning, Dubcek

was to be Czechoslovakia's Imre Nagy; it remained only to find the Czechoslovak Janos Kadar.

It is unwise for small nations to allow themselves the liberties their more powerful neighbors take as a matter of course. Hence, the Prague reply was once again soft and respectful in tone, full of assertions of friendship and loyalty to the cause of socialism and to the Soviet Union. It implicitly conceded Czechoslovakia's neighbors' rights to at least verbal intervention in Czechoslovakia's affairs, patiently reviewed the domestic evolution of the preceding months and the plans for the period ahead, and doggedly insisted that the Czechoslovak Communist Party was and would remain in control of Czechoslovakia. Beyond this, Dubcek would not retreat. The coldest words of the Prague reply came in this sentence: "We think that the common cause of socialism is not advanced by the holding of conferences at which the policy and activity of one of the fraternal parties is judged without the presence of their representatives."

The Czechoslovak reply reminded the Soviet leaders that on October 30, 1956, at the height of the Hungarian Revolution, the Soviet Government had declared publicly that socialist countries "can build their mutual relations only on the basis of complete equality, respect of national integrity, national independence, and sovereignty and mutual non-interference in their internal affairs." But the Czechoslovak reply omitted to mention that, five days after the issuance of that 1956 statement, Soviet troops invaded Hungary and overthrew that nation's legal government.

By July 18, with the publication of the Warsaw letter, Moscow and its allies had almost completed the creation of the political and psychological atmosphere needed for some kind of intervention in Czechoslovakia. Their preference was for a rerun of the 1956 Hungarian scenario with troops entering in response to an appeal by "honest Communists" in Prague. Only one more item of stage-setting was needed, some piece of seemingly tangible evidence that the "imperialist forces" were about to strike. *Pravda,* on July 19, remedied the omission in two articles. One unveiled what were claimed to be secret Pentagon and CIA documents plotting the overthrow of the Czechoslovak regime. The second reported that a secret cache of American arms had been found in Czechoslovakia near the West German border, weapons to be used by "Sudeten revanchists and advocates of the restoration of the old order in Czechoslovakia." It was an obvious plant. The Soviet secret service had more than enough American arms as well as collaborators in Czechoslovakia to arrange this transparent provocation. When the Czechoslovak Interior Ministry confirmed the *Pravda* report, it wondered out loud how the Russians had learned about the find before any public announcement, implying its belief that the cache had more to do with the Soviet Union than with the United States. But the stage had been set in those tension-filled days of mid-July, and the order could have been given at any moment for the invasion and occupation of Czechoslovakia.

Why did the Soviet leaders hesitate and finally decide not to move in July? One reason must certainly have been divisions in their own ranks—the fear of the consequences of invasion. Kadar, for all his brave words on July 3, was reluctant to see a military resolution of the problem and kept urging a continuation of the search for a political solution.

A second reason was the widespread support Dubcek enjoyed among foreign Communists. By mid-July, the Kremlin could have no doubt that Czechoslovakia had the sympathy not only of Rumania and Yugoslavia but of almost all the Western European Communist parties, of the Japanese Communists, and of the normally pro-Soviet Communist Party of India. The Communist leaders of Italy and France, Luigi Longo and Waldeck Rochet, even flew to Moscow in this period to warn the Russians of the damage any military move against Prague would do to Communist strength in Western Europe. The French Communists, seeking to avert an armed showdown, issued a call for an all-European meeting of Communist parties to discuss the Czechoslovak crisis. The idea of a meeting was finally abandoned when it became plain that both Prague and Moscow disliked the idea. By July 20, however, the Kremlin had been put on notice that an invasion of Czechoslovakia would fracture world Communist unity more drastically than ever before in history. The invasion of Hungary in 1956 had enjoyed almost unanimous support from the Communists of the world; an invasion of Czechoslovakia in 1968, it was plain, would be denounced by important and influential Communist parties in many lands.

The most important reason for the Kremlin hesitation was the political unity of the Czechoslovak people, the evident nearly unanimous support Dubcek enjoyed at home. The "honest Communists" whom Moscow hoped would challenge Dubcek decided that discretion was the wisest course as they observed the storm of nationalistic emotion raging about them. Dubcek demonstrated that he knew how to put pressure on the conservatives. Moscow's letter had been addressed to the Central Committee in the hope that that body might override the liberal-dominated Presidium. But when the Central Committee met, its members found in attendance several dozen liberals elected by regional conferences as delegates to the scheduled September Party Congress. In addition, just outside the meeting place, Dubcek representatives sat all day at a table piled high with petitions of support coming in from meetings occurring all over the country. This was an old Khrushchev tactic, often used by that once powerful leader to pack and dominate a potentially rebellious Central Committee. The tactic worked in Prague. Knowing that if they spoke up in support of Moscow, they would be denounced to the nation as traitors, the pro-Soviet members of the Central Committee remained silent. Dubcek announced to the world that his policy had been supported unanimously. For the moment, Moscow's attempt to divide and conquer had failed.

The Kremlin struck back immediately. It announced that it wanted to meet with the Czechoslovak leaders on an unprecedented basis—the entire Politburo of the Soviet Communist Party sitting down with the entire Presidium of the Czechoslovak Communist Party. It proposed the Soviet cities of Moscow, Kiev, or Lvov as the meeting place. The Soviet strategy was plain enough. United by traditional Party discipline, the Politburo members would speak as one man while exerting pressure on the less disciplined and badly divided Czechs and Slovaks to break up over internal squabbles that Moscow could then exploit. But the immediate reaction in Czechoslovakia emphasized another point—undisguised worry that, if Prague's leaders went to the Soviet Union, the liberals among them would be seized and held prisoner. Dubcek made plain to Moscow that the meeting would have to be held in Czechoslovakia. On Monday night, July 22, tension was eased slightly by the announcement that the Soviet Politburo and the Czechoslovak Presidium had agreed to meet soon in Czechoslovakia. It promised to be an even more unprecedented meeting than originally planned. Never before had the entire Soviet Politburo contemplated being outside the Soviet Union at one time.

As the world waited for the fateful meeting, Moscow stepped up the war of nerves. Scheduled visits of large groups of Soviet tourists to Czechoslovakia had been canceled, it was announced. Then came word that, at the height of the Soviet harvest, Soviet reservists had been called up and transport vehicles requisitioned for maneuvers of troops all along the western Soviet Union, including the area adjoining Czechoslovakia. Meanwhile, day after day, the Soviet press and the press of Eastern Europe thundered against the Czechoslovak heresies. Academician Konstantinov returned to *Pravda*'s

pages to assail Cestmir Cisar again; Yuri Zhukov, the top
Pravda foreign affairs commentator, pronounced anathema
on the "false slogan" of socialist democracy. An author signing himself S. Selyuk sought to make *Pravda*'s readers shake
in their boots by revealing that the heretics in Prague were
even suggesting that minorities in the Communist Party be
allowed to express their opinions publicly. Every day, this
propaganda barrage hammered away at the idea that Czechoslovak talk of democracy was only a screen for imperialist
subversion, for West German conquest, and for increasing
danger to the Soviet Union. At the grass roots of Soviet
society, thousands of meetings were taking place daily, in
factories, schools, and military units, to alert the Soviet
people to the "menace" in Czechoslovakia and to evoke
resolutions of support for the Warsaw letter and the harsh
line it represented.

I was in Czechoslovakia in the last week of July, when this
campaign of intimidation—designed to create an atmosphere
of despair among the Prague leaders when they met with the
Soviet Politburo—was at its height. The stolidity of the
Czechoslovak people was never more useful. Prague itself
was the most normal of cities. There was no significant food
hoarding or any other symptom of panic. The local hippies
were selling tabloid newspapers extolling the virtues of local
pop music singers and bands. The hotels were crowded with
tourists, and on the streets one could meet and debate with
East Germans and citizens of other neighboring Communist
states. On television, innocent Soviet tourists caught vacationing in Czechoslovakia during the crisis and obviously
uninformed about what had been happening were interviewed nightly. Had they seen any signs of a counterrevolution? Had they been treated with anything but the greatest
courtesy and friendship? To these and similar questions the
unknowing Russians replied with vigorous negatives, going
on to extol the virtues of Czechoslovak-Soviet friendship

they had experienced. Television was also used to inform the Czechoslovak people obliquely that the Russians were demanding the right to station troops in the country in order to "defend" it against "West German imperialism." Television viewers saw the defenses in the West and heard the commanders of the border troops declare proudly that they were ready for any eventuality. A viewer did not have to be very sophisticated to understand that the message being directed to Moscow was that Prague did not want Soviet troops stationed in Czechoslovakia even under the pretext of defense against West Germany.

By July 26, tension was at a new high in Prague as the nation waited for the promised meeting of the Czechoslovak and Soviet ruling bodies. The previous day had brought the news that Vaclav Prchlik had been removed from his influential post in the Central Committee apparatus. Officially, all that had happened was the scheduled abolition of the department he headed, but there were few who did not see this removal as a concession to Moscow, a blow at the man who had called publicly for changes in the Warsaw Pact. That same day, the reports from Moscow told of Yuri Zhukov's virulent *Pravda* article, with its claim that events in Czechoslovakia had gone from "first, 'criticism' of the socialist structure, then arguments for 'democratic socialism' to finally the factual call for a revolution with the goal of revenge for the 1948 revolution and restoration of the bourgeois society." Were Dubcek and his colleagues buckling under the remorseless Soviet pressure? Something had to be done to demonstrate the national will for resistance.

The intellectuals around *Literarni Listy* stepped into the breach. On Friday, July 26, a special four-page issue of the paper came out. It was devoted to one article: a flaming assertion of Czechoslovak nationalism by playwright Pavel Kohout. Within a matter of hours, anyone walking the streets of Prague or watching the local television broadcasts could see that this fervently nationalistic document had articulated the nation's thoughts. A huge signature campaign endorsing the article dominated the country's life that weekend. But could a wall of signatures stop Soviet tanks?

"This nation's history in past centuries is a history of slavery," Kohout's appeal to the Presidium declared.

> Except for two short intervals, we were condemned to creating our national existence illegally. Indeed several times we were on the brink of extinction. . . . The moment has arrived when after centuries our country has again become the cradle of hopes, and not only of our hopes. The moment has come when we can prove to the world that socialism is the only true alternative for all civilized mankind.
>
> We expected that all members of the socialist camp particularly would welcome this fact with sympathy. Instead we are being accused of treason. We are handed ultimatums by comrades who continue steadily showing their ignorance of our evolution and our situation. We are accused of crimes we did not commit. We are suspected of intentions we do not have and never had.
>
> The threat of an unjust punishment hangs over us. And whatever shape it may assume, it may rebound like a boomerang also on our judges, destroy our effort and—above all—leave a tragic blot on the idea of socialism anywhere in the world for years to come.

Then Kohout turned his words directly to the Presidium:

> Comrades, it is your historic task to avert this danger. It is your mission to convince the leaders of the Soviet Communist Party that the process of revival in this country must proceed to its end in a way that is in keeping with the interests of all our countries and in the interest of progressive forces on every continent.
>
> All we are working for can be summarized in these four words: SOCIALISM! ALLIANCE! SOVEREIGNTY! FREEDOM! . . .

It would be tragic if the personal feelings of any individual among you were to prevail over the responsibilities that at this time you carry for the 14,361,000 people to whom you yourselves belong.

Act, explain, but in unity and without concessions defend the road on which we have embarked and from which we will never depart alive. In the next few days we shall follow your talks with suspense, from hour to hour. We are impatiently awaiting your reports. Think of us! Write on our behalf a fateful page of the history of Czechoslovakia. Write it with deliberation, but above all with courage!

To fail this unique opportunity would be our misfortune and our shame! We trust you!

A nation had found its voice. But, simultaneously, the cynics in Prague were saying, "We will fight to the last drop of ink."

11

The Deception of August

Every Czechoslovak schoolboy knows the story of how, in 1415, the great Bohemian religious reformer, Jan Hus, met his untimely end. Trusting in the safe conduct promised him by King Sigismund, Hus left the safety of his native land and traveled to the Council of Constance. Once there, he was arrested, tortured, and finally burned at the stake as a heretic. That historic memory caused the national dismay and outcry against the prospect of the entire Czechoslovak leadership's going to Moscow, Kiev, or Lvov to meet with the Soviet Politburo. The same memory inspired similar dread on July 28, when it finally became known that the meeting would begin the next day at the tiny town of Cierna nad Tisou in eastern Slovakia, virtually at the Soviet border in an area where Czechoslovakia, the Soviet Union, and Hungary adjoin each other. One Czech told me bitterly that Sunday night, "The place will be swarming with Soviet troops and tanks. It will be the simplest thing in the world to kidnap Dubcek and his comrades. We've been tricked again. It's the Jan Hus story all over again."

Not only memories of Jan Hus's fate created apprehension throughout Czechoslovakia as the conferees gathered at Cierna. Over 1 million Czechs and Slovaks had signed petitions backing Pavel Kohout's flaming appeal to the Presidium, but could the representatives of a tiny nation stand up to the bullying that the Kremlin oligarchs were sure to attempt? Fears were raised still higher the day before the meeting began, when Prague radio and other news channels suddenly broadcast a *Ceteka* statement saying that authorized sources, whose identity was not given, had repudiated Prchlik's July 15 press conference statements. It was not true, the *Ceteka* release went on, that no Czechoslovak authority knew the number of Warsaw Pact troops on the nation's soil, as Prchlik had charged, nor was he correct in claiming that only Soviet officers command the Warsaw Pact troops. Was this major concession only the beginning of surrender? On the Monday morning that the talks began, dispatches from Moscow told of a major article in *Pravda* that reviewed in great detail Czechoslovakia's heavy economic dependence on the Soviet Union. Here was a blatant threat of economic strangulation if Prague did not bow. Would not worse threats be used in the privacy of the conference? The nation worried and waited. This period of tense anxiety lasted much longer than had originally been expected, for the conferees met at Cierna for four days, not for one day as the public had assumed. Until the end of the meetings, there was no official word of what was going on, only rumors, many of them spiced and spurred with panic.

What did happen at the Cierna meetings where almost all the members of the Soviet Politburo and all the Czechoslovak Presidium members met in unprecedented session? We have a great deal of information about the atmosphere there. We know, for example, that on each of those four mornings a red, yellow, and green Soviet diesel engine pulled fifteen green sleeping cars containing the Kremlin party the short distance across the border from the town of Chop in the Soviet Ukraine and pulled the cars back again each night. We know that the talks took place in a railwaymen's club, which had been hastily and completely refurnished just before the conference began. We know that there were several crises during the talks, particularly on Wednesday, the third day, when one crisis was resolved in a long private meeting between Brezhnev and Dubcek. But by nightfall on that day the crisis had resumed. A scheduled ceremonial banquet was peremptorily and suddenly canceled, and newsmen called together for a press briefing by the top Soviet and Czechoslovak negotiators were told there would be no news conference that night. We know that on Tuesday, July 30, with customary Soviet tact, *Pravda* in Moscow printed a letter signed by ninety-nine Prague workers, members of a factory people's militia unit, who denounced their countrymen's demands for withdrawal of Soviet troops from Czechoslovakia. However, the complete story of what actually went on in the four days of intensive talks, days of severe moral and political struggle, is still locked in the memories of the participants and the secret archives of both countries.

There is a sort of official Soviet version of the story of Cierna, but how trustworthy it is is not clear. This version was published in *Pravda* on August 22, immediately after the invasion, when the Kremlin had no reason to suppose that Dubcek or any of his independent colleagues would ever have a chance to tell their side of the story. According to this belated *Pravda* account, the Czechoslovak Presidium did split at the Cierna meeting, and "at the same time that a minority of Presidium members headed by A. Dubcek spoke from openly right opportunistic positions, the majority took a principled line and asserted the necessity of a decisive struggle against the reactionary anti-socialist forces, against the scheming of reaction." At another point in the same article, *Pravda* asserted that the representatives of Prague gave assurances "that they will take urgent concrete measures for stabilizing the situation in the country, for strengthening and defending the socialist conquests." Later, the East German press and informants in Prague asserted that Dubcek and his comrades had agreed at Cierna to a secret list of conditions: to restoring press censorship, to halting genuinely independent political activity that might threaten the Communist Party power monopoly, and the like. Premier Cernik denied later that any secret commitments had been accepted, but again his credibility cannot be taken for granted. It should be noted, however, that in October, 1968, a high-ranking American intelligence official stated that his information indicated that the Czechoslovak Presidium had presented a common front to the Russians at Cierna, despite severe internal differences.

Of none of this was there a hint in the Czechoslovak leaders' statements when the Cierna meeting broke up. Rather, the participants tried, in formal speeches to the public and in informal words to newsmen privately, to convey the impression that a great victory had been scored, that the Russians and their allies had been bested. "We shall not depart from the path on which we have set out. We shall continue to go forward on it consistently," President Svoboda said in the first post-Cierna speech to the nation. The next day, August 2, Dubcek took to the airwaves to address his people:

> I state frankly that you can be completely satisfied with the results and the spirit of the negotiations. We kept the promises which we had given you, and we returned with the same conviction with which we departed for the talks: to continue consistently on the road which the Czechoslovak Communist Party and all our people took last January. There can be no other alternative for our nation and the working people of our Czecho-

slovak socialist fatherland. Speaking of these results, which are satisfactory for us, one must frankly point to the good will and the efforts of the Soviet friends to understand our problems and also to respect our specific conditions as well as the inalienable right of any party to settle its affairs independently. The Soviet comrades were able to satisfy themselves during the talks that we are defending the principles of socialism jointly and that it is our wish to contribute to the strengthening of the socialist movement. It is our international duty to continue to demonstrate by our actual conduct that we are never going to deviate from the path of socialism, for socialism has the support of the decisive majority of our people, Communists and non-Communists, and of the entire National Front. . . .

In this connection, I wish to stress that our army is not only a firm component in the defense of our socialist community but also a sufficient guarantee of the defense of our state frontiers, and, by the same token, of the frontiers of socialism.

I was asked on my return to the airport if our sovereignty was threatened. Let me say frankly that it is not. We need friendship and good relations with the U.S.S.R. precisely in the interests of sovereignty and precisely in the interests of the development of our process of democratization. I want to stress the need for the people of our country to maintain their prudent and statesmanlike attitude. There must be no misuse of various spontaneous actions and meetings for expressions of various anti-socialist and anti-Soviet sentiments.

When Dubcek said these words, intended to reassure his people and yet plainly implying limits on free speech, he was well aware that there was much unrest in the country. The communiqué issued at the end of the Cierna meeting had been singularly uninformative. Its only new information had been an announcement that the five nations that had signed the ultimatum-like Warsaw letter and Czechoslovakia would meet in Bratislava the following Saturday. Word had already gotten out the day before Dubcek spoke that both sides at Cierna had agreed to end their open polemics. Czecho-

slovak journalists had already been told they must be careful what they wrote about the neighboring Communist
countries. A disturbed Czechoslovakia asked itself why its
friends Yugoslavia and Rumania would not be present at
Bratislava. Were more unpleasant surprises on the way? On
Thursday, August 1, the night the Cierna meeting ended,
thousands of angry and suspicious Prague residents gathered
in the Old Town Square, creating a situation that forced
Josef Smrkovsky, despite his own weariness, to address them.
When the crowd demanded to hear from Dubcek personally,
obviously not believing Smrkovsky's reassurances, Smrkovsky
pleaded, "I ask you, comrades, be so kind as to leave Dubcek
alone a bit! That comrade sleeps only three hours a day.
What he has got to carry in his head and on his shoulders
. . . nobody can even imagine. I can assure you that Comrade Dubcek would tell you in his Slovak the same things I
have said in my Prague Czech, for we both speak the same
language."

The Bratislava meeting began and ended in one day.
Present were all the disputants, Dubcek and Smrkovsky,
Brezhnev and Kosygin, Ulbricht, Gomulka, Kadar, and
Zhivkov. There was much handshaking, embracing, kissing
on the cheek, and presentation of flowers, as though these
were old friends joined together for comradely reunion un-
marred by differences. Prague passed the word that the meeting had been held merely to soothe Russia's defeated allies,
that the Warsaw letter was now dead and would not be discussed, and that Czechoslovakia's internal affairs would not
be treated. The communiqué that emerged from Bratislava
was a masterpiece of Communist gobbledygook, subject to
many possible interpretations. It was clear enough from the
document that Czechoslovakia had obligated itself not to
make a separate deal with West Germany, not to depart from
the common enmity with Israel, and not to leave the Soviet
bloc's Comecon economic organization. There was mysterious

reference to a high-level economic meeting, a theme first introduced at the Dresden conference the previous March. On internal affairs, there was a bow to the need for taking account of specific national conditions, and it was to this that Prague pointed as confirmation of its claim that it had succeeded in safeguarding Czechoslovak independence. On that same day, August 3, it was announced that the last Soviet troops had finally left Czechoslovakia.

Enormous relief struggled with frank incredulity in the minds of many Czechs and Slovaks in the days following the Cierna and Bratislava talks. So they had been spared after all! There had been no repetition of Munich, and the Soviet troops had left the country. But how could such a miracle have happened? How could a giant nation like the Soviet Union surrender to a tiny state like Czechoslovakia? In the rumors that abounded, an explanation frequently offered was in terms of the intervention of Yugoslavia's Tito, Rumania's Ceausescu, and the leaders of the French and Italian Communist parties. Letters from these men, so the story went, had persuaded Brezhnev to reverse himself at the key moment at Cierna. Many in the older generation were covered with shame when they heard this story. They remembered how ardent and vigorous a role Czechoslovakia had played in the anti-Tito campaign of the late 1940's and early 1950's. Yet Tito had forgiven everything and had come to Czechoslovakia's aid when help was desperately needed.

Skeptics did not share the general elation. They pointed to some of the language in the Bratislava statement that Dubcek had signed and wondered aloud how such language could be considered compatible with the democratization begun in January. Here are the words that bothered these worriers: "Unshakable fidelity to Marxism-Leninism, education of the popular masses in the spirit of the ideas of socialism, proletarian internationalism, irreconcilable struggle against bourgeois ideology, against all anti-socialist forces is the guarantee

of success in strengthening the position of socialism and in
rebuffing the efforts of the imperialists."

As day after day passed without any major change in
course, even the skeptics began to believe in the "Miracle at
Cierna." The new, still cautious, confidence grew sharply on
August 9, when Marshal Tito arrived in person and received
a tumultuous, historic welcome from tens of thousands of
Prague's grateful citizens. His stay was short. The communiqué issued when he departed was worded very generally,
but the fact of firm Yugoslav support for Czechoslovakia's
course and for the principle of nonintervention in Czechoslovakia's affairs was clear. As Tito left, it became known
that far-reaching plans for Czechoslovak-Yugoslav economic
cooperation were under consideration: joint export of
capital goods to third countries, the beginning of efforts
to create a common binational bank; import of tens of
thousands of Yugoslav workers plus Yugoslav construction
materials to aid the labor-short and material-short Czechoslovak building industry; Czechoslovak investment in Yugoslav industrial and tourist projects. Some began to consider
aloud the possibility of reviving the pre–World War II
Little Entente, a military and political alliance of Czechoslovakia, Yugoslavia, and Rumania.

Domestically, too, those first days after Bratislava brought
nothing drastically different from what had become the new
norm. Prague's own recently created version of Hyde Park,
Myslbek Park in the center of the city, functioned vigorously
and freely. Magazines such as *Reporter* and *Literarni Listy*
continued to express heterodox views. Thus, a commentator
writing in the August 8 *Literarni Listy* analyzed the "sources
of error of Soviet policy in Czechoslovakia and vis-à-vis
Czechoslovakia." The author declared that "Soviet policy is
founded primarily not on the analysis of social forces and
currents but on personalities. After citing examples such as
Nkrumah and Sukarno, the article noted, "It was not by

accident that Antonin Novotny more than once dropped a
hint that it was not in Prague that decisions were taken regarding the First Secretary or the President" of Czechoslovakia. The friends of Lieutenant General Prchlik, still
incensed by the anonymous *Ceteka* attack on him on July
28, were active on his behalf. On August 8, *Ceteka* announced that three Communist Party organizations in Prague
had separately nominated the general for the new Central
Committee to be elected at the Fourteenth Party Congress
scheduled for September 9. The next day, *Ceteka* itself issued
a public statement on the Prchlik case. It apologized for
having circulated the anonymous attack on him and said it
would not issue any other similar unsigned articles. Meanwhile, a campaign was under way against the People's Militia,
especially the ninety-nine members of it who had signed the
July 30 anti-Dubcek letter in *Pravda*. Petitions calling for
the abolition of the People's Militia were circulating and receiving many signatures. New Communist Party rules were
issued, rules that provided far more latitude for the expression of dissenting minority views by Communist Party members in Czechoslovakia than was true anywhere else in the
Soviet orbit. Work continued, too, on the formation of
workers' councils in different factories. These councils,
modeled somewhat after a Yugoslav innovation, were part of
Ota Sik's blueprint for reorganizing and revitalizing Czechoslovakia's economy.

Against this background of continuing freedom, not too
many people were disturbed by the arrival on August 12 of
Walter Ulbricht in Karlovy Vary for a one-day visit with
Dubcek. As might be expected by a man who had lead the
pre-Cierna offensive against Czechoslovakia, Ulbricht received a cool and correct welcome. The usual informed
sources reported that Ulbricht was concerned about signs
that Prague was seeking an accommodation with West Germany in order to get the badly needed large loan. They also

reported that two different interpretations of the Bratislava statement appeared in the negotiations. Dubcek's view that Bratislava had legalized Czechoslovakia's road to socialism was countered by Ulbricht's opinion that Bratislava was important mainly for its demand that all parties at the talks meet their international obligations as members of the Soviet bloc. Few seemed to have thought the latter point was important. After all, Ulbricht even submitted to questions at a press conference. He assured his auditors that East Germany had full democracy and no censorship. He dismissed a question about the July Warsaw letter with the comment that it had been agreed "not to talk about the past."

On August 14, two days after Ulbricht's short visit, the storm clouds reappeared in both Moscow and Prague. In the Soviet capital, newspaper polemics which had stopped barely two weeks earlier and were supposedly banned by the Cierna agreement, resumed. *Literaturnaya Gazeta* blasted *Literarni Listy* for "attacking the principles of Marxism-Leninism and for slanderous sallies against the U.S.S.R." The Czech weekly, Moscow's organ complained, "presents the concern of the Soviet people about the threat to peace in Europe as a certain effort to interfere in the internal affairs of a brotherly country."

In Prague that same day, the Presidium issued a statement that was notably conservative in tone and disturbing to those who had been fully reassured by the Svoboda, Dubcek, and Smrkovsky pronouncements in the first days of August. The Presidium's focus was on "violations of law and order" in recent political demonstrations in Prague. It accused unnamed groups of having "molested peaceful citizens under the pretext of joining their discussions." The same statement condemned the appeals being made for the abolition of the People's Militia and came to the defense of the ninety-nine militia members who had signed the July 30 letter in Prague. Particularly disturbing to liberals was the Presid-

ium's argument that the people's militia was not only part
of the country's defense force but also a guarantor of the
"socialist" character of Czechoslovakia. This guarantor was
the most pro-Soviet organized group in the country. Inevitably, men recalled the Presidium's condemnation of the
"2,000 Words" manifesto at the end of June. Were Dubcek
and his colleagues retreating again under Soviet pressure?
Or were there secret agreements at Cierna and Bratislava
about which the people of Czechoslovakia had been told
nothing? Anxiety was rekindled in many hearts and minds.
Yet there was no sign of panic.

At this point, only six days of freedom and full sovereignty
remained for Czechoslovakia, but no ordinary Czech or
Slovak knew that. There were, of course, abundant official
reports of the maneuvers of Warsaw Pact troops near Czechoslovakia's borders to the west, north, and east. But by now
the country had gotten used to such maneuvers. Even people
inclined to worry had been reassured by the departure from
Czechoslovakia of all the Warsaw Pact troops that had come
for the June "maneuvers." It seemed unreasonable to many
that there could be any imminent danger of Moscow's striking militarily. After all, the Russians had not struck when
they had their own armed forces within the country. Moreover, it was August, vacation time, and the minds of many
Czechs and Slovaks were on such questions as where they
should go for a swim or how long a hike they should take.
Even for those inclined to worry, there was reassurance in
what seemed to be a major change in East German policy.
On August 9, Ulbricht had publicly shifted his position toward Bonn, making his most conciliatory speech in years
with regard to West Germany. How ridiculous it seemed to
worry about an invasion of Czechoslovakia at a time when
even "frozen Walter" was thawing and beginning to woo
the West Germans. Some watchers in foreign intelligence
agencies were lulled during this period. They knew, for ex-

ample, that most of the members of the Soviet Politburo were out of Moscow and on vacation. Surely no crisis could be brewing under such conditions. Even at the highest levels of the United States Government, concern about Czechoslovakia was diminished. Negotiations in mid-August were going well for a Johnson-Kosygin summit meeting to discuss limitations of missiles. In the atmosphere then existing, President Johnson may even have thought of winding up his Presidency with a triumphal visit to Moscow, a signal that he had finally ended the cold war. No doubt such dreams included speculation that the Russians might help end the Vietnam conflict. Who could seriously expect an invasion of Czechoslovakia in these conditions?

The evidence is strong, in short, that one of the most successful and most complex political, military, and diplomatic deceptions in history was effectively carried out in these days. In retrospect, it seems most likely that in Soviet minds Czechoslovakia's fate was already sealed at the time of Cierna and Bratislava. The decision not to strike then was probably adopted for two reasons: First, the people of Czechoslovakia were at a fever pitch of nationalism, and any attempt to invade their country would have run a serious risk of meeting determined resistance that could have led to a wider conflict, which Moscow wanted to avoid. Second, world attention was focused on Czechoslovakia at the time of Cierna and Bratislava, and an invasion in the midst of parleys would have seemed the worst kind of treachery. On both scores, therefore, it was preferable to strike somewhat later, assuring surprise and confusion in Czechoslovakia and outside it and minimizing both possible armed Czechoslovak resistance and undesirably vigorous foreign reaction.

Dubcek and his colleagues can hardly have been entirely lulled. Reading between the lines of the August 14 Presidium statement reveals that they were afraid that excesses in Czechoslovakia might yet bring the Russians and their allies back. When the invasion did come, it became plain that certain nonmilitary preparations had been made, but one searches in vain for any sign of military preparation, for any serious consideration of armed resistance. The men in Prague seem to have been convinced they could fight only with moral and political weapons, that armed defense of Czechoslovakia would ultimately be futile while exacting a heavy cost in lives and property. In making that decision, they were ignoring some lessons from history. The Finns had successfully defended their national existence in the "winter war" of 1940–41, though Finland was far weaker and had a much smaller population than Czechoslovakia had in 1968. Stalin did not dare invade Yugoslavia at any time during his 1948–53 war against Tito, in large part because he knew the Yugoslavs would fight. When the Czechoslovak leaders made their decision to not even attempt armed resistance, their fellow Communists in distant Vietnam were demonstrating that a much larger and better equipped enemy could be fought to a standstill and a stalemate.

The great unanswered question about Czechoslovakia's fate in 1968 is whether the invasion would have taken place had Moscow been put on notice that the people of Czechoslovakia would fight. The suggestion has been made, for example, that Dubcek could have taken a different tack on the Soviet claim that Czechoslovakia needed better defenses against West Germany. Instead of asserting that his forces were adequate, Dubcek might have concurred with the Soviet fear and used that supposed need as the pretext for calling up several hundred thousand reservists, if only for extended maneuvers. But had Dubcek tried to do this, he undoubtedly would have met opposition from the pro-Soviet members of his own Presidium, and there is no reason to suppose that he could trust all his own generals. On August 15, in fact, the Czechoslovak Defense Ministry's Military Council associated itself publicly with the earlier anonymous *Ceteka-*

distributed attack on Prchlik, who was accused of having released secret information about the Warsaw Pact. The generals went on to deny Prchlik's assertion that Soviet troops and allied troops had come to Czechoslovakia in May or June without Prague's knowledge. "Leading officials of the state and of the Czechoslovak army command had full knowledge of the number of allied troops and ordnance on Czechoslovak territory during the entire exercise," the statement declared. Apparently, none of those issuing the statement felt it necessary to explain why, if this were true, the Czechoslovak people had been systematically misinformed during the period from May to July. In Moscow, in all probability, the Military Council's attack on Prchlik was read as further assurance that the invaders would not have to fight when they crossed the borders of Czechoslovakia.

Little time remained, but the play went on in Prague. On August 15, Rumania's Nicolae Ceausescu arrived to sign a friendship treaty. He got a warm welcome. It was not up to the standards of the enthusiastic greeting given Tito, but it was far, far better than Ulbricht's chilly reception. The next day, August 16, *Pravda* rejoined the polemics as Yuri Zhukov announced that the Bratislava statement was no mere "mirage" fit only for the archives but a meaningful document that the outspoken Prague press was violating. Nevertheless, he maintained security, insisting that "it is the affair of the Czechoslovak comrades themselves" to bring "elementary order" into what that country's press printed. On August 17, leading journalists met with members of the Czechoslovak Presidium and apparently were told they must not resume full-fledged polemics with Moscow. Apparently, the theory was that the Soviet articles were an effort to exert pressure in favor of Prague's conservatives, a sort of psychological offensive in preparation for the Czechoslovak Party Congress scheduled to open September 9. Prague's newspapers and other media did moderate their tone substantially, but on that same day, August 17, *Pravda* reprinted an article from the Hungarian Communist Party organ hinting that what was happening in Czechoslovakia was similar to what had happened in Hungary in 1956. On August 18, *Pravda* had two articles about Czechoslovakia, one informing its readers that "imperialist reaction" had "strengthened its hostile campaign against the Communist Party of Czechoslovakia" and the other reporting that Moscow's friends in Prague were living "in a state of moral terror." On August 19, Radio Prague announced that the Czechoslovak Army would hold maneuvers in the western part of the country—that is, the area furthest from the Soviet border—on August 21 and 22. That same morning, President Ludvik Svoboda had an hour-long meeting with six Czech and Slovak Roman Catholic bishops, the first such gathering since the Communist take over of February, 1948. Prague newspapers on that day, following the new policy of restraint, contained no anti-Soviet polemics. Instead, they made their points obliquely by printing long excerpts from Soviet newspaper articles attacking the post-Cierna political developments in Czechoslovakia. *Pravda* did not reciprocate the restraint but continued its campaign against Prague. Juxtaposed on the same page so that their connection could not be missed, *Pravda* printed two articles. One painted a dismaying picture of the wickedness and efficiency of the CIA in overthrowing governments through subversion; the locale of the article was nominally Africa, but the point was plain enough. The other article, date-lined Prague, reported that "the enemies of the working class in Czechoslovakia continue openly and insolently to attack its socialist conquests. Unfortunately, these attacks do not meet the necessary rebuff."

Preparations for the invasion moved into high gear on August 19 and 20. Some sources have reported that on August 19 President Johnson received a note from Premier Kosygin agreeing to a two-power summit meeting; this agreement was apparently part of the grand deception. That night, Dubcek received a very different note from Brezhnev, accusing him of breaking the promises Czechoslovakia had given at Cierna. But even then there was no threat of invasion. *Pravda*, the next morning, practically signaled what was about to come. Its front page editorial declared that the Communist parties considered it their duty "to insure that imperialist intrigues are nipped in the bud." The editorial concluded with assurance that the Communist Party was leading the laboring masses to "new victories of peace, democracy, national independence, and socialism." In Prague itself that morning, the conservative editor of *Rude Pravo* had done his part to help provide a justification for the coming Soviet invasion. In a front page signed editorial, Oldrich Svestka supported many of the themes advanced earlier in *Pravda*. The progressives were "making life miserable for honest officials and Party members," he charged, adding that "demagogic slogans" being advanced could be turned against the Party itself. Another article in the same issue charged that a "secret committee" had been established to direct the fight against the People's Militia.

Other Czechoslovak collaborators were active in the hours before the Soviet and satellite troops crossed the nation's borders, particularly in the Ministry of Interior. There, most of the middle-level leaders of the secret police were still holdovers from the Novotny era, men who feared and hated the changes Dubcek had brought and who looked to the Soviet Union to help restore "the good old days." The key figure among these men was Deputy Interior Minister Viliam Salgovic. At 4 P.M., on the afternoon of August 20, he called a meeting at which he divulged the plans for the invasion to his confederates and assigned tasks to them. One group was to surround Western embassies as well as those of Yugoslavia and Rumania. Their mission was to prevent any of their fellow citizens from taking refuge in these buildings. Moscow was anxious to avoid a repetition of what had happened in Budapest in November, 1956, when Premier Imre Nagy and many of his associates found temporary sanctuary from the Soviet invaders in the Yugoslav embassy. Another group of secret policemen was assigned to the radio stations and was instructed to prevent any official statement opposing the invasion from being broadcast, if one were issued. Behind Salgovic stood a group of Soviet secret police operatives, agents of Moscow's feared K.G.B. (Committee for State Security), who had flown in secretly on August 17. Once the invasion began, the Soviet secret police and their colleagues, the traitors in the Czechoslovak secret police, worked closely together.

That afternoon in Moscow, the Soviet Communist Party Central Committee met for a secret meeting. The great majority of its members—including Brezhnev, Kosygin, and Podgorny—were flown in from their vacation sites. The decision to invade had been made earlier, but those who had made the decision felt the need for prior endorsement by the Central Committee, and they got it promptly. The last formality was out of the way. At 11 P.M. Central European Time, August 20, 1968, Czechoslovakia was invaded from the east, north, and south—from East Germany, Poland, the Soviet Union, and Hungary. The effort to provide the "necessary rebuff" had begun.

III

AFTERMATH

12

The Invasion

Memorandum to the Soviet Soldier Fulfilling His International Duty on Czechoslovak Territory

Soviet soldier!

Perform your sacred international duty with courage and determination against all who resist. Counterrevolutionaries will attempt to provoke armed conflicts. Do not fall victim to these provocations. Employ your weapons only if the enemy uses arms first.

As a fighter for a just cause you must be able to differentiate between foes and friends. . . . Remember that you represent the great Soviet people and its heroic armed forces.

Act in a dignified and honorable way. You have come to aid friends. Respect their national traditions and their culture. Do not violate state property or the private property of citizens of the Czechoslovak Socialist Republic.

Soviet soldier! Always be alert and ready to give battle. . . .

We perform an important historic mission and each one of us must accomplish it to the end. . . .

Political Directorate of the High Command.

Presumably, similar instructions were also issued to the East German, Polish, Hungarian, and Bulgarian soldiers among the hundreds of thousands of troops who invaded Czechoslovakia at 11 P.M. on the night of August 20, 1968.

The Soviet soldiers did not always obey orders. Sometimes they panicked when faced by nonviolent resistance and shot wildly, murdering unarmed citizens. The "Battle of the Prague Radio Center," early Wednesday morning, August 21, 1968, provides a typical example of how Czechoslovakia got its first invasion martyrs.

The streets of Prague were crowded with the city's young people on the first morning of the invasion. Many had rushed to the Radio Center, knowing it was the nerve center of the nation. When tanks appeared in the street leading to the center, hundreds of young people massed to block off their approach, forming a wall of flesh before the mechanized monsters. The tanks stopped. In the time thus gained, more obstacles were added: overturned buses and other motor vehicles. While the confrontation went on, Radio Prague broadcast a running description of the scene. Through the loud-speakers on the street, it pleaded with the youngsters, "Keep calm. Let your weapon be passive resistance. Don't be provoked into bloodshed. That's what they're waiting for. Don't be provoked."

The young people tried to argue with the tank crews, to tell them in Russian that they should go back home. Then the tanks began shooting, first overhead and then at the crowd. As the bullets killed and wounded, Molotov cocktails appeared in the hands of some of the members of the crowd, and they were hurled at the tanks. Soon some Soviet tanks were on fire, and some Soviet soldiers, too, were victims.

There were similar incidents elsewhere—in Prague's Wenceslas Square, in Bratislava, and in other communities. Before the invasion was twelve hours old, Czechoslovak blood had been spilled on Czechoslovak soil, the blood of patriots trying to defend their country, usually without weapons in their hands. That blood unified the nation in hate.

*   *   *

In the fourth week of August, 1968, Prague became the graffiti, pop art, and poster capital of the world.

"Ivan, go home. Natasha has sexual problems." "Socialism, yes; occupation, no." "The Russian National State Circus has arrived, complete with performing gorillas." "What do you say at home to your mother about our dead?" "Great exhibition of Soviet arms and equipment—open 24 hours a day in Wenceslas Square—nothing to pay (except perhaps your life)." "This is not Vietnam." "Home, dogs." In a typical poster on the city's walls, a Czechoslovak Red Riding Hood looked up at a Soviet wolf with a submachine gun under his arm and said, "What great big eyes you've got, Grandma." "Big eyes, hell. I can't even see well enough to find my way home," the Soviet wolf replied.

Prague was completely under Soviet occupation, with Soviet tanks and troops everywhere. Many of the Soviet tanks carried chalked or painted swastikas and the injunction "Ivan, go home." Under the eyes of the Soviet occupiers, each day thousands of anti-Soviet newspapers and leaflets were given out, while pedestrians with transistor radios listened on the streets to anti-Soviet broadcasts. It was normal for a Soviet tank to be surrounded by angry Czechs seeking to persuade the crew, in stilted school-acquired Russian, that the invaders should go home since they had no business in Czechoslovakia. Many of the invaders, lithe peasant youngsters of 18 or 19 in many cases, could find nothing better to say than that they were following orders to help the Czechoslovak comrades stamp out counterrevolution and turn back a West German invasion. Prague's residents finally reacted to this stupidity by setting up prominently in the center of the city a large multiplication table—complete from $1 \times 0 = 0$ to $10 \times 10 = 100$. They addressed the elementary school lesson to General Ivan Pavlovsky, commander of the occupation troops.

All Czechoslovakia at this time was a country whose major city streets had no identification, while the direction signs on its roads were gone or pointed in the wrong direction. Only one direction sign was correct. That sign said: "Moscow —1,500 kilometers."

Czechoslovakia was occupied, but dozens of Western reporters and cameramen roamed the country each day, observing the events and sending out their stories and pictures. Free world embassies in Prague issued visas, and Czechoslovak citizens wishing to leave the country did so, while others returned from abroad to join their families and friends. The invasion had found five thousand American tourists in Czechoslovakia, plus hundreds of delegates attending the International Geological Congress in Prague. They all left safely.

At times during this bizarre period, experienced diplomats and international political observers wondered if they were dreaming. But it was all real enough. What the world saw in Czechoslovakia was the outcome of an enormously successful and precisely executed invasion by hundreds of thousands of troops and thousands of tanks. However, there had been a historic political miscalculation.

Soviet military planning had been excellent. The troops and vehicles that poured across the border at some eighteen or twenty points around Czechoslovakia met no resistance, and there is no record that even a single shot was fired by any border guard. Faultless, too, was the airborne invasion, in which dozens of huge Soviet *Antonov-12* four-engine turboprop transports brought thousands of troops and dozens of light tanks into Czechoslovakia's chief airports. The sporadic resistance that finally did emerge during the first few days—mostly from angry teen-agers—had only political, not military, importance. In a nation of over 14 million, about 70 people were killed and 1,000 wounded in shooting frays resulting from popular resistance to the swift military conquest and ensuing occupation. The Czechoslovak Army, considered by many to be the best fighting force in Eastern Europe, remained in its barracks and never fired a shot.

Moscow thought its political planning had been equally thorough and—a victim of its own propaganda—believed most Czechoslovaks would rally around a pro-Soviet regime as soon as it was formed. Yakov Malik, Soviet delegate at the United Nations, revealed the essence of the Kremlin blueprint on the night of August 21, when he told the U.N. Security Council, "The armed units of the Socialist countries, as is known, entered the territory of the Czechoslovak Socialist Republic on the basis of the request of the Government of this state, which applied to the allied governments for assistance with armed forces." It is indicative of the confusion prevailing in Moscow twenty-four hours after the invasion began that Ambassador Malik had to utter this lie. He knew the plan had miscarried, but he had no later, more appropriate instructions.

Moscow had a three-tiered political blueprint and contingency plan to accompany the detailed military dispositions. Ideally, it hoped that a special Czechoslovak Presidium meeting on the evening of the invasion would depose Dubcek as First Secretary and Cernik as Premier, replacing them with Presidium member Drahomir Kolder and Party Secretary Alois Indra, respectively. There were even plans for the "new government" to put Dubcek, Smrkovsky, and their

comrades on trial for "treason" and to execute them quickly
as convicted traitors. In East Berlin, *Neues Deutschland,*
Ulbricht's Party organ, had already set the type to announce
that Czechoslovakia had new leaders who had proclaimed a
Revolutionary Workers and Peasants Government and had
asked for the entrance of Soviet and allied troops to defeat
the revisionists and imperialist agents.

Moscow's planners realized that it might be impossible
to get a Presidium majority for Dubcek's ouster in time.
Hence, there was a fallback plan, a call for Soviet intervention by pro-Soviet leaders in Prague. The impression that
those leaders were acting as the government of Czechoslovakia would be given by transmitting the intervention appeal
over the news wires of *Ceteka.* Finally, if all else failed, Soviet troops would seize Dubcek, Cernik, Smrkovsky, Cisar,
and the other leading liberals. President Svoboda then would
be persuaded or forced to give his approval to a new Soviet-
approved government. The world and the Czechoslovak
people would be confronted with a *fait accompli,* which
would at least have the veneer of constitutional legality.
There seemed no reason to doubt that Svoboda would go
along with this scheme. At 72, he appeared to be hardly in
physical shape to give much resistance to pressure, and at
the Cierna conference three weeks earlier he had been the
most outspoken of Prague's delegates in insisting on the
necessity of always going hand in hand with the Soviet
Union. But Murphy's Law—"Anything that can go wrong
will go wrong, and at the most inconvenient time"—inter-
vened.

The first blow came when the plotters in the Presidium
were unable to depose Dubcek at the angry meeting the
afternoon, evening, and night of August 20. The formal
policy issues that were to be raised to get rid of Dubcek
were provided in a thirteen-page report on the internal
situation, which Kolder and Indra had drawn up. In effect,

it recommended that the Presidium adopt precisely the measures demanded in the Warsaw letter, the ultimatum Moscow and its allies had sent a month earlier.

At 11:30 P.M., as the bitter debate raged, Premier Cernik went to call Defense Minister Dzur. He was pale when he returned ten minutes later and announced, "The armies of the five countries have crossed the frontiers of the republic and are occupying us." Amid the confusion, Dubcek cried out, "It is a tragedy. I did not expect this to happen. I had no suspicion, not even the slightest hint that such a step could be taken against us." At that moment, Dubcek may well have been thinking of Hungary's Janos Kadar with whom he had conferred secretly a few days earlier but from whom he had gotten no intimation of the coming military blow. Tears were coming down Dubcek's face when he added, "I have devoted my entire life to cooperation with the Soviet Union, and they have done this to me. It is my personal tragedy."

In this emotionally-charged atmosphere, Dubcek and some of his colleagues drafted the Presidium's proclamation on the invasion. The proclamation almost did not reach the Czechoslovak people, for a powerful pro-Soviet conspirator was waiting at a key spot. This was Karel Hoffman, the 44-year-old Director of Communications. His reaction to receipt of the Presidium's proclamation was to attempt to prevent its broadcast and then to try to shut down all of Czechoslovakia's legal radio stations. But Hoffman's treacherous intent was so apparent that his subordinates rebelled. Frantic telephoning in those early morning hours finally apprised Josef Smrkovsky of the situation, and he overruled the traitor.

At 1:50 A.M., on August 21, Radio Prague began broadcasting the news of the invasion in a proclamation that declared: "This happened without the knowledge of the President of the Republic, the Chairman of the National Assembly, the Premier, or the First Secretary of the Czecho-slovak Communist Party Central Committee." This was a clear hint that these officials believed that among their colleagues in other high Government and Party offices there were men who had had advance knowledge of the invasion. The proclamation continued with an appeal "to all citizens of our republic to maintain calm and to offer no resistance to the troops on the march. Our army, security corps, and people's militia have not received the command to defend the country." The proclamation then came to the central point: "The Czechoslovak Communist Party Central Committee Presidium regards this act as contrary not only to the fundamental principles of relations between Socialist states but also as contrary to the principles of international law." The highest political body of Czechoslovakia had defied the Soviet Union, denounced the invasion, and appealed to the nation's population and to the world to resist the occupation by all means short of armed force.

The first fallback plan also failed. The plotter assigned to get the "cry for help" transmitted by *Ceteka* was Miroslav Sulek, the head of *Ceteka*. But when he sought to get the document transmitted, his teletype operators refused to send it.

Thus it was that, six and a half hours after the invasion began, the Kremlin was forced to improvise, to announce the obliteration of the sovereignty of an allied state, a member of the Warsaw Pact. No Soviet leader sought to gain public credit for the move, and the Soviet Foreign Ministry remained publicly mute. Instead, *Tass* informed the world that "Party and Government leaders of the Czechoslovak Socialist Republic have asked the Soviet Union and other allied states to render the fraternal Czechoslovak people urgent assistance, including assistance with armed forces." Neither then nor later were the identities of these "Party and Government leaders of the Czechoslovak Socialist Re-

public" revealed. Those widely suspected of being guilty
of this treachery later denied vigorously that they had called
for the intervention, resulting in the bitter Czechoslovak
joke that hundreds of thousands of Soviet and other foreign
troops had come to their country "to look for the people who
sent for them."

Reflecting the continued early confidence of the Kremlin
that it would soon have its own obedient government in
power in Prague, the *Tass* communiqué asserted that the
invading troops would be removed as soon as "the lawful
authorities find that further presence of these armed units
there is no longer necessary."

Only a few hours after the Czechoslovak Presidium's proclamation had been issued, Soviet troops finally did seize
Dubcek, Premier Cernik, and many of their colleagues.
Armed soldiers invaded Dubcek's room in the Central Committee building, tore a telephone out of his hands, hand-
cuffed him, and marched him off a prisoner. Smrkovsky, a
veteran of Communist prisons, was also arrested at the same
time. He took the precaution of taking three lumps of sugar
from a tea tray with him, murmuring from experience, "I
am going to need this." Twelve hours after the invasion
began, the First Secretary of the Czechoslovak Communist
Party, the Premier of Czechoslovakia, and the Chairman of
the Czechoslovak National Assembly had been flown to
Slovakia and imprisoned near the town of Sliac, a spa, in a
barn guarded by Soviet troops. Dubcek was later to tell
friends that he considered himself virtually dead, being de-
spairingly confident he had been chosen to share the fate
Imre Nagy had suffered a decade earlier.

At this point, two vital factors went wrong. First, President Svoboda, though virtually a prisoner in Hradcany
Castle on the hill overlooking Prague, refused to lend constitutional sanction to the coup. Moscow's demands were
pressed upon Svoboda by a delegation of conservatives con-

sisting of Indra, Presidium member Jan Piller, and Party Secretary Jozef Lenart. But unlike the ailing President Eduard Benes twenty years earlier, the 72-year-old veteran obstinately refused to give his signature. "Get out," he told his callers. When Soviet representatives appeared to press him, he demanded that Dubcek and the legal government be restored in office. Second, it quickly became apparent that Prague had made some important preparations for a possible invasion. It had been anticipated that foreign troops might seize radio and television facilities and newspaper printing plants. Radio and television transmitters had been hidden, along with secret presses. Some lives were lost in the fighting as Soviet troops shut down the regular broadcasting stations, but soon a network of "free" radio stations filled the air with the news the Russians wanted to suppress and also guided the national resistance effort.

It is probably impossible to overestimate the political importance of the electronic web of unity that the secret radio stations cast over Czechoslovakia that week. The broadcasts constantly gave evidence that the nation had not been conquered and had not capitulated, despite the occupation soldiers and tanks. They prevented panic, fought disorganization, and kept national morale high. Since everyone knew that those who were broadcasting might be arrested or killed at any minute, the personnel of the "free, legitimate radio" set individual examples of courage for all to emulate. The broadcasts gave specific instructions about how the invaders should be resisted. They broadcast eyewitness accounts of the chief events. They exposed collaborators and gave warning of Soviet efforts to arrest key groups of citizens. They provided evidence of the country's continuing unity, combating rumors that the Slovaks had defected and informing the public as to which national leaders had remained faithful and which had proved to be traitors. The radio stations' slogan, "We are with you. Be with us," provided a new symbol of the national determination to resist.

The Soviet occupiers mounted a counterpropaganda effort, of course. But the Soviet-operated "Radio Vltava," probably located in Dresden, was no match for the free transmitters. The Soviet performance might have been better if the announcers on "Radio Vltava" had not spoken such bad Czech and such bad Slovak. So great was the initial Soviet propaganda confusion that some leaflets dropped by Soviet planes and helicopters over Prague turned out to be printed in Slovak rather than in Czech, the language of most Prague residents.

These errors were proof that the Soviet authorities had been forced to improvise because matters were not going according to plan. Moscow had assumed that Czechoslovakia would awaken on Wednesday morning, August 21, and learn from the regular radio and television stations that a new Communist Party leadership had taken over and invited the "fraternal" troops to enter. Another miscalculation by Moscow was the assumption that traitorous Prague secret police agents would prevent the broadcasters from turning the population against the invaders. For this reason, the entering troops had not been ordered to seize the radio and television stations as their first priority. By the time the decision was made to seize these installations, radio and television broadcasts had already mobilized the nation to moral and psychological resistance. The Soviet troops sent to seize the radio and television stations in Prague did not even know their location and had to ask Soviet embassy personnel and Czechoslovak traitors where to find the studios. The decision to order the invading troops not to fire except in extreme emergency was consistent with the faulty assumptions about what the political situation would be Wednesday morning. Moscow also wanted to create as few martyrs as possible.

With each passing hour on that fateful Wednesday morning, the political situation became worse for the Soviet invaders and their allies. An outraged population woke to find its country occupied and its independence violated. The resulting rage and anger—expressed first by those hurling rocks and Molotov cocktails at tanks—solidified the nation as never before. Workers, intellectuals, and peasants were as one. Despite Moscow's best efforts, there were victims, and hence martyrs, killed by Soviet guns. Twenty-four hours after the invasion began, the Kremlin knew it had blundered. It had neither a compliant government nor a compliant people in Czechoslovakia.

The international repercussions also rained blows on Moscow. An effort had been made to minimize those repercussions. As soon as was consistent with security, Soviet ambassadors in countries all over the world had delivered messages intended to reassure the governments receiving them. In Washington, for example, at about 8:30 P.M. on August 20—two and one half hours after the invasion began—Soviet Ambassador Anatoly F. Dobrynin met with President Johnson in the White House. He assured the President that the invasion was an "internal" matter of the Communist world and posed no threat or danger to anyone. Later that same evening, the ambassador spent fifteen minutes with Secretary of State Dean Rusk, who had heard news of the invasion while testifying before the Democratic Party's platform committee. During that appearance, the Secretary of State had emphasized the Administration's accomplishments in improving Soviet-American relations and in getting concrete agreements with Moscow. President Johnson confined himself that night to calling an emergency meeting of the National Security Council. Not until the next day did he denounce the invasion. Two months later, U.S. Ambassador to the United Nations J. R. Wiggins inferentially explained this cautious behavior. "It is no secret that an announcement was ready with reference to the anti-ballistic discussions at the very moment" the invasion began, Ambassador Wiggins revealed. Perhaps President Johnson hoped that unhappy night that a miracle might yet make it possible for him to meet with Premier Kosygin, but no miracle occurred. The President may have felt guilty that he could do and say so little to help the brave people of Czechoslovakia. Not so Senator Eugene McCarthy, the "peace candidate" for the Democratic Party's nomination for the Presidency; he said that the President had given Czechoslovakia excessive importance by calling the night session of the National Security Council. But this was going too far, and even many of Senator McCarthy's supporters expressed their shock at his callous remarks.

For days after the invasion, a mounting wave of fear and anger swept the world. At a special session of the U.N. Security Council on the evening of August 21, for example, the Czechoslovak representative, Jan Muzik, officially transmitted his Government's protest. He was able to do this against Soviet protests because thirteen of the fifteen Security Council members—including such recipients of Soviet largesse as Algeria, India, and Pakistan—voted to put the Czechoslovak crisis on the agenda. Only Hungary voted with Moscow's representative in the negative. In Yugoslavia, President Tito called the invasion "a heavy blow inflicted on the socialist and progressive forces in the world." Rumania's Ceausescu told a crowd of ten thousand demonstrators in Bucharest, "the armed intervention in Czechoslovakia is a big mistake and a severe danger for peace in Europe and for socialism in the world." Later, huge demonstrations in the streets of Belgrade and Bucharest protested against the invasion and in favor of Czechoslovak freedom. The Italian pro-Communist newspaper *Paesa Sera* called the invasion "a present to our enemies." The French Communist Party expressed "surprise and severe disapproval" of the invasion. These were merely first reactions. Other and stronger protests were to come from many countries and Communist parties in the days that followed. Of the important Communist parties, only that of North Vietnam expressed full and immediate support of the invasion.

Against this background, there began a fantastic political race. The competition pitted the Soviet occupation authorities against the pro-Dubcek leaders of the Czechoslovak Communist Party who remained free. Moscow's urgent problem was how to achieve some kind of political arrangement that would end its acute embarrassment and yet assure a properly subservient Czechoslovakia. It could always establish a military government, of course, but that would represent a political defeat. A military regime would give the lie to the fictions that had been used to justify the invasion. It would also intensify foreign Communist horror at what had been done. Yet even at the end of the first twenty-four hours after the invasion, Moscow was still reasonably confident. That "old fool Svoboda" was being difficult, but no doubt he could be made to see reason. At any rate, *Pravda,* on August 22, printed a long justification of the invasion—an article that made plain that Dubcek, Presidium member Frantisek Kriegel, Deputy Premier Ota Sik, and Foreign Minister Jiri Hajek would be completely unacceptable in any future Prague ruling group.

The Czechoslovak Communists still free to act saw their problem as two-fold. First, they had to retain the loyalty of the Czechoslovak people by showing they stood at the head of the national resistance to the invasion. Second, as representatives of the Dubcek majority of the Party, they had to protect the legitimacy of their position against the potential challenge of the Kolder-Indra-Bilak-Svestka group. At any time, the pressures on President Svoboda might prove too much for the old man, and he might surrender. How, then, could a legal situation be created in which surrender by

Svoboda would not be disastrous? The way to do this, it was realized, was to hold a special emergency meeting of the Fourteenth Communist Party Congress as soon as possible, rather than waiting almost three weeks until September 9. The delegates had all been elected earlier. The problem was how to bring them together for a legal session in a country honeycombed with Soviet and satellite troops whose commanders wanted very badly to prevent such a Congress.

Both groups moved on August 22. The Russians kept up the pressure on the obdurate President Svoboda but simultaneously tried to mobilize their sympathizers in the upper levels of the Czechoslovak Communist Party. A small group of conservatives did meet under Soviet military protection, but they could not even agree among themselves as to who should be their leader. Finally, a directing trio consisting of Kolder, Indra, and Slovak Party chief Vasil Bilak was elected.

Efforts to install these men as Czechoslovakia's leaders were frustrated on the day of their election, when the underground free Czechoslovak Communist Party assembled about a thousand elected delegates for a secret Party Congress held at the huge C.K.D. factory in Prague. The delegates came in rough, workers' clothes and mingled with the genuine workers coming to work. Those who were well known were disguised—some as ambulance attendants, some as patients being moved by ambulance. As a further security measure to confuse Soviet intelligence, several other simulated congresses took place simultaneously at other large factories.

The People's Militia guarded the actual meeting, which elected a new liberal leadership headed by Dubcek and deputized Professor Venek Silhan, an economist, to substitute for Dubcek while he was unable to fulfill his functions. The Congress issued an ultimatum to the Soviet troops, demanding they withdraw in twenty-four hours or face a general strike. A one-hour general strike that day had already shown the nation's unity. But the Congress, though a great success for the moment, had an important defect: It had little Slovak representation because the Soviet troops had been able to stop most Slovak delegates from getting to Prague. Nevertheless, the organizers of the Congress could view their feat with satisfaction. The large number of delegates that had attended and accomplished their business without Soviet interference provided an impressive sign of the nation's solidarity. It would, after all, have taken only a single informer to bring Soviet troops swooping down on the plant to arrest all the participants. A new Party organization with a good claim to legitimacy had been created, one that might lead the nation's struggle for freedom in the days ahead.

On the following morning, August 23, Moscow recognized the seriousness of the situation that had evolved in Prague. President Svoboda was flown to the Soviet capital to negotiate directly with the Soviet leaders in the Kremlin. He was received with full honors and was driven through streets crowded with tens of thousands of workers released from factories to pay tribute to him. By now, the Kremlin must have been frantic to break the impasse and to throw a veneer of normality and legality over what it had done. Svoboda had even been allowed to address the Czechoslovak nation over the free radio network before he left, assuring his people that he would be back in one day and would serve their interests. It was an incredible spectacle: the 72-year-old head of a fully occupied nation demanding and receiving the right to negotiate on nominally equal terms with the top leaders of the nation whose troops physically controlled his invaded country.

The world political storm roaring around them had moved the Kremlin leaders to this extremity. By August 23, virtually all the Western European Communist parties plus the Japanese Communist Party had made their opposition plain. Similar opposition had been expressed also by several of the international Communist front organizations, notably the

World Federation of Trade Unions. Never in history had
Moscow and its allies been so nearly isolated in the world
Communist movement. That very day, Fidel Castro approved the invasion, but in such a way as to undercut completely the Soviet case. The invasion was indeed necessary
to prevent imperialism from taking over in Prague, Castro
averred, but the action had "not the slightest trace of legality" and involved a "flagrant" violation of Czechoslovakia's
sovereignty. The invasion, Castro added, "unquestionably
entailed a violation of legal principles and international
norms that, having often served as a shield for the peoples
against injustice, are highly esteemed by the world."

In Czechoslovakia itself, during those first few days the
spirit of resistance also hardened, strengthened by the news
from the "free" radio stations that a large part of the outside world—Communists and non-Communists alike—was outraged by what had happened. But the Czechs and Slovaks
knew they could expect no armed aid from the outside, while
armed resistance—now that the invaders had their troops,
tanks, and aircraft in every major area of the country—would
only precipitate a blood bath that would not expel the invaders. These considerations turned the population toward the
world's most remarkable example of national resistance by
means short of shooting. Psychological and political war-
fare was waged by a militarily conquered people against their
conquerors—a peaceful liberation struggle that had the
potential to explode into armed resistance with all the disastrous political consequences Moscow dreaded. So the anti-
Soviet posters and graffiti went up on the walls; the swastikas
appeared on the tanks; the young people argued with the
troops; the places where individual resisters had been killed
immediately became honored national shrines. And Soviet
troops, with rare exceptions, did not shoot.

The Soviet leaders and their puppets in the other states
participating in the invasion also had to cope with political

difficulties in their own lands. A major propaganda campaign
had been conducted for months to prepare Soviet citizens,
Poles, East Germans, and the others for the invasion, but
that campaign had by no means been fully successful. Only
the very bravest citizens of these police states dared protest
openly. Seven Moscow intellectuals—including Pavel Litvinov and Mrs. Yuli Daniel—who tried to demonstrate in
Red Square and got beaten up and arrested for their pains,
Soviet intellectuals who refused to vote for resolutions supporting the invasion or to sign statements of similar import,
East German youths who passed out leaflets denouncing
this act of aggression or who painted Dubcek's name in large
letters on the walls of buildings, prominent Polish writers
who wrote letters of protest—these and similar active dissidents were an infinitesimal minority. There was much
hidden unhappiness and questioning, however, because the
aggression involved was simply too patent to be missed by
intelligent and educated people. Soviet and Eastern European propaganda had for years denounced the United States
presence in Vietnam as "imperialist aggression." What
should one call the presence of Soviet and other Communist
troops in Czechoslovakia?

Soviet and puppet Eastern European propaganda media
tried to combat the skepticism. They wrote of an alleged
army of forty thousand counterrevolutionaries set to strike
within Czechoslovakia. They conjured up myths of Zionist
plots and West German conspiracies. However, those who
directed this brainwashing exercise were themselves dissatisfied with their effort. Symptomatic of Kremlin propaganda
insecurities was the decision shortly after the invasion to resume Soviet jamming of Voice of America broadcasts. For
the previous five years, Soviet leaders had felt secure enough
to permit their people to listen to what the United States had
to say. But less than twelve hours after the invasion began,

jamming was resumed, and more than two months later it was continuing.

Moreover, it was much more difficult for the propaganda chiefs to justify the 1968 invasion of Czechoslovakia than the 1956 invasion of Hungary. Their audiences in 1968 were far better educated, much more sophisticated, and more acquainted with foreign countries through personal travel than were the 1956 audiences, composed of masses still emerging from the intellectual anesthesia of the Stalin period. For Russians, too, the Czechs and Slovaks were fellow Slavs, not the Magyars of Hungary with their incomprehensible language. In Budapest in 1956, there had been a violent anti-Communist revolution with Communists being killed and Marxist literature being burned. Nothing of the sort was taking place in Czechoslovakia. As a result of these factors, with every day that passed without a political settlement in Czechoslovakia, but with continuing effective nonviolent resistance, the task of keeping the blinders on the people in the Soviet Union and in the puppet Eastern European states became ever more difficult.

All these considerations reinforced the invaders' search for an exit from this catastrophic, unexpected situation. They could not stop Czechoslovak Foreign Minister Jiri Hajek, who had been vacationing in Yugoslavia on August 20, from flying to New York and stating Czechoslovakia's case before the United Nations. But they could, and did, veto the U.N. Security Council resolution condemning the invasion. They could try to silence the hidden radio stations. Soon, however, they ran into determined resistance. A high-ranking official of the Czechoslovak Interior Ministry, Dr. Jan Zaruba, committed suicide rather than hand over secret information on the location of the transmitters. Czechoslovak railroad men, in response to orders from those same radio stations, delayed for days the arrival of a train loaded with radio-location equipment needed to find the secret broadcasters. In retaliation, Soviet broadcasts to Slovakia began seeking to stir up Slovak separatist sentiments, as the Kremlin played with the idea of creating a separate Slovakia, either as an "independent state" such as Hitler had created thirty years earlier or as a new, sixteenth component republic of the Soviet Union.

In Moscow, the decisive battle raged—a moral and political struggle between President Svoboda and the whole might and power of the Kremlin leadership. Svoboda incarnated the whole issue of legality, and only with his consent could the Russians hope for a settlement that might take world pressure off them and induce the Czechoslovak people to reconcile themselves to a new situation. When the Russians tried to threaten the stubborn old man, he replied with a counter threat: He would commit suicide and provide Czechoslovakia with a martyr even exceeding Jan Masaryk in emotional appeal. When the Russians offered bribes in the form of massive economic aid, Svoboda rejected them contemptuously, as he rejected offers to make him Premier or to replace Dubcek with some other figure who might be mutually satisfactory. Similarly, the Czechoslovak President proved impervious to threats that his country's national existence would be ended by imposing a pattern similar to that Hitler had used in 1938–39. Stolidly he persisted in his basic demand: The legal Party and Government leaders of Czechoslovakia—Dubcek, Cernik, Smrkovsky, and their comrades—must be recognized in their posts, brought to Moscow, and admitted to the negotiations as full-fledged and free members of Czechoslovakia's delegation. Under growing pressure from world public opinion and from Czechoslovakia's resistance, the Russians surrendered. Dubcek and his colleagues, many of them despairing and suffering from the physical and psychological shocks of their brutal arrest and imprisonment, were flown to Moscow. The Kremlin made no announce-

ment of their arrival, but it conceded an essential point: It
agreed to their continued tenure in their posts and recognized their right to negotiate for Czechoslovakia. Svoboda
had saved his comrades' lives and, for the moment, some
important shreds of his nation's remaining sovereignty and
independence. But the Russians were successful in insisting
that conservatives such as Bilak, Svestka, Indra, and Piller
also join the Prague negotiating team in the Kremlin.

Even after the arrival of Dubcek and the others, the negotiations were still hardly between equals. The experience of
Frantisek Kriegel—Presidium member, Chairman of the National Front, physician, veteran Communist, and Jew—suggests the atmosphere of these bizarre talks. Kriegel had been
arrested with, imprisoned with, and flown to Moscow with
Dubcek. But when he appeared at the enlarged negotiations
with the Czechoslovak team, the Russians barred him. "What
is this Jew from Galicia doing here?" an angry Leonid I.
Brezhnev demanded. This was more than simple anti-Semitism or even anger at Kriegel's liberal stance in the Presidium. Kriegel, who had been born in Stanislav in Galicia
when it was part of Austro-Hungary before World War I,
had dared to speak somewhat favorably about the "2,000
Words" manifesto at the end of June. He had also urged his
Presidium comrades to initiate contacts with Peking in an
effort to get Chinese Communist support against the Soviet
pressure. The vindictive Russians not only barred him from
the negotiations but, knowing he was a diabetic, kept him on
short insulin rations. This had a predictably devastating impact on his physical condition. Later, when the Czechoslovak
delegates were at Moscow airport about to embark for Prague,
they discovered that Kriegel was not with them. Staging a
sit-down strike, they refused to return without him. Only
after a two-hour impasse did the Soviet authorities finally
deliver Kriegel to the airport and permit him to leave with
his colleagues. One of the conservatives, Indra, did not re-

turn then. Reportedly, he suffered a heart attack when told in Moscow he would have to go back to the country he had tried to betray. He did not actually return to Prague, therefore, until late September.

In a speech two days after the return from Moscow, Smrkovsky called the days of his imprisonment and the Kremlin negotiations "the most difficult I have ever lived through in my life." He recalled that he and his comrades "had to act and decide in the shadow of tanks and aircraft stationed on our territory," that "our contacts with home were limited; we possessed extremely little or almost no information, and more than once we had to depend more on our faith in the firm attitude of our peoples than on actual knowledge of the situation." He revealed that he and his comrades wondered whether they really had a mandate to speak for Czechoslovakia, whether any agreement they signed would be regarded by their people and history as "a betrayal." He added that in the negotiations, "I beg you to believe that we did not keep silent, that we clashed sharply and repeatedly both with our partners and among ourselves, and that we used every available argument accessible to us." He hinted that he and his colleagues knew in Moscow of "certain difficulties into which the external military intervention had become involved politically. We knew that the world sympathized with us but that the great powers would accept a compromise solution rather than anything." He spoke of the "tragedy of small nations whose fatherland lies in a particularly sensitive place on this continent . . . the tragedy of the efforts for new socialist achievement, the tragedy of those who are trying to march in front, the tragedy of the attempts by peoples setting great noble aims for themselves." His point, of course, was that he, Dubcek, and the others in Moscow had been forced to accept what the Peking *People's Daily* accurately called "a deal made at bayonet point," a compromise heavily weighted in favor of those whose tanks and planes had cast such dark shadows over the negotiations.

The agreement reached after those four days of hard bargaining in Moscow and announced on the night of August 26 had five main points. First, both sides agreed that the chief, immediate necessity was "the realization of the decisions jointly accepted at Cierna and Tisou and of the propositions and principles formulated by the conference at Bratislava." But the only decision publicly announced at the end of the Cierna conference was the decision to hold the Bratislava meeting. Thus, the Moscow communiqué contained seeming admission that Prague had accepted obligations at Cierna that it had not revealed to its people.

Second, the Soviet side expressed its "understanding and support" of the Czechoslovak Communist Party positions arising from "the decisions accepted at the January and May plenums . . . with the goal of perfecting the methods of directing society, developing socialist democracy, and strengthening the socialist structure on the basis of Marxism-Leninism." But this conspicuously omitted the April plenum. Was the Action Program adopted there dead?

Third, agreement had been reached on measures to obtain "the quickest normalization of the situation," and the Czechoslovak side had agreed that all Party and Government efforts in that country "will be directed to guaranteeing effective measures serving socialist power, the directing role of the working class and the Communist Party, the interests of developing and strengthening friendly relations with the peoples of the Soviet Union and the entire socialist commonwealth."

Fourth, the Soviet authorities affirmed their readiness for

> . . . the broadest and most sincere cooperation on the basis of mutual respect, equality, territorial integrity, independence,

and socialist solidarity. The troops of allied countries, tempo-
rarily entering Czechoslovak territory, will not interfere in the
internal affairs of the Czechoslovak Socialist Republic. Agreement was reached on the conditions for withdrawal of these
troops from Czechoslovak territory in relation to the normalization of the situation there.

Fifth, the Czechoslovak representatives declared they had
not asked the United Nations to consider "the so-called problem of the situation in Czechoslovakia" and demanded removal of this matter from the Security Council agenda.

A wave of indignation and anger swept over Czechoslovakia when the communiqué was announced. The document's
delicate wording implied that much had been surrendered
and that much else, including even the withdrawal of Soviet
troops, had been left to the whim and good will, if any, of
Moscow. It was not difficult to read between the lines and see
that the document required censorship of press, radio, and
television, an end to really independent political activities,
and a purge of liberals and others Moscow did not like—men
like Kriegel, Foreign Minister Hajek, whose U.N. testimony
was repudiated by the communiqué, Deputy Premier Ota
Sik, whom *Pravda* had accused earlier of seeking to rein-
troduce capitalism in Czechoslovakia under the guise of
economic reform, and others. Had not Dubcek and his colleagues really capitulated completely? The sophisticated saw
that Moscow had imposed or come close to imposing the
terms demanded in the Warsaw letter of July. They also
realized there must be a secret agreement for virtually
permanent stationing of Soviet troops in Czechoslovakia,
nominally to protect the country against West Germany,
actually to insure Moscow against any repetition of the
revolt it had faced from January 5 to August 20. Later, it became known that these and other concessions had actually
been agreed to in a secret protocol imposed on the Czecho-

slovaks in Moscow. The belief that the country had been betrayed again was widespread in those first days after the agreement of August 26. The open resistance continued despite the initial appeals of the returned leaders for what they called "realism" in a difficult situation.

In despair, many concluded that all had been lost, that Czechoslovakia was about to be forced to return to the worst days of the past, complete with secret police terror, mass political trials, and the loss of all the gains made since 1954, under Novotny as well as under Dubcek. Thousands of Czechoslovaks, caught abroad vacationing in Rumania, Yugoslavia, and the West, halted preparations to return home. Some decided to become refugees and settle in the West permanently; others suspended judgment, waiting to see if their worst fears would be confirmed. Inside Czechoslovakia, thousands began preparing to emigrate, especially many intellectuals. The most frightening rumors swept the country: All who had supported the Action Program would now suffer Soviet revenge; Premier Cernik had urged the intellectuals to flee, declaring that since he could not guarantee his own safety, his Government could guarantee no one's safety. It was a new crisis of confidence, psychologically more severe because of the continued presence of foreign troops than the one in mid-July, which had forced rejection of the Warsaw ultimatum.

Haggard, bone-tired from his ordeal, looking as if he might drop from exhaustion at any moment, Alexander Dubcek sought to counter this black mood when he faced his nation again on August 27. His halting speech betrayed his fatigue, and he did not try to disguise the fact that a bitter dose had been forced on Czechoslovakia. He spoke of the nation's basic institutions' operating "in a situation and a reality not dependent on our will alone." He pleaded for trust "even though we might be forced to take some temporary measures that limit the extent of democracy and freedom of opinion we had already achieved and which we would not have taken under normal circumstances." He was asking the nation to accept as gracefully as possible the yoke that had been imposed upon it. In return, if normalization and consolidation could be achieved quickly, he offered the hope of "realizing in this new situation the program of our Communist Party on which we decided in January, April, and all other meetings." There was the core of his strategy: to retrieve as much as possible from the disaster, to exploit to the limit whatever narrow room for maneuver remained. As Smrkovsky pointed out even more bluntly in his speech two days later, Czechoslovakia was still governed by its own officials, its own Communist Party, and its own Government—a far better situation than if it had had an outright occupation regime imposed upon it. The nation must bow to superior force but, in the tradition of the Good Soldier Schweik, it might have a better tomorrow if it countered that superior force with ingenuity and intelligence.

Moscow's leaders read these speeches, too, and understood what was implied between the lines as well as said openly. They understood that they had suffered a partial and unprecedented setback in reinstating Dubcek and his comrades, that they must expect future resistance. But the Kremlin Politburo knew that Soviet troops controlled Czechoslovakia and that Dubcek and his associates would have to impose many unpopular measures on their people. Inevitably, Dubcek's forced moves would arouse resentment and weaken his political position. Then there would be opportunity to dispose of the Dubcek leadership and install a more compliant and cooperative group, perhaps even the original Kolder-Indra clique. Moreover, with the agreement signed, Moscow had genuinely popular Czechoslovak leaders actively appealing to the country's people to end the open psychological and political resistance. The gamble paid off in early September when all Czechoslovakia seemed to be embarked upon a gigantic clean-up campaign, erasing and washing off the graffiti, the drawings, the slogans, and all the other visible signs of the defiance of late August. For use abroad, Moscow had a legal document, a signed Czechoslovak-Soviet agreement. This might induce foreign Communist critics to moderate their attacks and concede that Moscow had ended the incident correctly even if those dissenters still disliked the original invasion. To some critics, Moscow turned a sterner face. The probability seems high that the Kremlin used the language of force toward Rumania, warning that Bucharest would suffer the fate of Prague if Ceausescu did not curb his violent tongue and stop inflaming anti-Soviet passions in his country. The threats worked. Almost overnight, Rumanian newspapers started reporting Czechoslovak developments without emotion and without exhortation. Ceausescu himself began a barnstorming speech tour of the country, emphasizing the need for national unity and assuring the minority Hungarians, Germans, and others that they were full-fledged, equal citizens of Rumania. The impression given was that cold fear—though not cowardice—had replaced passionate anger in this most exposed of the independent Communist states.

As he resumed the reins of power, Dubcek found himself under heavy pressure from two different directions. In Moscow, the Soviet press each day denounced the continued activity of "subversive elements," "imperialist agents," and the like. These were brutal reminders that the Kremlin expected quick action to impose what Yuri Zhukov of *Pravda* had earlier called "elementary order" in Czechoslovakia. Among his own people, Dubcek found himself surrounded by disillusionment, fear, and open questioning. As late as August 28, the Czechoslovak National Assembly bravely defied Moscow. It passed a resolution calling the occupation "illegal" and a violation of "the United Nations Charter and the Warsaw Treaty." It demanded that all communications media be allowed to resume normal, free activities and that all persons illegally arrested by foreign or Czechoslovak security agents since the invasion be released. It also called for uncompromising adherence to the original Action Program and the democratization program at its core. In Slovakia, a special Congress of the Communist Party ousted First Secretary Vasil Bilak, who was a Soviet collaborator, and replaced him with Gustav Husak, former prisoner and a pioneer in the liberation drive at its beginning in January, 1968. Premier Cernik, for his part, underlined his intention to retain maximum independence. As one of his first moves on returning to Prague, he dismissed Miroslav Sulek, the treacherous *Ceteka* Director who had tried unsuccessfully to have the news agency send out the conservatives' "cry for help" on the terrible night of August 20. But Cernik had to accept the "resignation" of his Interior Minister, Josef Pavel, who had no stomach for working with Moscow's secret police and who was unacceptable to the latter as well. Pavel's replacement, the regional Party official Jan Pelnar, was not known as a conservative, however.

Very quickly, Dubcek's effort to overcome the crisis of confidence focused on one issue: What was the legal status of the extraordinary Fourteenth Party Congress held secretly on August 22 in defiance of Soviet guns? It had elected a new Party Presidium and Central Committee. What authority, if any, did these bodies possess? Moscow, of course, had made clear to Dubcek that it wanted this meeting annulled as illegal. The Slovak Party Congress that elected Husak concurred because of Soviet pressure and because of nationalist feeling that a Congress without a full Slovak representation could not be accepted.

Practically, Dubcek had no alternative to nullifying the "illegal" Fourteenth Congress, but he did so in a way he hoped would be most reassuring to the nation. At an enlarged meeting of the old Central Committee on August 31, that body incorporated eighty new members—all persons elected as delegates to the Fourteenth Congress and therefore overwhelmingly Dubcek supporters. It also elected a new Party Presidium of twenty-one members, excluding one liberal (Kriegel), two conservatives (Kolder and Svestka), and one man who had wavered between the two sides (Emil Rigo). In addition, the conservative Frantisek Barbirek was demoted to candidate status. Of the six members retained, four (Dubcek, Cernik, Smrkovsky and Spacek) were liberals, and two (Bilak and Piller) were conservatives. Among the fifteen new full-ranking Presidium members, the most prominent were President Svoboda, new Slovak Party chief Husak, liberal Party Secretary Zdenek Mlynar, and Prague Party chief Bohumil Simon, whose organization had carried out the "illegal" Fourteenth Congress. Two aspects about this new Presidium were most significant: It contained a large majority of Dubcek supporters, and it gave increased representation to the Slovaks. It was a Presidium of conciliation between the nation's two peoples and a body that the Czechoslovak populace could assume would, with few exceptions, fight for the national interest from a liberal point of view, as much as possible. Many in the country noted that seven of the fifteen new members had first been elevated to the Presidium at the "illegal" Fourteenth Congress. This move made clear that that meeting had not been held in vain. It was announced that Oldrich Svestka had been removed as editor of *Rude Pravo,* thus confirming another decision of the "illegal" Congress. Behind these personnel changes, one could see the influence of Dubcek's thesis that a disciplined and courageous nation might yet salvage more than a little from the disaster. Whatever the facts of power, this was not a Presidium of willing puppets.

What made the August 31 Prague Communist Party reshuffle even more remarkable was the fact that it came the day after President Johnson had startled the world with a warning that a new Soviet invasion might soon be under way. The United States had heard "rumors" to this effect, the President declared, adding a hint that, if such new aggression occurred, the United States might not stand idle as it had on August 20. Rumania, still resistant to Soviet pressure, though less strident than earlier, was evidently the potential Soviet victim President Johnson had in mind when he declared, "So let no one unleash the dogs of war." As the tragic month of August ended, an anxious world felt that the foundations of international order might be falling into ruin. In Rumania and Yugoslavia, urgent preparations were being made to resist with every weapon should Soviet armies cross the borders. The Czechoslovak capitulation would not be repeated.

13

The Schweikism
of Autumn

Prague's U Kalicha restaurant treasures its image as a haunt of Jaroslav Hasek's immortal character, the Good Soldier Schweik. One of the cartoons on U Kalicha's walls sums up, perhaps better than any other comment, the essentials of Czechoslovakia's reaction during the period September–December, 1968, to its new servitude. The cartoon depicts the obviously weary and bedraggled Schweik declaring, "I've had five pints of beer, a couple of sausages, and a roll. I'll just have a plum brandy, and then I must go because I'm under arrest." Czechoslovakia was "under arrest" in these months, but the saucy impudence with which it defied some of Moscow's most urgent wishes amazed both Communists and anti-Communists. On November 30, 1968, *Pravda* was still playing what had become an old and familiar tune, bitter complaint about the heresies of Prague's journalists. A modern Rip Van Winkle who had gone to sleep in mid-

August and awakened in late November would never have guessed from *Pravda*'s grumbling that, during his slumber, Czechoslovakia had been invaded by hundreds of thousands of troops, many of whom still remained.

However, to recognize that the Czechoslovak autumn provided an amazing example of Schweikism in action is not to imply that the invasion had no consequences. On the contrary, the Dubcek leadership had to register a melancholy list of concessions and retreats. Soviet bayonets were still poised, and Soviet Deputy Foreign Minister Vasily Kuznetsov, who settled down in Prague to gather information and to supervise the occupation, skilfully turned that physical power into daily political pressure for the implementation of Moscow's demands. A recital of the key moves away from the spirit and substance of the pre-invasion period is sobering.

On September 13, the National Assembly passed almost without debate a series of measures providing for "temporary" censorship of the press and for equally "temporary" restrictions on the freedom of assembly, while banning political groups that were outside the framework of the Communist Party-dominated National Front. In October, Premier Kosygin came to Prague to sign a treaty "legalizing" the occupation. The treaty provided for the "temporary" stationing of Soviet troops in Czechoslovakia, nominally to protect the country against "West German imperialism." But neither a time limit on the stay of the Soviet troops nor a limit on the number of "protectors" who might be brought into the country was specified. In early November, the Prague Government, presumably under Soviet pressure, banned two magazines, *Reporter* and *Politika,* thereby reviving year-old memories of the time the Novotny Government banned *Literarni Noviny* to silence the writers.

There were personnel changes, too, during these months. Foreign Minister Hajek paid for his temerity in assailing the invasion before the United Nations and "resigned" after a vicious personal attack on him by *Izvestia,* which incorrectly implied that he was a Jew who had changed his name. Deputy Premier Ota Sik also "resigned" and took up residence in Switzerland. The directors of Czechoslovakia's television and radio, Jiri Pelikan and Zdenek Hejzlar—victims of Moscow's fury at the media's gigantic contribution to the nation's short period of unfettered free speech—lost their jobs. Some officials who had proved to be traitors on August 20 and 21 were fired too, however.

In these months, Dubcek, Premier Cernik, and other leaders—notably Slovak Communist Party First Secretary Gustav Husak, who showed special and surprising enthusiasm for the task—delivered innumerable speeches in which they preached "realism" and friendship for the Soviet Union, while denouncing Ivan Svitak and other "extremists" of the pre-invasion period—that is, the persons who had acted on a literal interpretation of the earlier talk about democracy and free speech. Thousands of Czechs and Slovaks left the country legally after August, and other thousands who had been abroad on vacation at the time of the invasion simply did not come back. In late November, the frontier barriers were installed again, when the liberal pre-invasion foreign travel regulations—one of the major gains of the Czechoslovak spring—were changed to make them far less permissive.

The ideological near-capitulation of the Czechoslovak Communist Party to the military realities took place in mid-November at a stormy Central Committee meeting. Radically different currents of opinion clashed there. The debaters ranged from would-be quislings, such as former Foreign Minister Vaclav David and other members of the pro-Soviet faction organized at a meeting in the Liben district in Prague in early October, to obdurate, unreformed liberals, such as Frantisek Kriegel, who had remained Central Committee members though forced to leave their former, high posts. Apparently reliable reports indicate that Dubcek flew to Warsaw to meet with Leonid I. Brezhnev and get the latter's approval for the final Central Committee resolution. Indicative of the new atmosphere was the fact that that resolution was not published in full; the parts that were made public showed the unmistakable retrogression that had taken place.

Much of the resolution was devoted to self criticism, to a *mea culpa* in analyzing what had happened between January and August 20. The Communist Party had not been prepared with solutions for the new problems that Novotny's removal brought, the resolution acknowledged; there had been pressure from the right wing, and the Party itself had been divided on the question of tactics to meet the new situation. The resolution continued:

> This introduced significant elements of spontaneity into the process of development, and this was not always successfully dealt with in the further development.
>
> This situation began to be utilized by forces trying to weaken the Communist Party of Czechoslovakia, to undermine its directive position in society, to weaken different decisive links of the socialist state, and, finally, to weaken the international ties of the Party and state in the framework of the community of socialist countries.
>
> Reference is made here first of all to tactics of putting forward one-sided, perverted evaluations, deliberate misinformation, of advancing—without account of the abilities of the Party and society—more and more problems while demanding that correct solutions and decisions for them be found immediately.
>
> All such tactics were used not only by right opportunists, but also by anti-socialist forces which succeeded in penetrating some means of mass information and misusing their great influence.
>
> Neither the Czechoslovak Communist Party Presidium nor the Government had a carefully thought out system for directing the press, radio, and television. Censorship was abolished. However, the influence of the negative activity of mass media was not analyzed, and it was underestimated. . . .

The means of mass information were gradually converted into an uncontrolled force. . . .

As a result of all these influences, especially in February, March, and early April, a situation was created in which different forms of pressure took place, at a time when there existed much confusion of views in the Party and in society. Criticisms were often turned against the entire Party rather than against those individuals who were actually guilty. Sweeping, unjust accusations were directed against the Party and state apparatus and the organs of power, especially against the security and justice organs, for errors committed during the 1950's. These accusations implicated the overwhelming majority of honest workers who had nothing to do with these deformations. This destroyed the activity of important organs of political power. . . .

The complexities in the Party's development were caused by the rightist forces and opportunist tendencies. The latter replaced justified criticisms of deformations in the execution of the Party's directive role by the concept of partnership, viewed as a free play of political forces in which the application of the weapons of power at the present stage of political struggle was considered unacceptable. Utilizing the false slogan of absolute democracy, they underestimated the class aspects of socialist democracy and tolerated and supported the unhealthy splintering of the political system and social organizations. They emphasized one-sidedly the independence of different component parts of the political system from the Communist Party of Czechoslovakia and its policy. They underestimated the danger of anti-socialist forces and took a negative attitude toward ideological struggle against those forces. They took a subjective and negligent position toward the foreign political aspects of the development of socialism in Czechoslovakia, for example toward the influence of the class struggle on an international scale, toward the aspiration of imperialism to misuse the processes taking place in Czechoslovakia, toward the international interests of the world socialist community of which Czechoslovakia is an inseparable part.

Those holding these views were given extraordinary and disproportionate opportunities to speak out in the press. As a result, the impression arose that these views represented the official policy of the Communist Party of Czechoslovakia. This objectively played into the hands of anti-socialist forces and disoriented a section of the members of the Party and of society.

Against the background of this analysis, the resolution gave this view of the functions of the press:

> The responsible workers of the means of mass information must orient the press to the formation of a principled ideological unity of socialist forces and speak out in principled fashion against all expressions of bourgeois ideology. They must rebuff extremist, foreign, and harmful views which could weaken the socialist development of Czechoslovakia. The urgent task of the means of mass information is actively to make possible understanding of the mutually connected international development, of the struggle between socialism and imperialism, and of the fact that our country is a firm component part of the socialist system.
>
> The press, radio, and television are first of all the instruments for carrying into life the policies of the Party and state.

In line with this shift by the Party leadership toward greater orthodoxy and more submission to Moscow, the same Central Committee meeting took a major step toward reducing Alexander Dubcek's power and status. He remained First Secretary, but the Executive Committee—a new body—became the supreme Communist Party agency. Composed of eight of the twenty-one Presidium members, the Executive Committee included Premier Cernik, Gustav Husak, Josef Smrkovsky, Ludvik Svoboda, Evzen Erban, Stefan Sadovsky, and Lubomir Strougal as well as Dubcek. Strougal —a former Minister of Interior under Novotny—made the largest personal gain at this meeting. He succeeded to the posts of Presidium member and Party Secretary vacated by the resignation of a key liberal, Zdenek Mlynar. Strougal was also named head of a new Central Committee bureau for the Czech lands, created in lieu of a separate Czech Communist Party parallel to the Slovak Communist Party. On October 28, Czechoslovakia had been legislatively turned into a federation of Czechs and Slovaks with parallel government and administrative hierarchies, but, reportedly, Soviet objections prevented the same parallelism from being introduced into the Communist Party organization.

There could have been no talk of Schweikism in post-invasion Czechoslovakia if the sequence of events summarized above had been the entire story. It was not, however. On the contrary, the enforced submission of the nation's leadership to many aspects of Soviet dictation took place simultaneously with the population's continued moral and political resistance. The occupying troops were made to know in many ways that they were hated and unwelcome. At times, the resistance flared into open and violent demonstrations of undisguised anti-Soviet feeling.

The psychological impact of the invasion and of the heroic though nonviolent opposition that followed unified the Czechoslovak peoples. Intellectuals, students, workers, farmers—all forgot their old mutual suspicions and animosities in outrage against what must have seemed to many a repetition of the nation's conquest by Hitler. The sentiments of most Czechs and Slovaks were probably accurately articulated in early September by the Slovak writer Pavel Stevcek when he wrote in *Kulturny Zivot:*

> The times in which we are being forced to live are not the times of words, and particularly not the times of free words. Therefore, let us declare, while still we may, that we shall not forget. We shall not forget that the tracks of their tanks have crushed the old tradition of sincere friendship, a friendship which had its heroic history, its moral laws and rules. We shall not forget Danka Kasanova, whom they murdered, nor the dozens of other victims who were criminally slain. We shall not

forget that they even ordered us to wash the blood off the paving, to level the grave mounds, and to blot out signs. These are crimes and wrongs which are not subject to historical rehabilitation. We ought to promise, for the second time, to preserve the original meaning and significance of words for the future, in our hearts and minds, if we are not allowed to do so in writing: breach of faith, aggression, invasion, treason, the criminal killing of innocent people, etc. As you can see, we have already been forced to euphemize these facts, and now one must speak of entry, stay, placement, and it is only good that we need not write about a friendly visit by troops of the five Warsaw Pact countries. . . . We will certainly not be permitted to write accurately; well, at least let us read accurately.

A few weeks after this was published, it was no longer possible to print anything so brutally frank. Nevertheless, the Czechoslovak press, radio, and television continued to be surprisingly bold and ingenious in articulating the nation's real thoughts. Thus, there frequently were polemics in the Czechoslovak media against the misrepresentations of the situation in the country by the Soviet and satellite press. A Soviet "white book" claiming to give a lengthy justification for the invasion became a particular target of Czechoslovak attacks. All the nation's media joined to present detailed refutations of this document. The Czechoslovak Academy of Sciences joined the fray, and its damning analysis was printed. Moreover, Czechoslovak editors and writers found innumerable sly ways to express their feelings. Very quickly, they renewed their *expertise* in the use of Aesopian language that was easily understood by readers, listeners, and viewers. This kind of defiance would have been much more difficult if the old system of precensorship—with a "reliable" censor examining every item before publication—had been instituted, but it was not. Instead, the new censorship was self-censorship based on instructions about what might be printed. The stick behind the instructions was the threat that a periodical violating them would have its publication halted. Thus, editors had to decide how bold they would be and what risks they would take. The lengths to which some editors were willing to go was illustrated by a cartoon that appeared in *Reporter* and that contributed to the enforced suspension of the publication. Originally printed in the Soviet humor magazine *Krokodil* in 1957, the cartoon showed a Western European ambassador leaving the White House and being helped into his outer garb while a bystander commented, "He's got his clothes back, but he had to leave his sovereignty behind." *Reporter* also printed, contrary to direct official orders, portions of speeches made in the National Assembly during the debate on the treaty permitting Soviet troops to remain indefinitely in Czechoslovakia. Some of the material printed stated the legal case against the treaty. That *Reporter* was forced to suspend publication after such transgressions is hardly surprising. The surprise is that it was able to publish such material in the first place. The essence of Czechoslovak Schweikism was reflected in the official decision to permit *Reporter* to resume publication, a decision taken after the editors threatened to challenge their shutdown in court. At the end of November, acting in the same Schweikian tradition, a portion of the Czechoslovak press publicly protested against the appearance of *Zpravy* (News), a Czech-language newspaper issued by the Soviet occupation forces. *Zpravy* had no license, as required by law, and represented interference in the internal affairs of Czechoslovakia, contrary to the provisions of both the August 26 Moscow agreement and the treaty legalizing the stay of Soviet troops in the country. An official protest to Moscow through diplomatic channels followed. On December 4, Prague radio and television reported that the Czechoslovak Ministry of Interior was impeding efforts of the General Prosecutor to ban the paper. The revelation was an ominous sign of splits in the Prague leadership, as well as a warning of the existence of a major group of Czechoslovak officials willing to serve Moscow in the Novotny tradition.

There were other, more dramatic, expressions of the nation's resentment besides the *Zpravy* case. During the celebration of Czechoslovakia's fiftieth anniversary, on October 28 and 29, and on the fifty-first anniversary of the Bolshevik Revolution, on November 7, there were mass anti-Soviet demonstrations in the streets of Prague, Bratislava, Brno, and other Czechoslovak cities. There were shouts of "Russians go home!" "We want freedom!" "Masaryk, Masaryk," and the like. In the first demonstrations, copies of *Pravda* were burned, and in the second wave of demonstrations, Soviet flags were publicly burned. Later in November, tens of thousands of Czech and Slovak students conducted a four-day sit-in in colleges and high schools to express their resentment at the Soviet occupation and their demand for freedom. The sympathy of the population with the students was shown by the dozens of trucks sent from factories to bring them food free of charge. On each of these occasions, many observers inside and outside Czechoslovakia awaited with apprehension possible violent action by Soviet troops against the dissidents. Some even feared the reinvasion of Czechoslovakia by the tens of thousands of soldiers who had left the country after the signing of the treaty legalizing the continued stay of Soviet troops, but the occupying soldiers remained quietly in their camps, and the only force used against the demonstrators was by Czechoslovak police who, particularly on November 7, employed clubs, tear gas, and water cannon. The police did their duty reluctantly, and there was no outcry of protest comparable to that aroused in October, 1967—during the Novotny era—by the police brutality then directed against Prague students.

The avowed Soviet goal in Czechoslovakia was "normalization." *Pravda,* on October 3, supplied a definition of the term: "Real normalization—this is the guarantee of actual

measures directed toward strengthening socialism, people's
power, the directing role of the working class, and the Communist Party in the life of society, and for the further development of friendly relations with the peoples of the Soviet
Union and all the socialist community." Even in early December, 1968, there was no sign that such "normalization"
would soon be completed in Czechoslovakia, and no observer
—even in Moscow—could doubt that a majority of Czechoslovaks continued to resent the August invasion and the indefinite Soviet occupation. If the Soviet leaders who ordered
the invasion had thought it would bring a quick end to their
political troubles in Czechoslovakia, they had been mistaken;
in Czechoslovakia, at least, the result had been to make a
nation once friendly to the Soviet Union deeply aggrieved
and obsessed with a sense of having been ill used and betrayed.

Pressure from an angry and united nation helped
strengthen Dubcek and those of his colleagues in the leadership who sought to save as much as possible from the debacle of August. After their return from Soviet captivity,
Dubcek, Smrkovsky, and others had pledged that Czechoslovakia would not return to the old Novotny practices, that
the basic democratic principles of the post-January development and the April Action Program would be preserved.
Thus, as heavy Soviet pressure bore down on Dubcek for
concession after concession, for retreat after retreat, he gained
some leverage by pointing to the sentiments of the Czechoslovak people and to the dangers of going too far and too
fast toward re-Stalinization of Czechoslovakia. Presumably,
this leverage, helped him prevent the reinstitution of police
terror—the mass arrests of liberal journalists, politicians,
union leaders, and others whom the Soviet leaders would
rather have had removed from circulation and influence on
the public.

Thus, more than one hundred days after the invasion,

something of a stalemate existed in Czechoslovakia. Tens of thousands of Soviet troops were in the country, but for the most part they were kept out of sight, away from most of the population. President Ludvik Svoboda and Communist Party chief Alexander Dubcek still retained their offices and were individual symbols of the nation's drive for freedom, but they and the regime they headed were committed to a policy of full collaboration with the Soviet Union. The fruits of the implementation of that policy over the one hundred days had been what some called "salami tactics"— that is, the slicing away, one after another, of the liberties and privileges won between January 5 and August 20. But Czechoslovakia was still, in early December, 1968, the freest of the Soviet satellite states, the only such country in which anti-Soviet sentiments and the desire for freedom were widely articulated. The wounds caused by the invasion had not healed, and Czechs and Slovaks were united in a desire for freedom and an end to Soviet occupation. Yet the population was not prepared for a military struggle, fearing a terrible blood bath in which losses would be great and fruitless. Neither slaves nor free men, the Czechs and Slovaks could see no better alternative to their precarious position.

The pressures on the Czechoslovaks were clear enough. But why did Moscow accept what it must have regarded as an unsatisfactory equilibrium? The Kremlin had the military force to reinvade Czechoslovakia, do away with the Dubcek regime, and impose a puppet government. Moreover, as 1968 ended, it was evident that there were several thousand Czech and Slovak quislings, grouped together in the so-called Liben faction, who would gladly have provided the manpower for such a puppet regime. The encouragement Soviet officers in Czechoslovakia gave to the organizers of this conservative force and the approving publicity its activities received in the Soviet press suggested that this possibility was not far from the minds of Brezhnev and his colleagues.

In part, no doubt, the Kremlin hoped it could still whip Czechoslovakia into line by pressure applied over a period of time. The Soviet leaders must have reasoned that as the noose of restrictive measures settled more tightly about Czechoslovakia's throat, disillusionment with Dubcek, Svoboda, Smrkovsky, and their colleagues would increase to the point where they could be upset politically and replaced by others, who would fulfill Moscow's wishes more zealously. Gustav Husak's speeches suggested that he was inviting Moscow to install him in Dubcek's place. Soviet restraint indicated that the prestige of the Kremlin hawks had suffered from the unsatisfactory results of the August invasion and from the political miscalculations on which the hawks had based their policy proposal. The Soviet leaders must have reckoned with the possibility of genuine military resistance if the reinvasion drama were given a reprise in defiance of the August and October agreements. Czechoslovakia still had an army and an air force, which might not remain so passive a second time.

Foreign policy and Soviet domestic considerations must also have played major roles in Moscow's acceptance of less than complete victory. At home, the population had accepted the invasion, and millions had dutifully attended the meetings called to demonstrate "unanimous approval." After the invasion, only a half dozen or so brave Soviet dissidents—including Dr. Pavel Litvinov and Mrs. Yuli Daniel—had dared participate in a Red Square protest demonstration that was quickly and violently broken up. No doubt there was a sprinkling of other protests among intellectuals. Some reports mentioned a letter of apology that eighty Soviet writers, who did not dare reveal their names, had sent the Czechoslovak Writers Union. Such opposition was negligible, yet there were signs that the Kremlin feared deeper unease. The Soviet press in September went to great pains to explain the dangers of what was called the "quiet counterrevolution" and the need to suppress it as vigorously as the more militant type that had taken place in Budapest in 1956. For the most part, no doubt, the Kremlin could rely on primitive patriotism and on the argument that the invasion prevented Czechoslovakia from becoming a West German spearhead against the Soviet Union. Nothing like the anti-Vietnam War movement in the United States was sparked in the Soviet Union by the Czechoslovak invasion, but a reinvasion of Czechoslovakia might have caused more difficulty, especially because it would have amounted to a confession that the first effort had been bungled. The Kremlin did not want Soviet people thinking of Czechoslovakia as the Soviet Union's Bay of Pigs.

The propaganda and political cost of the invasion in the outside world had been very great indeed—both among Communist parties and in non-Communist nations with which Moscow wanted to have normal or good relations. Much Soviet energy during September, October, and November, 1968, went into trying to soothe the jangled nerves and indignant voices of the many upset foreigners. The partial success achieved in this effort would have been immediately dissipated if Czechoslovakia's limited remaining sovereignty had been violated again.

Moscow would have liked the outside world to grant it a free hand in Eastern Europe and to regard the Czechoslovak invasion as an "internal matter" of the Soviet bloc. It tried to claim even more in various formulations of the so-called Brezhnev doctrine, which was enunciated in the summer and fall of 1968, notably in *Pravda* on September 26. The doctrine holds that socialist states have only limited or conditional sovereignty, that the community of socialist states has the right to intervene in any Socialist state in which internal developments are endangering the survival of socialism. In practice, of course, this amounts to an assertion of the full right of the Soviet Union to intervene in any socialist state in which there are developments disapproved of by Moscow. The Brezhnev doctrine, taken literally, would sanction the reinvasion of Czechoslovakia at Moscow's discretion.

What prevented additional, direct Soviet action against Czechoslovakia—up to late December at least—was the massive negative reaction in the rest of the world to the original invasion and the likelihood of an even more massive negative reaction to a second invasion. In Western Europe and the United States, the original invasion tended to revitalize the North Atlantic Treaty Organization and to drive President de Gaulle and France closer to NATO. If the Soviet Union could flout world public opinion by marching into Czechoslovakia, might it not similarly invade Austria or Germany or Yugoslavia or Rumania? Such fears were heightened by Soviet insistence that the 1945 agreements ending World War II gave Moscow the right to invade West Germany whenever it thought "Nazi aggression" posed a new threat. Soviet press attacks on Yugoslavia and Rumania raised questions about whether the Brezhnev doctrine might be applied against those countries.

Other fears resulting from the invasion also boomeranged against the Kremlin. The view that the entry of large numbers of Soviet troops into Czechoslovakia had altered the military balance of power in Europe ended serious American discussions about pulling U.S. soldiers out of Europe. In addition, the West German regime moved to strengthen its military posture. Moscow's unhappiness about these developments was reflected in its accusation that NATO was trying to use Czechoslovakia as a pretext for speeding up the arms race. Whether the military balance of power had actually been altered was debatable, of course. Whatever the Kremlin gained by the new disposition of its own troops had to be weighed against the fact that for the time being Czechoslovak armed forces could no longer be trusted to serve the Soviet cause in the event of war with the West. On balance, the Soviet Union may have been weakened militarily by the political developments in Czechoslovakia and their military consequences.

The negative reaction of many Communist parties, especially those in Western Europe, to the invasion hardly gave support to men in the Kremlin who may have wanted to "finish the job" in Prague. But many Communist parties suffered serious internal disarray as a result of their members' different reactions to the invasion. Thus, the French Communist Party—whose leaders, along with those of Italy's Communists, were among the strongest voices condemning the invasion—had to deal with an important pro-Soviet faction whose leader, Jeanette Vermeersch, widow of the late Party chief Maurice Thorez, resigned rather than accept the Party line. The strength of the anti-invasion Communists was evident at a Budapest meeting in early October, when they forced indefinite postponement of the international Communist Congress originally scheduled to be held in Moscow on November 25. Six weeks later at another Budapest meeting, the Kremlin did win nearly unanimous agreement to hold the international conference in Moscow in May, 1969. To some extent, this acceptance of Moscow's will by the dissident Communist parties represented a weakening of their protest over Czechoslovakia. Yet it also had a measure of gain for Dubcek, for it implied that until May, 1969, at least the Kremlin would be well advised to proceed cautiously against Czechoslovakia, lest new aggression unleash a new burst of Communist anger that would scrap the May conference date as well.

The outcome of the August invasion was unsatisfactory for the Kremlin as well as for the people of Czechoslovakia. Brezhnev and his colleagues had paid a high price in international disfavor without extirpating the desire for freedom and the reawakened Czechoslovak nationalism that had been the main targets of the military blow. The Soviet leaders hesitated to use their power to rectify the situation. They feared that another military blow might exact even greater costs from them, costs taking the form of more vigorous Czechoslovak resistance, new questioning among the Soviet people, and increased alarm and disgust among Communists and non-Communists alike in the Free World.

The key question as 1968 closed was how long Czechoslovakia could keep up its Schweik-like behavior in the face of continued relentless Soviet pressure. Just before Christmas, Alexander Dubcek spoke of the use of "measures appearing undemocratic, but serving democracy to chase anarchist elements back." The threat was clear. Gustav Husak, who seemed to many the most ardent of the post-invasion turncoats, had begun a major public campaign to oust Josef Smrkovsky—the liberal leader who had retreated least before Soviet pressure—from his post as Chairman of the National Assembly. Husak claimed that Smrkovsky's post properly belonged to a Slovak, since President Svoboda and Premier Cernik—like Smrkovsky—were Czechs. But many suspected Husak of serving Moscow, whose wish to see Smrkovsky ousted was plain. The Russians, in an effort to gain popularity in Czechoslovakia, finally signed an economic-aid agreement in late December, but the studied vagueness of its terms and scope raised suspicions about how generous Moscow had been. At Christmas, *Literaturnaya Gazeta* in Moscow renewed Soviet complaints about revisionism in Prague and counterrevolutionary material in Prague newspapers. The complaints were a tribute to the continued resistance, but how long could it continue?

14

Final Reflections

The insecurity and the incompetence of the Brezhnev leadership in Moscow emerge vividly from the history of Czechoslovakia in 1968. Insecurity was the reason for the invasion decision. Prague had to be stopped from further progress toward democracy because it threatened the bureaucratic dictatorships in the Soviet Union and the satellite countries. The doom of the Dubcek experiment was probably sealed in early March, 1968, when the student demonstrators in Warsaw shouted "Long Live Czechoslovakia." The development of socialist democracy in Czechoslovakia had to be halted because it created pressure for similar development elsewhere in the Soviet bloc. From the point of view of the Moscow oligarchs, the invasion was a defensive move required to maintain their power.

In March, 1953, when Stalin died, his courtiers and underlings feared precisely such a sequence of events as actually occurred in Czechoslovakia after the fall of Novotny. This was indicated by the public warning against "panic and disarray" that was issued within hours of Stalin's death. A decade and a half ago, those fears were groundless because Russia had no tradition of democracy or of a free press that could take over in the period of confusion following a tyrant's demise. Stalin (presumably) died a natural death, rather than falling victim to the tensions of his society like Novotny. Nevertheless, the men in the Kremlin must have seen the Czechoslovak developments from January to August, 1968, as a small-scale model of what might happen in the Soviet Union. Certainly, many of the factors operative in Czechoslovakia in January, 1968, are still present in the Soviet Union: Moscow has never really come to terms with the Stalinist past and its many injustices. The kinds of pressures the Slovaks generated in Czechoslovakia now emanate in the Soviet Union from the Ukrainians, the Moslem peoples, the Balts, and other minorities. Soviet intellectuals are subject to controls and repressions more severe than at any time since the Stalin era. Soviet workers and farmers have lower living standards than the people of any Western industrialized nation and much lower than those of the Czechs and Slovaks. Thus, every theme sounded in Prague during the months of rising ferment set off sensitive and painful resonances in Moscow's domain. Fear of these resonances caused the Soviet leaders to decide that their empire could not exist 95 per cent slave and 5 per cent free. They moved to obliterate the small percentage of burgeoning freedom.

Soviet miscalculations that contributed so greatly to the Arab-Israeli war in June, 1967, and its outcome had hinted much about incompetence in the Kremlin. Those hints were fully confirmed by the political debacle Moscow suffered in Czechoslovakia after the invasion. One could find excuses to explain why the primarily Russian and Ukrainian ruling elite in Moscow misjudged the fighting will and ability of distant Arabs and Israelis, but those excuses cannot be applied to the monumental failure to anticipate how the Czechs and Slovaks—two Slavic peoples with many cultural and historic ties to the Russians and the Ukrainians—would react to the crude violation of their national sovereignty. The leaders who have shown twice in two years such gross inability to understand the psychology and motivation of other nations command more than enough nuclear weapons to devastate the earth. The thought is not reassuring.

Another level of Kremlin incompetence was exposed by the Czechoslovak events. Vital Soviet national interests were harmed by the Politburo's handling of the Prague renaissance. One must assume that the rulers in Moscow are patriots who wish to increase their nation's security and economic welfare, as well as to maintain themselves in power. However, the Czechoslovak policy followed by this group, composed mainly of frightened old men, tended in an opposite direction. This emerges plainly from the negative consequences of the Czechoslovak invasion for what must have been policy goals of the Moscow leadership.

It is at least as important to the Soviet Union as to the United States that the proliferation of nuclear weapons end and that no more nations join the group of nuclear powers. The immediate impact of the invasion was to darken considerably the prospect for general adoption of a nuclear nonproliferation treaty. In the United States, ratification of the treaty was discouraged by Richard M. Nixon during his campaign for the Presidency. Nixon made no secret of the fact that he was motivated by the invasion of Czechoslovakia. Important also was the added strength the Czechoslovak invasion gave to the treaty's opponents in such countries as Japan, India, West Germany, and Israel. By proving the Soviet Union's willingness to use its military power in defiance of all international law, agreements, treaties, and even the United Nations Charter, Moscow implied that it still believed that might makes right and played into the hands of those people in non-nuclear countries who believe that their nations require nuclear weapons to guard against dictation by the nuclear powers. Would Czechoslovakia have been invaded if it had had its own atomic and hydrogen bombs? This question was asked by many people all over the world after August 20. To many, the answer seemed so obviously negative that it made irrefutable the case for non-nuclear nations, acquiring nuclear capabilities. It is conceivable, therefore, that an ultimate result of the Czechoslovak invasion will be the acquisition of nuclear weapons by West Germany, India, Japan, Israel, and other countries Moscow would prefer to have remain outside the nuclear club. The prospect that a nuclear West Germany may be one of the ultimate consequences of the invasion makes a special mockery of the Kremlin claim that it had to act against Czechoslovakia in order to protect the Soviet Union against West Germany.

Even more immediately adverse to Soviet interests is the acceleration the invasion gave the missile race. The forces urging the United States to build anti-missile missiles received powerful assistance from the invasion, while plans for beginning talks to halt the missile race were set back by months if not by years. The invasion increased American suspicion of Soviet intentions, and helped Richard M. Nixon make political capital during the 1968 election campaign, with his call for attaining American military superiority, rather than accepting mere parity with the Soviet Union. The new stage of the arms race will cost the Soviet Union, as well as the United States, dearly, while adding still further to their mutual insecurity. The Soviet Union will have to spend billions of additional rubles that otherwise could go to improving its people's relatively low living standards. Premier Kosygin realized this very well, and he seemed almost frantic in November, 1968, as he sought to induce American officials to begin missile limitation talks at the summit or lower levels as soon as possible. But by then it was clear that key Washington decisions would have to await Nixon's inauguration. In the lost months, the technicians made further progress in both defensive and offensive missiles, including the fractional orbital bombs, the multiple independently-targeted re-entry vehicles (MIRVS), and the other nightmarish wonders of the arms race.

Finally, given the malignant character of China's hatred for the Soviet Union, it is of primary importance for Moscow to try to keep the Peking regime as weak and politically isolated as possible. The Czechoslovak invasion and its consequences worked in precisely the opposite direction. The Czechoslovak invasion and the Brezhnev doctrine reminded Mao Tse-tung that his nation faced similar dangers. It required only elementary prudence to see that he would be wise to try to end the chaos the cultural revolution had brought to China and to mend some of his country's fences abroad. In the months after the invasion of Czechoslovakia, Mao suddenly turned toward repression of the Red Guards and other disorderly elements, while unexpectedly inviting the Nixon Administration to begin a dialogue with China. In Yugoslavia, dismay caused by the invasion prompted a new look at China and study of whether it might be possible to improve relations with Peking as a counterweight to the menace from Moscow. The possibility that Czechoslovakia marked the beginning of a new series of Soviet aggressions prompted people influential in Washington to reexamine the question of Washington-Peking relations with similar ideas in mind. More and more, the logic of balance of power politics suggested that the West would be wise to strengthen China as an offset to Soviet strength and scorn for the rights of other nations.

These results of the invasion came from the blow inflicted upon the vision of the future that had earlier been held by many of the West's most influential policy-makers. The vision

was of a growing *détente* with Moscow—the natural result
of increasing Soviet affluence and of the growing convergence
of Soviet and American societies and interests. It was thought
that Moscow had mellowed and softened and no longer
practiced Stalinism at home or sought aggrandizement
abroad. Much of such thinking assumed that the Russian
bear had shed his claws and had become an affectionate cub
with whom it was possible to play safely. This picture of a
changed Soviet Union led many—before the invasion—to re-
ject the notion that Moscow would move militarily against
Prague. The slogan of the purveyors of good cheer and complacency was "1968 is not 1956." This analysis was proven
inaccurate by the invasion. The Russian bear still had claws
and could be very nasty, and the bear's idea of maintaining
the *status quo* had no room for any real growth of Czechoslovak—or other satellite—independence and democracy. The
observers who were not surprised by events in Czechoslovakia were those who had grasped the implications of the increasingly Stalinist cultural and political internal policies
followed by the Brezhnev leadership since the Sinyavsky-
Daniel trial in early 1966.

Having exaggerated the degree of Soviet mellowing before the invasion, the West was in danger of overestimating
Moscow's return to Stalinism. This was particularly true
because the Nixon Administration was on the Washington
horizon, a new government headed by a politician who had
built his career on professional anti-Communism. The reality
in Moscow was that of a confusion of voices, of a divided
ruling committee whose members had sharply differing prior-
ities and values. The West would be criminally negligent,
in the wake of Czechoslovakia, if it did not look to its defenses and take precautions against possible further Kremlin adventures. But the West would be equally negligent if
it rebuffed Moscow's efforts to renew the *détente* and to
retreat from the kind of international lawlessness implied

by the invasion. The Kremlin was canny enough not to close the door to mutually beneficial agreements with the United States even at the height of the Vietnam War. Improvement of East-West relations in the future would not be a betrayal of Czechoslovakia or even a sign of approval of what Moscow did to that country. The lessening of cold war tensions had played a great role in making possible the "Czechoslovak spring," and a lessening of tensions in the future would again give rulers in Prague an opportunity to widen the constricted area of freedom that Moscow now permits the Czechs and Slovaks.

The rulers in Moscow were well aware of the damage their Czechoslovak adventure had done to their foreign-policy position. Their efforts to minimize this damage were nowhere more evident than in Moscow's behind-the-scenes efforts to help the Johnson Administration in Asia during the last months of 1968. It was a poorly disguised secret in Washington during that period that Soviet influence had played a positive role in relation to the Vietnam peace talks and to the North Korean decision to release the crew of the *Pueblo*. Some cynics argued that there had been a Washington-Moscow deal, that Washington's mild reaction to the Czechoslovak invasion had been rewarded by Kremlin aid in getting the American–North Vietnamese peace talks in Paris expanded to include Saigon and the Vietcong and in inducing North Korea to accept an American "confession," which was promptly repudiated by the U.S. Government, as an adequate price for freeing the *Pueblo* sailors. Such cynicism was probably excessive. Washington did almost nothing about the invasion of Czechoslovakia mainly because of its Vietnam preoccupation but also in part because of the Johnson Administration's anger at Prague's long and important role in supplying Hanoi and the Vietcong. The end result however, was not unlike what might have been agreed to in a formal arrangement, had there been one. The reality behind these developments was the sense of common interest in Washington and Moscow in the need to avoid a clash that might lead to mutual thermonuclear suicide.

*   *   *

In post-invasion Czechoslovakia, "extremists" have been blamed for the Soviet invasion: If the journalists had not spoken so freely and written so bluntly, if non-Communist political organizations had not tried to organize, if nothing had been said about Czechoslovakia's grievances against Moscow, then the troops would not have marched—according to the approved argument. But if democratic socialism is to have real meaning, then it must give its people at least as much freedom as is given by democratic capitalism. The United States has a Communist Party; the American press covers the entire spectrum of political opinion. People who believe that socialism is superior to capitalism ought to be the first to protest against limits to freedom in a socialist society that do not exist in a democratic capitalist society. The people of Canada and Mexico have little hesitancy about often expressing a sense of grievance against, or dissatisfaction with, the United States. Why should the people of Czechoslovakia be any less free to express their disenchantment with the Soviet Union? Democratic socialism is meaningless without a broad range of freedoms for the people. If a state wants to create a democratic socialism, it cannot dole out only a little freedom.

The real culprits for denying Czechoslovakia its freedom in 1968 were the rulers in Moscow, not the alleged "extremists" in Prague. The mistake the "extremists" made was simply in believing that they were living in a genuinely sovereign state as guaranteed by the United Nations Charter and by numerous Soviet and international Communist pronouncements. They discovered too late that Moscow regarded Czechoslovakia's sovereignty as a façade that could be discarded whenever necessary. They can hardly be blamed for the error. After all, until the moment of the invasion, Soviet diplomats and Soviet newspapers would have vigorously denied as an "imperialist slander" a suggestion that Czechoslovakia was inferior in rights and privileges to, say, the Central African Republic, Gabon, or Kenya.

Insofar as there are Czechoslovaks who really bear much responsibility for the invasion, it is the conservatives, who misinformed the Kremlin on the real political situation. But attention must also be directed at Dubcek, Smrkovsky, and their fellow leaders, who also bear some responsibility. To say this is not to deny these individuals' good intentions, their fortitude, and even their heroism at key points during the period January–August, 1968. These men promised to tell their people the truth, but they never frankly discussed the Soviet threat with their nation before August 20. They vacillated between abject surrender—on the issue of the June "maneuvers" that permitted the Soviet and satellite armies to conduct a dress rehearsal for the invasion—and defiance—when they refused to attend the Warsaw Conference in July. By completely ruling out the possibility of armed resistance to an invasion, they threw away the one possibility they had of preventing the entry of the "fraternal armies." They sought to act like the Good Soldier Schweik when Jan Hus and Hus's military successor, Jan Zizka, were more appropriate models.

Yet the dilemma of the Dubcek group was real, and it is impossible not to feel sympathy for them. Czechoslovakia is a small country, and the Soviet Union alone—even without the satellite armies—could easily destroy any military resistance Prague mounted. No doubt Dubcek and his associates thought of appealing to the West, but there are hints that they feared that Czechoslovakia might precipitate a thermonuclear war. These men were veteran Communists. Given their backgrounds, they must have found it hard to realize that the Soviet Union, not the West, was the real enemy of Czechoslovakia and of democratic socialism. Dubcek deserves great credit for the remarkable way in which, within a few weeks after the beginning of 1968, he changed from a leader of the aggrieved Slovak minority into a truly national leader commanding the affection and respect of Czechs and Slovaks alike.

The Dubcek story has not ended as this is written. Future historians will have to provide a more balanced view of Dubcek than is possible in 1968. What is certain even now —so close to the dramatic events—is that the "Czechoslovak spring" of 1968 has marked a new milestone in the history of human freedom and particularly in the evolution of Communist parties and ideology toward greater humanism.

Czechoslovakia's transformation almost overnight from one of the most nearly Stalinist Communist nations into the leader of the drive toward greater freedom in the Soviet bloc surprised everyone—Communists and non-Communists, Czechoslovaks, Russians, Americans, Yugoslavs, Germans. The swiftness of the change suggests what enormous possibilities are hidden in the deceptive quiet of the Soviet Union and the orthodox Eastern European states. Whatever happens in Czechoslovakia in the future, there will be others in Czechoslovakia and elsewhere who will pick up the torch lit by Dubcek and his colleagues. The Czechoslovak story in 1968 demonstrates the strength of the forces of national independence and democracy in the face of overwhelming odds. The day will come when the peoples of the Soviet Union will honor Dubcek's Czechoslovakia for its contribution toward hastening the end of the bureaucratic neo-Stalinist dictatorship. That tyranny has outlived its time but stubbornly refuses to surrender the stage, hoping against hope for a political heart transplant that will rejuvenate its aging leaders and its obsolete ideas.

Index

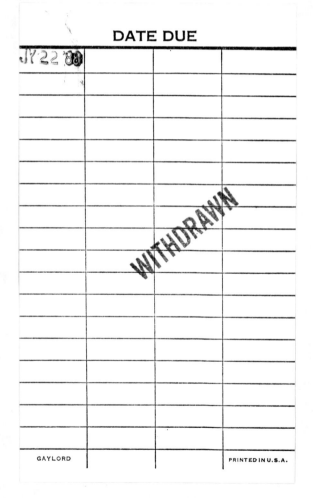